The Hitchhiker's Guide to Python
Best Practices for Development

Kenneth Reitz and Tanya Schlusser

Beijing · Boston · Farnham · Sebastopol · Tokyo

The Hitchhiker's Guide to Python

by Kenneth Reitz and Tanya Schlusser

Printed in the United States of America.

Published by O'Reilly Media, Inc., 1005 Gravenstein Highway North, Sebastopol, CA 95472.

O'Reilly books may be purchased for educational, business, or sales promotional use. Online editions are also available for most titles (*http://safaribooksonline.com*). For more information, contact our corporate/institutional sales department: 800-998-9938 or *corporate@oreilly.com*.

Editor: Dawn Schanafelt	**Indexer:** WordCo Indexing Services, Inc.
Production Editor: Nicole Shelby, Nicholas Adams	**Interior Designer:** David Futato
Copyeditor: Jasmine Kwityn	**Cover Designer:** Randy Comer
Proofreader: Amanda Kersey	**Illustrator:** Rebecca Demarest

September 2016:   First Edition

Revision History for the First Edition

2016-08-26:   First Release

See *http://oreilly.com/catalog/errata.csp?isbn=9781491933176* for release details.

978-1-491-93317-6

[LSI]

Dedicated to you

Table of Contents

Preface

Python is big. Really big. You just won't believe how vastly hugely mind-bogglingly big it is.

This guide is *not* intended to teach you the Python language (we cite lots of great resources that do that) but is rather an (opinionated) insider's guide to our community's favorite tools and best practices. The primary audience is new to mid-level Python programmers who are interested in contributing to open source or in beginning a career or starting a company using Python, although casual Python users should also find Part I and Chapter 5 helpful.

The first part will help you choose the text editor or interactive development environment that fits your situation (for example, those using Java frequently may prefer Eclipse with a Python plug-in) and surveys options for other interpreters that may meet needs you don't yet know Python could address (e.g., there's a MicroPython implementation based around the ARM Cortex-M4 chip). The second section demonstrates Pythonic style by highlighting exemplary code in the open source community that will hopefully encourage more in-depth reading and experimentation with open source code. The final section briefly surveys the vast galaxy of libraries most commonly used in the Python community—providing an idea of the scope of what Python can do right now.

All of the royalties from the print version of this book will be directly donated to the Django Girls (*https://djangogirls.org/*), a giddily joyous global organization dedicated to organizing free Django and Python workshops, creating open-sourced online tutorials, and curating amazing first experiences with technology. Those who wish to contribute to the online version can read more about how to do it at our website (*http://docs.python-guide.org/en/latest/notes/contribute/*).

Conventions Used in This Book

The following typographical conventions are used in this book:

Italic
> Indicates new terms, URLs, email addresses, filenames, and file extensions.

`Constant width`
> Used for program listings, as well as within paragraphs to refer to program elements such as variable or function names, databases, data types, environment variables, statements, and keywords.

`Constant width bold`
> Shows commands or other text that should be typed literally by the user.

`Constant width italic`
> Shows text that should be replaced with user-supplied values or by values determined by context.

 This element signifies a tip or suggestion.

 This element signifies a general note.

 This element indicates a warning or caution.

Safari® Books Online

 *Safari Books Online* is an on-demand digital library that delivers expert content in both book and video form from the world's leading authors in technology and business.

Technology professionals, software developers, web designers, and business and creative professionals use Safari Books Online as their primary resource for research, problem solving, learning, and certification training.

Safari Books Online offers a range of plans and pricing for enterprise, government, education, and individuals.

Members have access to thousands of books, training videos, and prepublication manuscripts in one fully searchable database from publishers like O'Reilly Media, Prentice Hall Professional, Addison-Wesley Professional, Microsoft Press, Sams, Que, Peachpit Press, Focal Press, Cisco Press, John Wiley & Sons, Syngress, Morgan Kaufmann, IBM Redbooks, Packt, Adobe Press, FT Press, Apress, Manning, New Riders, McGraw-Hill, Jones & Bartlett, Course Technology, and hundreds more. For more information about Safari Books Online, please visit us online.

How to Contact Us

Please address comments and questions concerning this book to the publisher:

O'Reilly Media, Inc.
1005 Gravenstein Highway North
Sebastopol, CA 95472
800-998-9938 (in the United States or Canada)
707-829-0515 (international or local)
707-829-0104 (fax)

We have a web page for this book, where we list errata, examples, and any additional information. You can access this page at *http://bit.ly/the-hitchhikers-guide-to-python*.

To comment or ask technical questions about this book, send email to *bookquestions@oreilly.com*.

For more information about our books, courses, conferences, and news, see our website at *http://www.oreilly.com*.

Find us on Facebook: *http://facebook.com/oreilly*

Follow us on Twitter: *http://twitter.com/oreillymedia*

Watch us on YouTube: *http://www.youtube.com/oreillymedia*

Acknowledgments

Welcome, friends, to *The Hitchhiker's Guide to Python*.

This book is, to the best of my knowledge, the first of its kind: designed and curated by a single author (myself—Kenneth), with the majority of the content provided by hundreds of people from all over the world, for free. Never before in the history of mankind has the technology been available to allow a beautiful collaboration of this size and scale.

This book was made possible with:

Community
  Love brings us together to conquer all obstacles.

Software projects
  Python, Sphinx, Alabaster, and Git.

Services
  GitHub and Read the Docs.

Lastly, I'd like to extend a personal thank you to Tanya, who did all the hard work of converting this work into book form and preparing it for publication, and the incredible O'Reilly team—Dawn, Jasmine, Nick, Heather, Nicole, Meg, and the dozens of other people who worked behind the scenes to make this book the best it could be.

## PART I

Getting Started

This part of the guide focuses on setting up a Python environment. It was inspired by Stuart Ellis's guide for Python on Windows (*http://www.stuartellis.eu/articles/python-development-windows/*), and consists of the following chapters and topics:

Chapter 1, Picking an Interpreter
  We compare Python 2 and Python 3, and share some interpreter options other than CPython.

Chapter 2, Properly Installing Python
  We show how to get Python, pip, and virtualenv.

Chapter 3, Your Development Environment
  We describe our favorite text editors and IDEs for Python development.

Picking an Interpreter

The State of Python 2 Versus Python 3

When choosing a Python interpreter, one looming question is always present: "Should I choose Python 2 or Python 3?" The answer is not as obvious as one might think (although 3 is becoming more compelling every day).

Here is the state of things:

- Python 2.7 has been the standard for a *long* time.
- Python 3 introduced major changes to the language, which some developers are unhappy with.[1]
- Python 2.7 will receive necessary security updates until 2020 (*https://www.python.org/dev/peps/pep-0373/*).
- Python 3 is continually evolving, like Python 2 did in years past.

You can now see why this is not such an easy decision.

---

[1] If you don't do much low-level networking programming, the change was barely noticeable outside of the print statement becoming a function. Otherwise, "unhappy with" is kind of a polite understatement—developers responsible for large, popular web, socket, or networking libraries that deal with unicode and byte strings had (or still have) *extensive* changes to make. Details about the change, direct from the first introduction of Python 3 to the world, start off with: "Everything you thought you knew about binary data and Unicode has changed." (*http://bit.ly/text-vs-data*)

Recommendations

The way we see it, a truly hoopy frood[2] would use Python 3. But if you can only use Python 2, at least you're still using Python. These are our recommendations:

Use Python 3 if…
- You love Python 3.

- You don't know which one to use.

- You embrace change.

Use Python 2 if…
- You love Python 2 and are saddened by the future being Python 3.

- The stability requirements of your software would be impacted.[3]

- Software that you depend on requires it.

So…3?

If you're choosing a Python interpreter to use, and aren't opinionated, then use the newest Python 3.x—every version brings new and improved standard library modules, security, and bug fixes. Progress is progress. So only use Python 2 if you have a strong reason to, such as a Python 2–exclusive library that has no adequate Python 3–ready alternative, a need for a specific implementation (see "Implementations" on page 5), or you (like some of us) love and are inspired by Python 2.

Check out Can I Use Python 3? (*https://caniusepython3.com/*) to see whether any Python projects you're depending on will block adoption of Python 3.

For further reading, try Python2orPython3 (*http://bit.ly/python2-or-python3*), which lays out some of the reasoning behind a backward-incompatible break in the language specification, and links to detailed specifications of the differences.

If you're a beginner, there are far more important things to worry about than cross-compatibility between all of the Python versions. Just get something working for the system you've got, and cross this bridge later.

---

2 Someone who's really amazingly together. We mean, who really knows where their towel is.

3 Here's a link to a high-level list of changes (*http://python3porting.com/stdlib.html*) to Python's Standard Library.

Implementations

When people speak of *Python*, they often mean not just the language but also the CPython implementation. *Python* is actually a specification for a language that can be implemented in many different ways.

The different implementations may be for compatibility with other libraries, or maybe for a little speed. Pure Python libraries should work regardless of your Python implementation, but those built on C (like NumPy) won't. This section provides a quick rundown on the most popular implementations.

 This guide presumes you're working with the standard CPython implementation of Python 3, although we'll frequently add notes when relevant for Python 2.

CPython

CPython (*http://www.python.org/*) is the reference implementation[4] of Python, written in C. It compiles Python code to intermediate bytecode which is then interpreted by a virtual machine. CPython provides the highest level of compatibility with Python packages and C extension modules.[5]

If you are writing open source Python code and want to reach the widest possible audience, use CPython. To use packages that rely on C extensions to function, CPython is your only implementation option.

All versions of the Python language are implemented in C because CPython is the reference implementation.

Stackless

Stackless Python (*https://bitbucket.org/stackless-dev/stackless/wiki/Home*) is regular CPython (so it should work with all of the libraries that CPython can use), but with a patch that decouples the Python interpreter from the call stack, making it possible to change the order of execution of code. Stackless introduces the contepts of *tasklets*, which can wrap functions and turn them into "micro-threads" that can be serialized to disk for future execution and scheduled, by default in round-robin execution.

---

4 The *reference implementation* accurately reflects the language's definition. Its behavior is how all other implementations should behave.

5 *C extension modules* are written in C for use in Python.

The greenlet library (*http://greenlet.readthedocs.org*) implements this same stack-switching functionality for CPython users. Much of the functionality has also been implemented in PyPy.

PyPy

PyPy (*http://pypy.org/*) is a Python interpreter implemented in a restricted statically typed subset of the Python language called RPython, making certain kinds of optimization possible. The interpreter features a just-in-time compiler and supports multiple backends, such as C, Common Intermediate Language (CIL) (*http://bit.ly/standard-ecma-335*), and Java Virtual Machine (JVM) bytecode.

PyPy aims for maximum compatibility with the reference CPython implementation while improving performance. If you are looking to increase performance of your Python code, it's worth giving PyPy a try. On a suite of benchmarks, it's currently over five times faster than CPython (*http://speed.pypy.org/*).

It supports Python 2.7, and PyPy3 (*http://pypy.org/compat.html*) targets Python 3. Both versions are available from the PyPy download page (*http://pypy.org/download.html*).

Jython

Jython (*http://www.jython.org/*) is a Python interpreter implementation that compiles Python code to Java bytecode which is then executed by the JVM. Additionally, it is able to import and use any Java class like a Python module.

If you need to interface with an existing Java code base or have other reasons for needing to write Python code for the JVM, Jython is the best choice.

Jython currently supports up to Python 2.7 (*http://bit.ly/jython-supports-27*).

IronPython

IronPython (*http://ironpython.net/*) is an implementation of Python for the .NET framework. It can use both Python and .NET framework libraries, and can also expose Python code to other languages in the .NET framework.

Python Tools for Visual Studio (*http://ironpython.net/tools/*) integrates IronPython directly into the Visual Studio development environment, making it an ideal choice for Windows developers.

IronPython supports Python2.7 (*http://ironpython.codeplex.com/releases/view/81726*).

PythonNet

Python for .NET (*http://pythonnet.github.io/*) is a package that provides near seamless integration of a natively installed Python installation with the .NET Common Language Runtime (CLR). This is the inverse approach to that taken by IronPython, meaning PythonNet and IronPython complement rather than compete with each other.

In conjunction with Mono (*http://www.mono-project.com/*), PythonNet enables native Python installations on non-Windows operating systems, such as OS X and Linux, to operate within the .NET framework. It can be run in addition to IronPython without conflict.

PythonNet supports from Python 2.3 up to Python 2.7; the installation instructions are on the PythonNet readme page (*http://pythonnet.github.io/readme.html*).

Skulpt

Skulpt (*http://www.skulpt.org/*) is a JavaScript implementation of Python. It has not ported all of the CPython standard library; the library has the modules math, random, turtle, image, unittest, and parts of time, urllib, DOM, and re. It is intended for use in teaching. There is also a way to add your own modules (*http://bit.ly/skulpt-adding-module*).

Notable examples of its use are Interactive Python (*http://interactivepython.org/*) and CodeSkulptor (*http://www.codeskulptor.org/demos.html*).

Skulpt supports most of Python 2.7 and Python 3.3. See the Skulpt GitHub page (*https://github.com/skulpt/skulpt*) for details.

MicroPython

MicroPython (*https://micropython.org/*) is an implementation of Python 3 optimized to run on a microcontroller; it supports 32-bit ARM processors with the Thumb v2 instruction set, such as the Cortex-M range used in low-cost microcontrollers. It includes these modules (*http://bit.ly/micropython-library*) from Python's Standard Library, plus a few MicroPython-specific libraries for board details, memory information, network access, and a modified version of the ctypes optimized for smaller size. It is not the same as the Raspberry Pi (*https://www.raspberrypi.org*), which has a Debian or other C-based operating system, with Python installed. The pyboard (*https://micropython.org/store/#/store*) actually uses MicroPython as its operating system.

From here on out, we're using CPython on a Unix-like system, on OS X, or on a Windows system.

On to installation—grab your towel!

## CHAPTER 2

Properly Installing Python

This chapter walks through CPython installation on the Mac OS X, Linux, and Windows platforms. Sections on packaging tools (like Setuptools and pip) are repetitive, so you should skip straight to the section for your particular operating system, and ignore the others.

If you are part of an organization that recommends you use a commercial Python distribution, such as Anaconda or Canopy, you should follow your vendor's instructions. There is also a small note for you in "Commercial Python Redistributions" on page 19.

 If Python already exists on your system, do not, on any account, allow anybody to change the symbolic link to the python executable to point at anything other than what it is already pointing at. That would be almost as bad as reading Vogon poetry (*https://en.wikipedia.org/wiki/Vogon#Poetry*) out loud. (Think of the system-installed code that depends on a specific Python in a specific place...)

Installing Python on Mac OS X

The latest version of Mac OS X, El Capitan, comes with its own Mac-specific implementation of Python 2.7.

You don't *need* to install or configure anything else to use Python. But we strongly recommend installing Setuptools, pip, and virtualenv before you start building Python applications for real-world use (i.e., contributing to collaborative projects). You'll learn more about these tools and how to install them later in this section. In particular, you should always install Setuptools, as it makes it much easier for you to use other third-party Python libraries.

The version of Python that ships with OS X is great for learning, but it's not good for collaborative development. The version shipped with OS X may also be out of date from the official current Python release, which is considered the stable production version.[1] So, if all you want to do is write scripts for yourself to pull information from websites, or process data, you don't need anything else. But if you are contributing to open source projects, or working on a team with people that may have other operating systems (or ever intend to in the future[2]), use the CPython release.

Before you download anything, read through the end of the next few paragraphs for notes and warnings. Before installing Python, you'll need to install GCC. It can be obtained by downloading Xcode (*http://developer.apple.com/xcode/*), the smaller Command-Line Tools (*https://developer.apple.com/downloads/*) (you need an Apple account to download it), or the even smaller osx-gcc-installer package (*http://bit.ly/osx-gcc-installer-package*).

 If you already have Xcode installed, do not install osx-gcc-installer. In combination, the software can cause issues that are difficult to diagnose.

While OS X comes with a large number of Unix utilities, those familiar with Linux systems will notice one key component missing: a decent package manager. Homebrew (*http://brew.sh/*) fills this void.

To install Homebrew, open Terminal or your favorite OS X terminal emulator and run the following code:

```
$ BREW_URI=https://raw.githubusercontent.com/Homebrew/install/master/install
$ ruby -e "$(curl -fsSL ${BREW_URI})"
```

The script will explain what changes it will make and prompt you before the installation begins. Once you've installed Homebrew, insert the Homebrew directory at the

---

1 Other people have different opinions. The OS X Python implementation is not the same. It even has some separate OS X–specific libraries. A small rant on this subject criticizing our recommendation is at the Stupid Python Ideas blog (*http://bit.ly/sticking-with-apples-python*). It raises valid concerns about collision of some names for people who switch-hit between OS X's CPython 2.7 and the canonical CPython 2.7. If this is a concern, use a virtual environment. Or, at the very least, leave the OS X Python 2.7 where it is so that the system runs smoothly, install the standard Python 2.7 implemented in CPython, modify your path, and never use the OS X version. Then everything works fine, including products that rely on Apple's OS X–specific version.

2 The best option is to pick Python 3, honestly, or to use virtual environments from the start and install nothing but virtualenv and maybe virtualenvwrapper according to the advice of Hynek Schlawack (*https://hynek.me/articles/virtualenv-lives/*).

top of your PATH environment variable.[3] You can do this by adding the following line at the bottom of your *~/.profile* file:

```
export PATH=/usr/local/bin:/usr/local/sbin:$PATH
```

And then to install Python, run this once in a terminal:

```
$ brew install python3
```

Or for Python 2:

```
$ brew install python
```

By default, Python will then be installed in */usr/local/Cellar/python3/* or */usr/local/Cellar/python/* with symbolic links[4] to the interpreter at */usr/local/python3* or */usr/local/python*. People who use the `--user` option to `pip install` will need to work around a bug involving distutils and the Homebrew configuration (*http://bit.ly/pip-install-bug*). We recommend just using virtual environments, described in "virtualenv" on page 12.

Setuptools and pip

Homebrew installs Setuptools and pip for you. The executable installed with pip will be mapped to `pip3` if you are using Python 3 or to `pip` if you are using Python 2.

With Setuptools, you can download and install any compliant[5] Python software over a network (usually the Internet) with a single command (`easy_install`). It also enables you to add this network installation capability to your own Python software with very little work.

Both pip's `pip` command and Setuptools's `easy_install` command are tools to install and manage Python packages. `pip` is recommended over `easy_install` because it can also uninstall packages, its error messages are more digestible, and partial package installs can't happen (installs that fail partway through will unwind everything that happened so far). For a more nuanced discussion, see pip vs easy_install (*http://bit.ly/pip-vs-easy-install*) in the Python Packaging User Guide (*https://packaging.python.org*), which should be your first reference for current packaging information.

---

3 This will ensure that the Python you use is the one Homebrew just installed, while leaving the system's original Python exactly as it is.

4 A symbolic link is a pointer to the actual file location. You can confirm where the link points to by typing, for example, `ls -l /usr/local/bin/python3` at the command prompt.

5 Packages that are compliant with Setuptools at a minimum provide enough information for the library to identify and obtain all package dependencies. For more information, see the documentation for Packaging and Distributing Python Projects (*https://packaging.python.org/en/latest/distributing.html*), PEP 302 (*https://www.python.org/dev/peps/pep-0302/*), and PEP 241 (*https://www.python.org/dev/peps/pep-0241/*).

To upgrade your installation of pip, type the following in a shell:

```
$ pip install --upgrade pip
```

virtualenv

virtualenv (*http://pypi.python.org/pypi/virtualenv*) creates isolated Python environments. It creates a folder containing all the necessary executables to use the packages that a Python project would need. Some people believe best practice is to install nothing except virtualenv and Setuptools and to then *always* use virtual environments.[6]

To install virtualenv via pip, run pip at the command line of a terminal shell:

```
$ pip3 install virtualenv
```

or if you are using Python 2:

```
$ pip install virtualenv
```

Once you are in a virtual environment, you can always use the command pip, whether you are working with Python 2 or Python 3, so that is what we will do in the rest of this guide. "Virtual Environments" on page 36 describes usage and motivation in more detail.

Installing Python on Linux

Ubuntu started releasing with only Python 3 installed (and Python 2 available via apt-get) as of Wily Werewolf (Ubuntu 15.10). All of the details are on Ubuntu's Python page (*https://wiki.ubuntu.com/Python*). Fedora's release 23 is the first with only Python 3 (both Python 2.7 and 3 are available on releases 20–22), and otherwise Python 2.7 will be available via its package manager.

Most parallel installations of Python 2 and Python 3 make a symbolic link from python2 to a Python 2 interpreter and from python3 to a Python 3 interpreter. If you decide to use Python 2, the current recommendation on Unix-like systems (see Python Enhancement Proposal [PEP (*https://www.python.org/dev/peps/pep-0394/*) 394]) is to explicitly specify python2 in your shebang notation (e.g., #!/usr/bin/env python2 as the first line in the file) rather than rely on the environment python pointing where you expect.

Although not in PEP 394, it has also become convention to use pip2 and pip3 to link to the respective pip package installers.

---

6 Advocates of this practice say it is the only way to ensure nothing ever overwrites an existing installed library with a new version that could break other version-dependent code in the OS.

Setuptools and pip

Even if `pip` is available through a package installer on your system, to ensure you get the most recent version, follow these steps.

First, download get-pip.py (*https://bootstrap.pypa.io/get-pip.py*).[7]

Next, open a shell, change directories to the same location as *get-pip.py*, and type:

```
$ wget https://bootstrap.pypa.io/get-pip.py
$ sudo python3 get-pip.py
```

or for Python 2:

```
$ wget https://bootstrap.pypa.io/get-pip.py
$ sudo python get-pip.py
```

This will also install Setuptools.

With the `easy_install` command that's installed with Setuptools, you can download and install any compliant[8] Python software over a network (usually the Internet). It also enables you to add this network installation capability to your own Python software with very little work.

`pip` is a tool that helps you easily install and manage Python packages. It is recommended over `easy_install` because it can also uninstall packages, its error messages are more digestible, and partial package installs can't happen (installs that fail partway through will unwind everything that happened so far). For a more nuanced discussion, see "pip vs `easy_install`" (*http://bit.ly/pip-vs-easy-install*) in the Python Packaging User Guide (*https://packaging.python.org*), which should be your first reference for current packaging information.

Development Tools

Almost everyone will at some point want to use Python libraries that depend on C extensions. Sometimes your package manager will have these, prebuilt, so you can check first (using `yum search` or `apt-cache search`); and with the newer *wheels* format (*http://pythonwheels.com/*) (precompiled, platform-specific binary files), you may be able to get binaries directly from PyPI, using `pip`. But if you expect to create C extensions in the future, or if the people maintaining your library haven't made wheels for your platform, you will need the development tools for Python: various C

---

7 For additional details, see the `pip` installation instructions (*https://pip.pypa.io/en/latest/installing.html*).

8 Packages that are compliant with Setuptools at a minimum provide enough information for it to identify and obtain all package dependencies. For more information, see the documentation for Packaging and Distributing Python Projects (*https://packaging.python.org/en/latest/distributing.html*), PEP 302 (*https://www.python.org/dev/peps/pep-0302/*), and PEP 241 (*https://www.python.org/dev/peps/pep-0241/*).

libraries, make, and the GCC compiler. The following are some useful packages that use C libraries:

Concurrency tools
- The threading library threading (*https://docs.python.org/3/library/threading.html*)
- The event-handling library (Python 3.4+) asyncio (*https://docs.python.org/3/library/asyncio.html*)
- The coroutine-based networking library curio (*https://curio.readthedocs.org*)
- The coroutine-based networking library gevent (*http://www.gevent.org/*)
- The event-driven networking library Twisted (*https://twistedmatrix.com/*)

Scientific analysis
- The linear algebra library NumPy (*http://www.numpy.org/*)
- The numerical toolkit SciPy (*http://www.scipy.org/*)
- The machine learning library scikit-learn (*http://scikit-learn.org/*)
- The plotting library Matplotlib (*http://matplotlib.org//*)

Data/database interface
- The interface to the HDF5 data format h5py (*http://www.h5py.org/*)
- The PostgreSQL database adapter Psycopg (*http://initd.org/psycopg/*)
- The database abstraction and object-relational mapper SQLAlchemy (*http://www.sqlalchemy.org/*)

On Ubuntu, in a terminal shell, type:

```
$ sudo apt-get update --fix-missing
$ sudo apt-get install python3-dev # For Python 3
$ sudo apt-get install python-dev  # For Python 2
```

Or on Fedora, in a terminal shell, type:

```
$ sudo yum update
$ sudo yum install gcc
$ sudo yum install python3-devel  # For Python 3
$ sudo yum install python2-devel  # For Python 2
```

and then pip3 install --user *desired-package* will be able to build tools that must be compiled. (Or pip install --user *desired-package* for Python 2.) You also will need the tool itself installed (for details on how to do this, see the HDF5 installation documentation (*https://www.hdfgroup.org/HDF5/release/obtain5.html*)). For PostgreSQL on Ubuntu, you'd type this in a terminal shell:

```
$ sudo apt-get install libpq-dev
```

or on Fedora:

```
$ sudo yum install postgresql-devel
```

virtualenv

`virtualenv` is a command installed with the virtualenv (*https://pypi.python.org/pypi/virtualenv*) package that creates isolated Python environments. It creates a folder containing all the necessary executables to use the packages that a Python project would need.

To install virtualenv using Ubuntu's package manager, type:

```
$ sudo apt-get install python-virtualenv
```

or on Fedora:

```
$ sudo yum install python-virtualenv
```

Or via `pip`, run `pip` at the command line of a terminal shell, and use the `--user` option to install it locally for yourself rather than doing a system install:

```
$ pip3 install --user virtualenv
```

or if you are using Python 2:

```
$ sudo pip install --user virtualenv
```

Once you are in a virtual environment, you can always use the command `pip`, whether you are working with Python 2 or Python 3, so that is what we will do in the rest of this guide. "Virtual Environments" on page 36 describes usage and motivation in more detail.

Installing Python on Windows

Windows users have it harder than other Pythonistas—because it's harder to compile anything on Windows, and many Python libraries use C extensions under the hood. Thanks to wheels (*http://pythonwheels.com/*), binaries can be downloaded from PyPI using `pip` (if they exist), so things have gotten a little easier.

There are two paths here: a commercial distribution (discussed in "Commercial Python Redistributions" on page 19) or straight-up CPython. Anaconda is much easier, especially when you're going to do scientific work. Actually, pretty much everyone who does scientific computing on Windows with Python (except those developing C-based Python libraries of their own) will recommend Anaconda. But if you know your way around compiling and linking, if you want to contribute to open source projects that use C code, or if you just don't want a commercial distribution (what you need is free), we hope you consider installing straight-up CPython.[9]

As time progresses, more and more packages with C libraries will have wheels on PyPI, and so can be obtained via `pip`. The trouble comes when required C library dependencies are not bundled with the wheel. This dependency problem is another reason you may prefer commercial Python redistributions like Anaconda.

Use CPython if you are the kind of Windows user who:

- Doesn't need Python libraries that rely on C extensions
- Owns a Visual C++ compiler (not the free one)
- Can handle setting up MinGW
- Is game to download binaries by hand[10] and then `pip install` the binary

If you will use Python as a substitute for R or MATLAB, or just want to get up to speed quickly and will install CPython later if necessary (see "Commercial Python Redistributions" on page 19 for some tips), use Anaconda.[11]

If you want your interface to be mostly graphical (point-and-click), or if Python is your first language and this is your first install, use Canopy.

If your entire team has already committed to one of these options, then you should go with whatever is currently being used.

To install the standard CPython implementation on Windows, you first need to download the latest version of Python 3 (*https://www.python.org/ftp/python/3.5.0/python-3.5.0.exe*) or Python 2.7 (*https://www.python.org/ftp/python/2.7.10/python-2.7.10.msi*) from the official website. If you want to be sure you are installing a fully up-to-date version (or are certain you really, really want the 64-bit installer[12]),

---

9 Or consider IronPython (discussed in "IronPython" on page 6) if you want to integrate Python with the .NET framework. But if you're a beginner, this should probably not be your first Python interpreter. This whole book talks about CPython.

10 You must know at least what version of Python you're using and whether you selected 32-bit or 64-bit Python. We recommend 32-bit, as every third-party DLL will have a 32-bit version and some may not have 64-bit versions. The most widely cited location to obtain compiled binaries is Christoph Gohlke's resource site (*http://www.lfd.uci.edu/~gohlke/pythonlibs/*). For scikit-learn, Carl Kleffner is building binaries using MinGW (*https://pypi.anaconda.org/carlkl/simple/*) in preparation for eventual release on PyPI (*https://pypi.python.org/pypi*).

11 Anaconda has more free stuff, and comes bundled with Spyder, a better IDE. If you use Anaconda, you'll find Anaconda's free package index (*https://repo.continuum.io/pkgs/*) and Canopy's package index (*https://www.enthought.com/products/canopy/package-index/*) to be helpful.

12 Meaning you are 100% certain that any Dynamically Linked Libraries (DLLs) and drivers you need are available in 64 bit.

then use the Python Releases for Windows site (*https://www.python.org/downloads/windows/*) to find the release you need.

The Windows version is provided as an MSI package. This format allows Windows administrators to automate installation with their standard tools. To install the package manually, just double-click the file.

By design, Python installs to a directory with the version number embedded (e.g., Python version 3.5 will install at *C:\Python35*) so that you can have multiple versions of Python on the same system without conflicts. Of course, only one interpreter can be the default application for Python file types. The installer does not automatically modify the PATH environment variable,[13] so that you always have control over which copy of Python is run.

Typing the full path name for a Python interpreter each time quickly gets tedious, so add the directories for your default Python version to the PATH. Assuming that the Python installation you want to use is in *C:\Python35*, you will want to add this to your PATH:

```
C:\Python35;C:\Python35\Scripts\
```

You can do this easily by running the following in PowerShell:[14]

```
PS C:\> [Environment]::SetEnvironmentVariable(
    "Path",
    "$env:Path;C:\Python35\;C:\Python35\Scripts\",
    "User")
```

The second directory (*Scripts*) receives command files when certain packages are installed, so it is a very useful addition. You do not need to install or configure anything else to use Python.

Having said that, we strongly recommend installing Setuptools, pip, and virtualenv before you start building Python applications for real-world use (i.e., contributing to collaborative projects). You'll learn more about these tools and how to install them later in this section. In particular, you should always install Setuptools, as it makes it much easier for you to use other third-party Python libraries.

---

13 The PATH lists every location the operating system will look to find executable programs, like Python and Python scripts like pip. Each entry is separated by a semicolon.

14 Windows PowerShell provides a command-line shell and scripting language that is similar enough to Unix shells that Unix users will be able to function without reading a manual, but with features specifically for use with Windows. It is built on the .NET Framework. For more information, see Microsoft's "Using Windows PowerShell." (*http://bit.ly/using-windows-powershell*)

Setuptools and pip

The current MSI packaged installers install Setuptools and pip for you with Python, so if you are following along with this book and just installed now, you have them already. Otherwise, the best way to get them with Python 2.7 installed is to upgrade to the newest release.[15] For Python 3, in versions 3.3 and prior, download the script *get-pip.py* (*https://bootstrap.pypa.io/get-pip.py*),[16] and run it. Open a shell, change directories to the same location as *get-pip.py*, and then type:

```
PS C:\> python get-pip.py
```

With Setuptools, you can download and install any compliant[17] Python software over a network (usually the Internet) with a single command (`easy_install`). It also enables you to add this network installation capability to your own Python software with very little work.

Both pip's `pip` command and Setuptools's `easy_install` command are tools to install and manage Python packages. `pip` is recommended over `easy_install` because it can also uninstall packages, its error messages are more digestible, and partial package installs can't happen (installs that fail partway through will unwind everything that happened so far). For a more nuanced discussion, see "`pip` vs `easy_install`" (*http://bit.ly/pip-vs-easy-install*) in the Python Packaging User Guide (*https://packaging.python.org*), which should be your first reference for current packaging information.

virtualenv

The `virtualenv` (*http://pypi.python.org/pypi/virtualenv*) command creates isolated Python environments. It creates a folder containing all the necessary executables to use the packages that a Python project would need. Then, when you activate the environment using a command in the new folder, it prepends that folder to your PATH environment variable—the Python in the new folder becomes the first one found, and the packages in its subfolders are the ones used.

To install virtualenv via `pip`, run `pip` at the command line of a PowerShell terminal:

```
PS C:\> pip install virtualenv
```

---

15 The installer will prompt you whether it's OK to overwrite the existing installation. Say yes; releases in the same minor version are backward-compatible.

16 For additional details, see the `pip` installation instructions (*https://pip.pypa.io/en/latest/installing.html*).

17 Packages that are compliant with Setuptools at a minimum provide enough information for the library to identify and obtain all package dependencies. For more information, see the documentation for "Packaging and Distributing Python Projects," (*https://packaging.python.org/en/latest/distributing.html*) PEP 302 (*https://www.python.org/dev/peps/pep-0302/*), and PEP 241 (*https://www.python.org/dev/peps/pep-0241/*).

"Virtual Environments" on page 36 describes usage and motivation in more detail. On OS X and Linux, because Python comes installed for use by system or third-party software, they must specifically distinguish between the Python 2 and Python 3 versions of pip. On Windows, there is no need to do this, so whenever we say pip3, we mean pip for Windows users. Regardless of OS, once you are in a virtual environment, you can always use the command pip, whether you are working with Python 2 or Python 3, so that is what we will do in the rest of this guide.

Commercial Python Redistributions

Your IT department or classroom teaching assistant may have asked you to install a commercial redistribution of Python. This is intended to simplify the work an organization needs to do to maintain a consistent environment for multiple users. All of the ones listed here provide the C implementation of Python (CPython).

A technical reviewer for the first draft of this chapter said we massively understated the trouble it is to use a regular CPython installation on Windows for most users: that even with wheels, compiling and/or linking to external C libraries is painful for everyone but seasoned developers. We have a bias toward plain CPython, but the truth is if you're going to be a *consumer* of libraries and packages (as opposed to a creator or contributor), you should just download a commercial redistribution and get on with your life—doubly so if you're a Windows user. Later, when you want to contribute to open source, you can install the regular distribution of CPython.

> It is easier to go back to a standard Python installation if you do not alter the default settings in vendor-specific installations.

Here's what these commercial distributions have to offer:

The Intel Distribution for Python
> The purpose of the Intel Distribution for Python (*https://software.intel.com/en-us/python-distribution*) is to deliver high-performance Python in an easy-to-access, free package. The primary boost to performance comes from linking Python packages with native libraries such as the Intel Math Kernel Library (MKL), and enhanced threading capabilities that include the Intel Threading Building Blocks (TBB) library (*http://bit.ly/intel-tbb-for-python*). It relies on Continuum's conda for package management, but also comes with pip. It can be

downloaded by itself or installed from *https://anaconda.org/* in a conda environment (*http://bit.ly/intel-python-beta*).[18]

It provides the SciPy stack and the other common libraries listed in the release notes (PDF) (*http://bit.ly/intel-python-release-notes*). Customers of Intel Parallel Studio XE get commercial support and everyone else can use the forums for help. So, this option gives you the scientific libraries without too much fuss, and otherwise is a regular Python distribution.

Continuum Analytics' Anaconda

Continuum Analytics' distribution (*https://www.continuum.io/downloads*) of Python is released under the BSD license and provides tons of precompiled science and math binaries on its free package index (*https://repo.continuum.io/pkgs/*). It has a different package manager than pip, called conda, that also manages virtual environments, but acts more like Buildout (discussed in "Buildout" on page 40) than like virtualenv—managing libraries and other external dependencies for the user. The package formats are incompatibile, so each installer can't install from the other's package index.

The Anaconda distribution comes with the SciPy stack and other tools. Anaconda has the best license and the most stuff for free; if you're going to use a commercial distribution—especially if you're already comfortable working with the command line already and like R or Scala (also bundled)—choose this. If you don't need all of those other things, use the miniconda distribution (*http://conda.pydata.org/miniconda.html*) instead. Customers get various levels of indemnification (related to open source licenses, and who can use what when, or whom gets sued for what), commercial support, and extra Python libraries.

ActiveState's ActivePython

ActiveState's distribution (*http://www.activestate.com/downloads*) is released under the ActiveState Community License and is free for evaluation only; otherwise it requires a license. ActiveState also provides solutions for Perl and Tcl. The main selling point of this distribution is broad indemnification (again related to open source licenses) for the more than 7,000 packages in its cultivated package index (*https://code.activestate.com/pypm/*), reachable using the ActiveState `pypm` tool, a replacement for `pip`.

Enthought's Canopy

Enthought's distribution (*https://store.enthought.com/downloads/*) is released under the Canopy Software License, with a package manager, `enpkg`, that is used

---

[18] Intel and Anaconda have a partnership (*http://bit.ly/announce-anaconda-intel*), and all of the Intel accelerated packages (*https://anaconda.org/intel*) are only available using conda. However, you can always `conda install` pip and use pip (or `pip install conda` and use conda) when you want to.

in place of `pip` to connect to Canopy's package index (*http://bit.ly/enthought-canopy*).

Enthought provides free academic licenses to students and staff from degree-granting institutions. Distinguishing features from Enthought's distribution are graphical tools to interact with Python, including its own IDE that resembles MATLAB, a graphical package manager, a graphical debugger, and a graphical data manipulation tool. Like the other commercial redistributors, there is indemnification and commercial support, in addition to more packages for customers.

## CHAPTER 3

Your Development Environment

This chapter provides an overview of the text editors, integrated development environments (IDEs), and other development tools currently popular in the Python edit → test → debug cycle.

We unabashedly prefer Sublime Text (discussed in "Sublime Text" on page 25) as an editor and PyCharm/IntelliJ IDEA (discussed in "PyCharm/IntelliJ IDEA" on page 31) as an IDE but recognize that the best option depends on the type of coding you do and the other languages you use. This chapter lists a number of the most popular ones and reasons for choosing them.

Python does not need build tools like Make or Java's Ant or Maven because it is interpreted, not compiled,[1] so we do not discuss them here. But in Chapter 6, we'll describe how to use Setuptools to package projects and Sphinx to build documentation.

We also won't cover version control systems, as these are language-independent, but the people who maintain the C (reference) implementation of Python just moved from Mercurial to Git (see PEP 512 (*https://www.python.org/dev/peps/pep-0512/*)). The original justification to use Mercurial, in PEP 374 (*https://www.python.org/dev/peps/pep-0374/*), contains a small but useful comparison between today's top four options: Subversion, Bazaar, Git, and Mercurial.

This chapter concludes with a brief review of the current ways to manage different interpreters to replicate different deployment situations while coding.

---

[1] If at some point you want to build C extensions for Python, check out "Extending Python with C or C++." (*https://docs.python.org/3/extending/extending.html*) For more details, see Chapter 15 of *Python Cookbook* (*http://bit.ly/python-cookbook*).

Text Editors

Just about anything that can edit plain text will work for writing Python code; however, choosing the right editor can save you hours per week. All of the text editors listed in this section support syntax highlighting and can be extended via plug-ins to use static code checkers (linters) and debuggers.

Table 3-1 lists our favorite text editors in descending order of preference and articulates why a developer would choose one over the other. The rest of the chapter briefly elaborates on each editor. Wikipedia has a very detailed text editor comparison chart (*https://en.wikipedia.org/wiki/Comparison_of_text_editors*) for those who need to check for specific features.

Table 3-1. Text editors at a glance

Tool	Availability	Reason to use
Sublime Text	• Open API/has free trial • OS X, Linux, Windows	• It's fast, with a small footprint. • It handles large (> 2 GB) files well. • Extensions are written in Python.
Vim	• Open source/donations appreciated • OS X, Linux, Windows, Unix	• You already love Vi/Vim. • It (or at least Vi) is preinstalled on every OS except Windows. • It can be a console application.
Emacs	• Open source/donations appreciated • OS X, Linux, Windows, Unix	• You already love Emacs. • Extensions are written in Lisp. • It can be a console application.
TextMate	• Open source/need a license • OS X only	• Great UI. • Nearly all interfaces (static code check/debug/test) come preinstalled. • Good Apple tools—for example, the interface to xcodebuild (via the Xcode bundle).
Atom	• Open source/free • OS X, Linux, Windows	• Extensions are written in JavaScript/HTML/CSS. • Very nice GitHub integration.

Tool	Availability	Reason to use
Code	• Open API (eventually)/free • OS X, Linux, Windows (but Visual Studio, the corresponding IDE, only works on Windows)	• IntelliSense (code completion) worthy of Microsoft's VisualStudio. • Good for Windows devs, with support for .Net, C#, and F#. • Caveat: not yet extensible (to come).

Sublime Text

Sublime Text (*http://www.sublimetext.com/*) is our recommended text editor for code, markup, and prose. Its speed is the first thing cited when people recommend it; the number of packages available (3,000+) is next.

Sublime Text was first released in 2008 by Jon Skinner. Written in Python, it has excellent support for editing Python code and uses Python for its package extension API. A "Projects" feature allows the user to add/remove files or folders—these can then be searched via the "Goto Anything" function, which identifies locations within the project that contain the search term(s).

You need PackageControl (*https://packagecontrol.io/installation*) to access the Sublime Text package repository. Popular packages include SublimeLinter, an interface to the user's selection of installed static code checkers; Emmett for web development snippets;[2] and Sublime SFTP for remote editing via FTP.

Anaconda (*http://damnwidget.github.io/anaconda/*) (no relation to the commercial Python distribution of the same name), released in 2013, by itself turns Sublime almost into an IDE, complete with static code checks, docstring checks, a test runner, and capability to look up the definition of or locate uses of highlighted objects.

Vim

Vim is a console-based text editor (with optional GUI) that uses keyboard shortcuts for editing instead of menus or icons. It was first released in 1991 by Bram Moolenaar, and its predecessor, Vi, was released in 1976 by Bill Joy. Both are written in C.

Vim is extensible via vimscript, a simple scripting language. There are options to use other languages: to enable Python scripting, set the build configuration flags when building from the C source to `--enable-pythoninterp` and/or `--enable-python3interp` before you build from source. To check whether Python or Python3 are enabled, type `:echo has("python")` or `:echo has("python3")`; the result will be "1" if True or "0" if False.

---

2 Snippets are sets of frequently typed code, like CSS styles or class definitions, that can be autocompleted if you type a few charaters and then hit the Tab key.

Vi (and frequently Vim) is available out of the box on pretty much every system but Windows, and there is an executable installer for Vim on Windows (*http:// www.vim.org/download.php#pc*). Users who can tolerate the learning curve will become extremely efficient; so much that the basic Vi key bindings are available as a configuration option in most other editors and IDEs.

 If you want to work for a large company in any sort of IT role, a functioning awareness of Vi is necessary.[3] Vim is much more featureful than Vi, but is close enough that a Vim user can function in Vi.

If you only develop in Python, you can set the default settings for indentation and line wrapping to values compliant with PEP 8 (*https://www.python.org/dev/peps/ pep-0008*). To do that, create a file called *.vimrc* in your home directory,[4] and add the following:

```
set textwidth=79    " lines longer than 79 columns will be broken
set shiftwidth=4    " operation >> indents 4 columns; << unindents 4 columns
set tabstop=4       " a hard TAB displays as 4 columns
set expandtab       " insert spaces when hitting TABs
set softtabstop=4   " insert/delete 4 spaces when hitting a TAB/BACKSPACE
set shiftround      " round indent to multiple of 'shiftwidth'
set autoindent      " align the new line indent with the previous line
```

With these settings, newlines are inserted after 79 characters and indentation is set to four spaces per tab, and if you are inside an indented statement, your next line will also be indented to the same level.

There is also a syntax plug-in called python.vim (*http://bit.ly/python-vim*) that features some improvements over the syntax file included in Vim 6.1, and a small plug-in, SuperTab (*http://bit.ly/supertab-vim*), that makes code completion more convenient by using the Tab key or any other customized keys. If you also use Vim for other languages, there is a handy plug-in called indent (*http://bit.ly/indent-vim*), which handles indentation settings for Python source files.

These plug-ins supply you with a basic environment for developing in Python. If your Vim is compiled with +python (the default for Vim 7 and newer), you can also use the plug-in vim-flake8 (*https://github.com/nvie/vim-flake8*) to do static code checks from within the editor. It provides the function Flake8, which runs PEP8 (*http:// pypi.python.org/pypi/pep8/*) and Pyflakes (*http://pypi.python.org/pypi/pyflakes/*), and

---

3 Just open the editor by typing vi (or vim) then Enter on the command line, and once inside, type :help then Enter for the tutorial.

4 To locate your home directory on Windows, open Vim and type :echo $HOME.

---

can be mapped to any hotkey or action you want in Vim. The plug-in will display errors at the bottom of the screen and provide an easy way to jump to the corresponding line.

If you think it's handy, you can make Vim call `Flake8` every time you save a Python file by adding the following line to your *.vimrc*:

```
autocmd BufWritePost *.py call Flake8()
```

Or, if you are already using syntastic (*https://github.com/scrooloose/syntastic*), you can set it to run Pyflakes on write and show errors and warnings in the quickfix window. Here's an example configuration to do that and also show status and warning messages in the status bar:

```
set statusline+=%#warningmsg#
set statusline+=%{SyntasticStatuslineFlag()}
set statusline+=%*
let g:syntastic_auto_loc_list=1
let g:syntastic_loc_list_height=5
```

Python-mode

Python-mode (*https://github.com/klen/python-mode*) is a complex solution for working with Python code in Vim. If you like any of the features listed here, use it (but be aware it will slow down Vim's launch a little bit):

- Asynchronous Python code checking (`pylint`, `pyflakes`, `pep8`, `mccabe`), in any combination
- Code refactoring and autocompletion with rope (*https://github.com/python-rope/rope*)
- Fast Python folding (you can hide and show code within indents)
- Support for virtualenv
- The ability to search through Python documentation and run Python code
- Auto PEP8 (*http://pypi.python.org/pypi/pep8/*) error fixes

Emacs

Emacs is another powerful text editor. It now has a GUI but can still be run directly in the console. It is fully programmable (Lisp), and with a little work can be wired up as a Python IDE. Masochists and Raymond Hettinger (*http://pyvideo.org/speaker/138/raymond-hettinger*)[5] use it.

---

5 We love Raymond Hettinger. If everyone coded the way he recommends, the world would be a much better place.

Emacs is written in Lisp and was first released in 1976 by Richard Stallman and Guy L. Steele, Jr. Built-in features include remote edit (via FTP), a calendar, mail send/read, and even a shrink (Esc, then x, then doctor). Popular plug-ins include YASnippet to map custom code snippets to keystrokes, and Tramp for debugging. It is extensible via its own dialect of Lisp, elisp plus.

If you are already an Emacs user, EmacsWiki's "Python Programming in Emacs" (*http://emacswiki.org/emacs/PythonProgrammingInEmacs*) has the best advice for Python packages and configuration. Those new to Emacs can get started with the official Emacs tutorial (*http://bit.ly/gnu-emacs-tutorial*).

There are three major Python modes for Emacs right now:

- Fabián Ezequiel Gallina's python.el, now bundled with Emacs (version 24.3+), implements syntax highlighting, indentation, movement, shell interaction, and a number of other common Emacs edit-mode features (*https://github.com/fgallina/python.el#introduction*).

- Jorgen Schäfer's Elpy (*http://elpy.readthedocs.org/*) aims to provide a full-featured interative development environment within Emacs, including debugging, linters, and code completion.

- Python's source distribution (*https://www.python.org/downloads/source/*) ships with an alternate version in the directory *Misc/python-mode.el*. You can download it from the Web as a separate file from launchpad (*https://launchpad.net/python-mode*). It has some tools for programming by speech, additional keystroke shortcuts, and allows you to set up a complete Python IDE (*http://www.emacswiki.org/emacs/ProgrammingWithPythonModeDotEl*).

TextMate

TextMate (*http://macromates.com/*) is a GUI with Emacs roots that works only on OS X. It has a truly Apple-worthy user interface that somehow manages to be unobtrusive while exposing all of the commands with minimal discovery effort.

TextMate is written in C++ and was first released in 2004 by Allan Oddgard and Ciarán Walsh. Sublime Text (discussed in "Sublime Text" on page 25) can directly import TextMate snippets, and Microsoft's Code (discussed in "Code" on page 29) can directly import TextMate syntax highlighting.

Snippets in any language can be added in bundled groups, and it can otherwise be extended with shell scripts: the user can highlight some text and pipe it as standard input through the script using the Cmd+| (pipe) key combination. The script output replaces the highlighted text.

It has built-in syntax highlighting for Apple's Swift and Objective C, and (via the Xcode bundle) an interface to xcodebuild. A veteran TextMate user will not have problems coding in Python using this editor. New users who don't spend much time coding for Apple products are probably better off with the newer cross-platform editors that borrow heavily from TextMate's best-loved features.

Atom

Atom (*https://atom.io/*) is a "hackable text editor for the 21st century," according to the folks at GitHub who created it. It was first released in 2014, is written in CoffeeScript (JavaScript) and Less (CSS), and is built on top of Electron (formerly Atom Shell),[6] which is GitHub's application shell based on io.js and Chromium.

Atom is extensible via JavaScript and CSS, and users can add snippets in any language (including TextMate-style snippet definitions). As you'd expect, it has very nice GitHub integration. It comes with native package control and a plethora of packages (2,000+). Recommended for Python development is Linter (*https://github.com/Atom Linter/Linter*) combined with linter-flake8 (*https://github.com/AtomLinter/linter-flake8*). Web developers may also like the Atom development server (*https://atom.io/packages/atom-development-server*), which runs a small HTTP server and can display the HTML preview within Atom.

Code

Microsoft announced Code in 2015. It is a free, closed source text editor in the Visual Studio family, also built on GitHub's Electron. It is cross-platform and has key bindings just like TextMate.

It comes with an extension API (*https://code.visualstudio.com/Docs/extensions/over view*)—check out the VS Code Extension Marketplace to browse existing extensions (*https://code.visualstudio.com/docs/editor/extension-gallery*)—and merges what its developers thought were the best parts of TextMate and Atom with Microsoft. It has IntelliSense (code completion) worthy of VisualStudio, and good support for .Net, C#, and F#.

Visual Studio (the sister IDE to the Code text editor) still only works on Windows, even though Code is cross-platform.

IDEs

Many developers use both a text editor and an IDE, switching to the IDE for larger, more complex, or more collaborative projects. Table 3-2 highlights the distinguishing

---

6 Electron is a platform to build cross-platform desktop applications using HTML, CSS, and JavaScript.

features of some popular IDEs, and the sections that follow provide more in-depth information on each one.

One feature frequently cited as a reason to go to a full IDE (outside of great code completion and debugging tools) is the ability to quickly switch between Python interpreters (e.g., from Python 2 to Python 3 to IronPython); this is available in the free version of all of the IDEs listed in Table 3-2, Visual Studio now offers this at all levels.[7]

Additional features that may or may not come free are tools that interface with ticketing systems, deployment tools (e.g., Heroku or Google App Engine), collaboration tools, remote debugging, and extra features for using web development frameworks such as Django.

Table 3-2. IDEs at a glance

Tool	Availability	Reason to use
PyCharm/Intellij IDEA	• Open API/paid professional edition • Open source/free community edition • OS X, Linux, Windows	• Nearly perfect code completion. • Good support for virtual environments. • Good support for web frameworks (in the paid version).
Aptana Studio 3 / Eclipse + LiClipse + PyDev	• Open source/free • OS X, Linux, Windows	• You already love Eclipse. • Java support (LiClipse/Eclipse).
WingIDE	• Open API/free trial • OS X, Linux, Windows	• Great debugger (web)—best of the IDEs listed here. • Extensible via Python.
Spyder	• Open source/free • OS X, Linux, Windows	• Data science: IPython integrated, and it is bundled with NumPy, SciPy, and matplotlib. • The default IDE in popular scientific Python distributions: Anaconda, Python(x,y), and WinPython.
NINJA-IDE	• Open source/donations appreciated • OS X, Linux, Windows	• Intentionally lightweight. • Strong Python focus.

---

7 *https://github.com/Microsoft/PTVS/wiki/Features-Matrix*

Tool	Availability	Reason to use
Komodo IDE	• Open API/text editor (Komodo Edit) is open source • OS X, Linux, Windows	• Python, PHP, Perl, Ruby, Node. • Extensions are based on Mozilla add-ons.
Eric (the Eric Python IDE)	• Open source/donations appreciated • OS X, Linux, Windows	• Ruby + Python. • Intentionally lightweight. • Great debugger (scientific)—can debug one thread while others continue.
Visual Studio (Community)	• Open API/free community edition • Paid professional or enterprise edition • Windows only	• Great integration with Microsoft languages and tools. • IntelliSense (code completion) is fantastic. • Project management and deployment assistance, including sprint planning tools and manifest templates in the Enterprise edition. • Caveat: cannot use virtual environments except in the Enterprise (most expensive) edition.

PyCharm/IntelliJ IDEA

PyCharm (*http://www.jetbrains.com/pycharm/*) is our favorite Python IDE. The top reasons are its nearly perfect code completion tools, and the quality of its tools for web development. Those in the scientific community recommend the free edition (which doesn't have the web development tools) as just fine for their needs, but not as often as they choose Spyder (discussed in "Spyder" on page 33).

PyCharm is developed by JetBrains, also known for IntelliJ IDEA, a proprietary Java IDE that competes with Eclipse. PyCharm (first released in 2010) and IntelliJ IDEA (first released in 2001) share the same code base, and most of PyCharm's features can be brought to IntelliJ with the free Python plug-in (*http://bit.ly/intellij-python*).

JetBrains recommends PyCharm for a simpler UI, or IntelliJ IDEA if you want to introspect into Jython functions, perform cross-language navigation, or do Java-to-Python refactoring. (PyCharm works with Jython but only as a possible choice for interpreter; the introspection tools aren't there.) The two are licensed separately—so choose before you buy.

The IntelliJ Community Edition and PyCharm Commuity Edition are open sourced (Apache 2.0 License) and free.

Aptana Studio 3/Eclipse + LiClipse + PyDev

Eclipse is written in Java and was first released in 2001 by IBM as an open, versatile Java IDE. PyDev (*http://pydev.org/*), the Eclipse plug-in for Python development, was released in 2003 by Aleks Totic, who later passed the torch to Fabio Zadrozny. It is the most popular Eclipse plug-in for Python development.

Although the Eclipse community doesn't push back online when people advocate for IntelliJ IDEA in forums comparing the two, Eclipse is still the most commonly used Java IDE. This is relevant for Python developers who interface with tools written in Java, as many popular ones (e.g., Hadoop, Spark, and proprietary versions of these) come with instructions and plug-ins for development with Eclipse.

A fork of PyDev is baked into Aptana's Studio 3 (*http://www.aptana.com/products/studio3.html*), which is an open source suite of plug-ins bundled with Eclipse that provide an IDE for Python (and Django), Ruby (and Rails), HTML, CSS, and PHP. The primary focus of Aptanta's owner, Appcelerator, is the Appcelerator Studio, a proprietary mobile platform for HTML, CSS, and JavaScript that requires a monthly license (once your app goes live). General PyDev and Python support is there, but is not a priority. That said, if you like Eclipse and are primarily a JavaScript developer making apps for mobile platforms with occasional forays into Python, especially if you use Appcelerator at work, Aptana's Studio 3 is a good choice.

LiClipse was born out of a desire to have a better multilanguge experience in Eclipse, and easy access to fully dark themes (i.e., in addition to the text background, menus and borders will also be dark). It is a proprietary suite of Eclipse plug-ins written by Zadrozny; part of the license fees (optional) go to keeping PyDev totally free and open source (EPL License; the same as Eclipse). It comes bundled with PyDev, so Python users don't need to install it themselves.

WingIDE

WingIDE (*http://wingware.com/*) is a Python-specific IDE; probably the second most popular Python IDE after PyCharm. It runs on Linux, Windows, and OS X.

Its debugging tools are very good and include tools to debug Django templates. WingIDE users cite its debugger, the quick learning curve, and a lightweight footprint as reasons they prefer this IDE.

Wing was released in 2000 by Wingware and is written in Python, C, and C++. It supports extensions but does not have a plug-in repository yet, so users have to search for others' blogs or GitHub accounts to find existing packages.

Spyder

Spyder (*https://github.com/spyder-ide/spyder*) (an abbreviation of Scientific PYthon Development EnviRonment) is an IDE specifically geared toward working with scientific Python libraries.

Spyder is written in Python by Carlos Córdoba. It is open source (MIT License), and offers code completion, syntax highlighting, a class and function browser, and object inspection. Other features are available via community plug-ins.

Spyder includes integration with pyflakes (*http://pypi.python.org/pypi/pyflakes/*), pylint (*https://www.pylint.org/*), and rope (*https://github.com/python-rope/rope*), and comes bundled with NumPy, SciPy, IPython, and Matplotlib. It is itself bundled with the popular Scientific Python distributions Anaconda, Python(x, y), and WinPython.

NINJA-IDE

NINJA-IDE (*http://www.ninja-ide.org/*) (from the recursive acronym: "Ninja-IDE Is Not Just Another IDE") is a cross-platform IDE designed to build Python applications. It runs on Linux/X11, Mac OS X, and Windows. Installers for these platforms can be downloaded from NINJA-IDE's website.

NINJA-IDE is developed in Python and Qt, open sourced (GPLv3 License), and is intentionally lightweight. Out of the box, its best-liked feature is that it highlights problem code when running static code checkers or debugging, and the ability to preview web pages in-browser. It is extensible via Python, and has a plug-in repository. The idea is that users will add only the tools they need.

Development slowed for a while, but a new NINJA-IDE v3 is planned for some time in 2016, and there is still active communication on the NINJA-IDE listserv (*http://bit.ly/ninja-ide-listserv*). The community has many native Spanish speakers, including the core development team.

Komodo IDE

Komodo IDE (*http://www.activestate.com/komodo-ide*) is developed by ActiveState and is a commercial IDE for Windows, Mac, and Linux. KomodoEdit (*https://github.com/Komodo/KomodoEdit*), the IDE's text editor, is the open source (Mozilla public license) alternative.

Komodo was first released in 2000 by ActiveState and uses the Mozilla and Scintilla code base. It is extensible via Mozilla add-ons. It suports Python, Perl, Ruby, PHP, Tcl, SQL, Smarty, CSS, HTML, and XML. Komodo Edit does not have a debugger, but one is available as a plug-in. The IDE does not support virtual environments, but does allow the user to select which Python interpreter to use. Django support is not as extensive as in WingIDE, PyCharm, or Eclipse + PyDev.

Eric (the Eric Python IDE)

Eric (*http://eric-ide.python-projects.org/*) is open source (GPLv3 licence) with more than 10 years of active development. It is written in Python and based on the Qt GUI toolkit, integrating the Scintilla editor control. It is named after Eric Idle, a member of the Monty Python troupe, and in homage to the IDLE IDE, bundled with Python distributions.

Its features include source code autocompletion, syntax highlighting, support for version control systems, Python 3 support, an integrated web browser, a Python shell, an integrated debugger, and a flexible plug-in system. It does not have extra tools for web frameworks.

Like NINJA-IDE and Komodo IDE, it is intentionally lightweight. Faithful users believe it has the best debugging tools around, including the ability to stop and debug one thread while others continue to run. If you wish to use Matplotlib for interactive plotting in this IDE, you must use the Qt4 backend:

```
# This must come first:
import matplotlib
matplotlib.use('Qt4Agg')

# And then pyplot will use the Qt4 backend:
import matplotlib.pyplot as plt
```

This link is to the most recent documentation for the Eric IDE (*http://eric-ide.python-projects.org/eric-documentation.html*). Users leaving positive notes on Eric IDE's web page are almost all from the scientific computation (e.g., weather models, or computational fluid dynamics) community.

Visual Studio

Professional programmers who work with Microsoft products on Windows will want Visual Studio (*https://www.visualstudio.com/products*). It is written in C++ and C#, and its first version appeared in 1995. In late 2014, the first Visual Studio Community Edition was made available for free for noncommercial developers.

If you intend to work with primarily with enterprise software and use Microsoft products like C# and F#, this is your IDE.

Be sure to install with the Python Tools for Visual Studio (PTVS) (*https://www.visualstudio.com/en-us/features/python-vs.aspx*), which is a checkbox in the list of custom installation options that is by default unchecked. The instructions for installing with Visual Studio or after installing Visual Studio are on the PTVS wiki page (*https://github.com/Microsoft/PTVS/wiki/PTVS-Installation*).

Enhanced Interactive Tools

The tools listed here enhance the interactive shell experience. IDLE is actually an IDE, but not included in the preceding section because most people do not consider it robust enough to use in the same way (for enterprise projects) as the other IDEs listed; however, it is fantastic for teaching. IPython is incorporated into Spyder by default, and can be incorporated into others of the IDEs. They do not replace the Python interpreter, but rather augment the user's chosen interpreter shell with additional tools and features.

IDLE

IDLE (*http://docs.python.org/library/idle.html#idle*), which stands for Integrated Development and Learning Environment (and is also the last name of Monty Python member Eric Idle), is part of the Python standard library; it is distributed with Python.

IDLE is completely written in Python by Guido van Rossum (Python's BDFL—Benevolent Dictator for Life) and uses the Tkinter GUI toolkit. Though IDLE is not suited for full-blown development using Python, it is quite helpful to try out small Python snippets and experiment with different features in Python.

It provides the following features:

- A Python shell window (interpreter)
- A multiwindow text editor that colorizes Python code
- Minimal debugging capability

IPython

IPython (*http://ipython.org/*) provides a rich toolkit to help you make the most out of using Python interactively. Its main components are:

- Powerful Python shells (terminal- and Qt-based)
- A web-based notebook with the same core features as the terminal shell, plus support for rich media, text, code, mathematical expressions, and inline plots
- Support for interactive data visualization (i.e., when configured, your Matplotlib plots pop up in windows) and use of GUI toolkits
- Flexible, embeddable interpreters to load into your own projects
- Tools for high-level and interactive parallel computing

To install IPython, type the following in a terminal shell or in PowerShell:

```
$ pip install ipython
```

bpython

bpython (*http://bpython-interpreter.org/*) is an alternative interface to the Python interpreter for Unix-like operating systems. It has the following features:

- Inline syntax highlighting
- Auto indentation and autocompletion
- Expected parameter list for any Python function
- A "rewind" function to pop the last line of code from memory and re-evaluate it
- The ability to send entered code to a pastebin (to share code online)
- The ability to save entered code to a file

To install bpython, type the following in a terminal shell:

```
$ pip install bpython
```

Isolation Tools

This section provides more details about the most widely used isolation tools, from virtualenv, which isolates Python environments from each other, to Docker, which virtualizes the entire system.

These tools provide various levels of isolation between the running application and its host environment. They make it possible to test and debug code against different versions of Python and library dependencies, and can be used to provide a consistent deployment environment.

Virtual Environments

A Python virtual environment keeps dependencies required by different projects in separate places. By installing multiple Python environments, your global *site-packages* directory (where user-installed Python packages are stored) can stay clean and manageable, and you can simultaneously work on a project that, for example, requires Django 1.3 while also maintaining a project that requires Django 1.0.

The virtualenv command does this by creating a separate folder that contains a softlink to the Python executable, a copy of pip, and a place for Python libraries. It prepends that location to the PATH upon activation, and then returns the PATH to its original state when deactivated. It is also possible to use the system-installed version of Python and system-installed libraries, via command-line options.

You can't move a virtual environment once it's created—the paths in the executables are all hardcoded to the current absolute path to the interpreter in the virtual environment's *bin/* directory.

Create and activate the virtual environment

Setup and activation of Python virtual environments is slightly different on different operating systems.

On Mac OS X and Linux.   You can specify the version of Python with the `--python` argument. Then, use the `activate` script to set the `PATH`, entering the virtual environment:

```
$ cd my-project-folder
$ virtualenv --python python3 my-venv
$ source my-venv/bin/activate
```

On Windows.   If you haven't already, you should set the system execution policies to allow a locally created script to run.[8] To do this, open PowerShell as an administrator, and type:

```
PS C:\> Set-ExecutionPolicy RemoteSigned
```

Reply Y to the question that appears, `exit`, and then, in a regular PowerShell, you can create a virtual environment like so:

```
PS C:\> cd my-project-folder
PS C:\> virtualenv --python python3 my-venv
PS C:\> .\my-venv\Scripts\activate
```

Add libraries to the virtual environment

Once you have activated the virtual environment, the first `pip` executable in your path will be the one located in the *my-venv* folder you just made, and it will install libraries into the following directory:

- *my-venv/lib/python3.4/site-packages/* (on POSIX[9] systems)
- *my-venv\Lib\site-packages* (on Windows)

When bundling your own packages or projects for other people, you can use:

---

8 Or if you prefer, use `Set-ExecutionPolicy AllSigned` instead.

9 POSIX stands for Portable Operating System Interface. It comprises a set of IEEE standards for how an operating system should behave: the behavior of and interface to basic shell commands, I/O, threading, and other services and utilities. Most Linux and Unix distributions are considered POSIX compatible, and Darwin (the operating system underneath Mac OS X and iOS) has been compatible since Leopard (10.5). A "POSIX system" is a system that is considered POSIX compatible.

```
$ pip freeze > requirements.txt
```

while the virtual environment is active. This writes all of the currently installed packages (which are hopefully also project dependencies) to the file *requirements.txt*. Collaborators can install all of the dependencies in their own virtual environment when given a *requirements.txt* file by typing:

```
$ pip install -r requirements.txt
```

pip will install the listed dependencies, overriding dependency specifications in subpackages if conflicts exist. Dependencies specified in *requirements.txt* are intended to set the entire Python environment. To set dependencies when distributing a library, it is better to use the install_requires keyword argument to the setup() function in a *setup.py* file.

 Be careful to not use pip install -r requirements.txt outside of a virtual environment. If you do, and anything in *requirements.txt* is a different version than the one installed on your computer, pip will overwrite the other version of the library with the one specified in *requirements.txt*.

Deactivate the virtual environment

To return to normal system settings, type:

```
$ deactivate
```

For more information, see the Virtual Environments docs (*http://bit.ly/virtualenv-guide*), the official virtualenv docs (*https://virtualenv.pypa.io/en/latest/userguide.html*), or the official Python packaging guide (*https://packaging.python.org*). The package pyvenv, which is distributed as part of the Python standard library in Python versions 3.3 and above, does not replace virtualenv (in fact, it is a dependency of virtualenv), so these instructions work for all versions of Python.

pyenv

pyenv (*https://github.com/yyuu/pyenv*) is a tool that allows multiple versions of the Python interpreter to be used at the same time. This solves the problem of having different projects that each require different versions of Python, but you would still need to use virtual environments if the dependency conflict was in the libraries (e.g., requiring different Django versions). For example, you can install Python 2.7 for compatibility in one project, and still use Python 3.5 as the default interpreter. pyenv isn't just limited to the CPython versions—it will also install PyPy, Anaconda, Miniconda, Stackless, Jython, and IronPython interpreters.

Pyenv works by filling a *shims* directory with a shim version of the Python interpreter and executables like pip and 2to3. These will be the executables found if the directory is prepended to the $PATH environment variable. A *shim* is a pass-through function that interprets the current situation and selects the most appropriate function to perform the desired task. For example, when the system looks for a program named python, it looks inside the *shims* directory first, and uses the shim version, which in turn passes the command on to pyenv. Pyenv then works out which version of Python should be run based on environment variables, *.python-version* files, and the global default.

For virtual environments, there is the plug-in pyenv-virtualenv (*https://github.com/yyuu/pyenv-virtualenv*), which automates the creation of different environments, and also makes it possible to use the existing pyenv tools to switch to different environments.

Autoenv

Autoenv (*https://github.com/kennethreitz/autoenv*) provides a lightweight option to manage different environment settings outside of the scope of virtualenv. It overrides the cd shell command so that when you change into a directory containing a *.env* file (e.g., setting the PATH and an environment variable with a database URL), Autoenv automagically activates the environment, and when you cd out of it, the effect is undone. It does not work in Windows PowerShell.

Install it on Mac OS X using brew:

```
$ brew install autoenv
```

or on Linux:

```
$ git clone git://github.com/kennethreitz/autoenv.git ~/.autoenv
$ echo 'source ~/.autoenv/activate.sh' >> ~/.bashrc
```

and then open a new terminal shell.

virtualenvwrapper

virtualenvwrapper (*http://bit.ly/virtualenvwrapper-docs*) provides a set of commands that extend Python virtual environments for more control and better manageability. It places all your virtual environments in one directory and provides empty hook functions that can be run before or after creation/activation of the virtual environment or of a project—for example, the hook could set environment variables by sourcing the *.env* file within a directory.

The problem with placing such functions with the installed items is that the user must somehow acquire these scripts to completely duplicate the environment on another machine. It could be useful on a shared development server, if all of the environments were placed in a shared folder and used by multiple users.

To skip the full virtualenvwrapper installation instructions (*http://bit.ly/virtualenvwrapper-install*), first make sure virtualenv is already installed. Then, on OS X or Linux, type the following in a command terminal:

```
$ pip install virtualenvwrapper
```

Or use `pip install virtualenvwrapper` if you are using Python 2, and add this to your *~/.profile*:

```
export VIRTUALENVWRAPPER_PYTHON=/usr/local/bin/python3
```

and then add the following to you *~/.bash_profile* or favorite other shell profile:

```
source /usr/local/bin/virtualenvwrapper.sh
```

Finally, close the current terminal window, and open a new one to activate your new profile, and virtualenvwrapper will be available.

On Windows, use virtualenvwrapper-win (*http://bit.ly/virtualenvwrapper-win*) instead. With `virtualenv` already installed, type:

```
PS C:\> pip install virtualenvwrapper-win
```

Then, on both platforms, the following commands are the most commonly used:

mkvirtualenv *my_venv*
:   Creates the virtual environment in the folder *~/.virtualenvs/my_venv*. Or on Windows, *my_venv* will be created in the directory identified by typing %USERPRO FILE%\Envs on the command line. The location is customizable via the environment variable $WORKON_HOME.

workon *my_venv*
:   Activates the virtual environment or switches from the current environment to the specified one.

deactivate
:   Deactivates the virtual environment.

rmvirtualenv *my_venv*
:   Deletes the virtual environment.

virtualenvwrapper provides tab-completion on environment names, which really helps when you have a lot of environments and have trouble remembering their names. A number of other convenient functions are documented in the full list of virtualenvwrapper commands (*http://bit.ly/virtualenvwrapper-command*).

Buildout

Buildout (*http://www.buildout.org/en/latest/*) is a Python framework that allows you to create and compose *recipes*—Python modules containing arbitrary code (usually system calls to make directories or to check out and build source code, and to add non-Python parts to the project, such as a database or a web server). Install it using pip:

```
$ pip install zc.buildout
```

Projects that use Buildout would include zc.buildout and the recipes they need in their *requirements.txt*, or would directly include custom recipes with the source code. They also include the configuration file *buildout.cfg*, and the *bootstrap.py* script in its top directory. If you run the script by typing python bootstrap.py, it will read the configuration file to determine which recipes to use, plus each recipe's configuration options (e.g., the specific compiler flags and library linking flags).

Buildout gives a Python project with non-Python parts portability—another user can reconstruct the same environment. This is different from the script hooks in Virtualenvwrapper, which would need to be copied and transmitted along with the *requirements.txt* file to be able to re-create a virtual environment.

It includes parts to install eggs,[10] which can be skipped in the newer versions of Python that use wheels instead. See the Buildout tutorial (*http://www.buildout.org/en/latest/docs/tutorial.html*) for more information.

Conda

Conda (*http://conda.pydata.org/docs/*) is like pip, virtualenv, and Buildout together. It comes with the Anaconda distribution of Python and is Anaconda's default package manager. It can be installed via pip:

```
$ pip install conda
```

And pip can be installed via conda:

```
$ conda install pip
```

The packages are stored on different repositories (pip pulls from *http://pypi.python.org*, and conda pulls from https://repo.continuum.io/), and they use different formats, so the tools are not interchangeable.

---

10 An *egg* is a ZIP file with a specific structure, containing distribution content. Eggs have been replaced by wheels as of PEP 427 (*https://www.python.org/dev/peps/pep-0427/*). They were introduced by the very popular (and now de facto) packaging library, Setuptools, which provides a useful interface to the Python Standard Library's distutils (*https://docs.python.org/3/library/distutils.html*). You can read all about the differences between the formats in "Wheel vs Egg" (*https://packaging.python.org/en/latest/wheel_egg/*) in the Python Packaging User Guide.

This table (*http://bit.ly/conda-pip-virtualenvl*) created by Continuum (the creators of Anaconda) provides a side-by-side comparison of all three options: conda, pip, and virtualenv.

conda-build, Continuum's analogue to Buildout, can be installed on all platforms by typing:

```
conda install conda-build
```

Like with Buildout, the conda-build configuration file format is called a "recipe," and the recipes are not limited to using Python tools. Unlike Buildout, the code is specified in shell script, not Python, and the configuration is specified in YAML,[11] not Python's ConfigParser format (*https://docs.python.org/3/library/configparser.html*).

The main advantage of conda over pip and virtualenv is for Windows users—Python libraries built as C extensions may or may not be present as wheels, but they are almost always present on the Anaconda package index (*http://docs.continuum.io/anaconda/pkg-docs*). And if a package is not available via conda, it is possible to install pip and then install packages hosted on PyPI (*https://pypi.python.org/pypi*).

Docker

Docker (*https://www.docker.com/*) helps with environment isolation like virtualenv, conda, or Buildout, but instead of providing a virtual environment, it provides a *Docker container*. Containers provide greater isolation than environments. For example, you can have containers running, each with different network interfaces, firewalling rules, and a different hostname. These running containers are managed by a separate utility, the Docker Engine (*https://docs.docker.com/engine/*), that coordinates access to the underlying operating system. If you're running Docker containers on OS X, Windows, or on a remote host, you'll also need Docker Machine (*https://docs.docker.com/machine/*), which interfaces with the virtual machine(s)[12] that will run the Docker Engine.

Docker containers were originally based on Linux Containers, which were themselves originally related to the shell command chroot (*https://en.wikipedia.org/wiki/Chroot*). chroot is kind of a system-level version of the virtualenv command: it makes it appear that the root directory (/) is at a user-specified path instead of the actual root, providing a completely separate user space (*https://en.wikipedia.org/wiki/User-space*).

---

11 YAML (*https://en.wikipedia.org/wiki/YAML*) YAML Ain't Markup Language, is a markup language intended to be both human-readable and machine-readable.

12 A *virtual machine* is an application that emulates a computer system by imitating the desired hardware and providing the desired operating system on a host computer.

Docker doesn't use chroot, and it doesn't even use Linux Containers anymore (allowing the universe of Docker images to include Citrix and Solaris machines), but the Docker Containers are still doing about the same thing. Its configuration files are called Dockerfiles (*https://docs.docker.com/engine/reference/builder/*), which build Docker images (*https://docs.docker.com/engine/userguide/containers/dockerimages/*) that can then be hosted on the Docker Hub (*https://docs.docker.com/docker-hub/*), the Docker package repository (like PyPI).

Docker images, when configured correctly, can take up less space than environments created using Buildout or conda because Docker users the AUFS (*https://docs.docker.com/engine/userguide/storagedriver/aufs-driver/*) union file system, which stores the "diff" of an image, instead of the whole image. So, for example, if you want to build and test your package against multiple releases of a dependency, you could make a base Docker image that contains a virtual environment[13] (or Buildout environment, or conda environment) containing all of the other dependencies. You'd then inherit from that base for all of your other images, adding only the single changing dependency in the last layer. Then, all of the derived containers will contain only the different new library, sharing the contents of the base image. For more information, see the Docker documentation (*https://docs.docker.com/*).

---

13 A virtual environment inside of a Docker container will isolate your Python environment, preserving the OS's Python for the utilities that may be needed to support your application—in keeping with our advice to not install anything via pip (or anything else) in your system Python directory.

## PART II

Getting Down to Business

We've got our towels, a Python interpreter, virtual environments, and an editor or IDE—we're ready to get down to business. This part does not teach you the language; "Learning Python" on page 303 lists great resources that already do that. Instead, we want you to come out of this part feeling froody, like a real Python insider, knowing the tricks of some of the best Pythonistas in our community. This part includes the following chapters:

Chapter 4, Writing Great Code
   We briefly cover style, conventions, idioms, and gotchas that can help new Pythonistas.

Chapter 5, Reading Great Code
   We take you on a guided tour of parts of our favorite Python libraries, with the hope that you'll be encouraged to do more reading on your own.

Chapter 6, Shipping Great Code
   We briefly talk about the Python Packaging Authority and how to load libraries to PyPI, plus options to build and ship executables.

## CHAPTER 4

Writing Great Code

This chapter focuses on best practices for writing great Python code. We will review coding style conventions that will be used in Chapter 5, and briefly cover logging best practices, plus list a few of the major differences between available open source licenses. All of this is intended to help you write code that is easy for us, your community, to use and extend.

Code Style

Pythonistas (veteran Python developers) celebrate having a language so accessible that people who have never programmed can still understand what a Python program does when they read its source code. Readability is at the heart of Python's design, following the recognition that code is *read* much more often than it is written.

One reason Python code can be easily understood is its relatively complete set of code style guidelines (collected in the two Python Enhancement Proposals PEP 20 and PEP 8, described in the next few pages) and "Pythonic" idioms. When a Pythonista points to portions of code and says they are not "Pythonic," it usually means that those lines of code do not follow the common guidelines and fail to express the intent in what is considered the most readable way. Of course, "a foolish consistency is the hobgoblin of little minds."[1] Pedantic devotion to the letter of the PEP can undermine readability and understandability.

---

1 Originally stated by Ralph Waldo Emerson in *Self-Reliance*, it is quoted in PEP 8 to affirm that the coder's best judgment should supercede the style guide. For example, conformity with surrounding code and existing convention is more important than consistency with PEP 8.

PEP 8

PEP 8 (*https://www.python.org/dev/peps/pep-0008/*) is the de facto code style guide for Python. It covers naming conventions, code layout, whitespace (tabs versus spaces), and other similar style topics.

This is highly recommended reading. The entire Python community does its best to adhere to the guidelines laid out within this document. Some projects may stray from it from time to time, while others (like Requests (*http://bit.ly/reitz-code-style*)) may amend its recommendations.

Conforming your Python code to PEP 8 is generally a good idea and helps make code more consistent when working on projects with other developers. The PEP 8 guidelines are explicit enough that they can be programmatically checked. There is a command-line program, pep8 (*https://github.com/jcrocholl/pep8*), that can check your code for conformity. Install it by running the following command in your terminal:

```
$ pip3 install pep8
```

Here's an example of the kinds of things you might see when you run pep8:

```
$ pep8 optparse.py

optparse.py:69:11: E401 multiple imports on one line
optparse.py:77:1: E302 expected 2 blank lines, found 1
optparse.py:88:5: E301 expected 1 blank line, found 0
optparse.py:222:34: W602 deprecated form of raising exception
optparse.py:347:31: E211 whitespace before '('
optparse.py:357:17: E201 whitespace after '{'
optparse.py:472:29: E221 multiple spaces before operator
optparse.py:544:21: W601 .has_key() is deprecated, use 'in'
```

The fixes to most of the complaints are straightforward and stated directly in PEP 8. The code style guide for Requests (*http://bit.ly/reitz-code-style*) gives examples of good and bad code and is only slightly modified from the original PEP 8.

The linters referenced in "Text Editors" on page 24 usually use pep8, so you can also install one of these to run checks within your editor or IDE. Or, the program auto pep8 can be used to automatically reformat code in the PEP 8 style. Install the program with:

```
$ pip3 install autopep8
```

Use it to format a file in-place (overwriting the original) with:

```
$ autopep8 --in-place optparse.py
```

Excluding the --in-place flag will cause the program to output the modified code directly to the console for review (or piping to another file). The --aggressive flag will perform more substantial changes and can be applied multiple times for greater effect.

PEP 20 (a.k.a. The Zen of Python)

PEP 20 (*https://www.python.org/dev/peps/pep-0020/*), the set of guiding principles for decision making in Python, is always available via `import this` in a Python shell. Despite its name, PEP 20 only contains 19 aphorisms, not 20 (the last has not been written down…).

The true history of the Zen of Python is immortalized in Barry Warsaw's blog post "import this and the Zen of Python." (*http://bit.ly/import-this-zen-python*)

The Zen of Python by Tim Peters[2]

Beautiful is better than ugly.
Explicit is better than implicit.
Simple is better than complex.
Complex is better than complicated.
Flat is better than nested.
Sparse is better than dense.
Readability counts.
Special cases aren't special enough to break the rules.
Although practicality beats purity.
Errors should never pass silently.
Unless explicitly silenced.
In the face of ambiguity, refuse the temptation to guess.
There should be one—and preferably only one—obvious way to do it.
Although that way may not be obvious at first unless you're Dutch.
Now is better than never.
Although never is often better than *right* now.
If the implementation is hard to explain, it's a bad idea.
If the implementation is easy to explain, it may be a good idea.
Namespaces are one honking great idea—let's do more of those!

For an example of each Zen aphorism in action, see Hunter Blanks' presentation "PEP 20 (The Zen of Python) by Example." (*http://artifex.org/~hblanks/talks/2011/ pep20_by_example.pdf*) Raymond Hettinger also put these principles to fantastic use in his talk "Beyond PEP 8: Best Practices for Beautiful, Intelligible Code." (*http:// bit.ly/beyond-pep-8*)

---

2 Tim Peters is a longtime Python user who eventually became one of its most prolific and tenacious core developers (creating Python's sorting algorithm, Timsort (*https://en.wikipedia.org/wiki/Timsort*)), and a frequent Net presence. He at one point was rumored to be a long-running Python port of the Richard Stallman AI program stallman.el. The original conspiracy theory (*https://www.python.org/doc/humor/#the-other-origin-of-the-great-timbot-conspiracy-theory*) appeared on a listserv in the late 1990s.

General Advice

This section contains style concepts that are hopefully easy to accept without debate, and often applicable to languages other than Python. Some of them are direct from the Zen of Python, but others are just plain common sense. They reaffirm our preference in Python to select the most obvious way to present code, when multiple options are possible.

Explicit is better than implicit

While any kind of black magic is possible with Python, the simplest, most explicit way to express something is preferred:

Bad	Good

`def make_dict(*args):`
`    x, y = args`
`    return dict(**locals())`
	`def make_dict(x, y):`
	`    return {'x': x, 'y': y}`

In the good code, x and y are explicitly received from the caller, and an explicit dictionary is returned. A good rule of thumb is that another developer should be able to read the first and last lines of your function and understand what it does. That's not the case with the bad example. (Of course, it's also pretty easy when the function is only two lines long.)

Sparse is better than dense

Make only one statement per line. Some compound statements, such as list comprehensions, are allowed and appreciated for their brevity and their expressiveness, but it is good practice to keep disjoint statements on separate lines of code. It also makes for more understandable diffs[3] when revisions to one statement are made:

Bad	Good
`print('one'); print('two')`	`print('one')` `print('two')`
`if x == 1: print('one')`	`if x == 1:` `    print('one')`

`if (<complex comparison> and`
`    <other complex comparison>):`
`    # do something`
	`cond1 = <complex comparison>`
	`cond2 = <other complex comparison>`
	`if cond1 and cond2:`
	`    # do something`

---

3 *diff* is a shell utility that identifies and shows lines that differ between two files.

Gains in readability, to Pythonistas, are more valuable than a few bytes of total code (for the two-prints-on-one-line statement) or a few microseconds of computation time (for the extra-conditionals-on-separate-lines statement). Plus, when a group is contributing to open source, the "good" code's revision history will be easier to decipher because a change on one line can only affect one thing.

Errors should never pass silently / Unless explicitly silenced

Error handling in Python is done using the try statement. An example from Ben Gleitzman's HowDoI package (described more in "HowDoI" on page 99) shows when silencing an error is OK:

```
def format_output(code, args):
    if not args['color']:
        return code
    lexer = None

    # try to find a lexer using the Stack Overflow tags
    # or the query arguments
    for keyword in args['query'].split() + args['tags']:
        try:
            lexer = get_lexer_by_name(keyword)
            break
        except ClassNotFound:
            pass

    # no lexer found above, use the guesser
    if not lexer:
        lexer = guess_lexer(code)

    return highlight(code,
                     lexer,
                     TerminalFormatter(bg='dark'))
```

This is part of a package that provides a command-line script to query the Internet (Stack Overflow, by default) for how to do a particular coding task, and prints it to the screen. The function format_output() applies syntax highlighting by first searching through the question's tags for a string understood by the lexer (also called a *tokenizer*; a "python", "java", or "bash" tag will identify which lexer to use to split and colorize the code), and then if that fails, to try inferring the language from the code itself. There are three paths the program can follow when it reaches the try statement:

- Execution enters the try clause (everything between the try and the except), a lexer is successfully found, the loop breaks, and the function returns the code highlighted with the selected lexer.

- The lexer is not found, the ClassNotFound exception is thrown, it's caught, and nothing is done. The loop continues until it finishes naturally or a lexer is found.

- Some other exception occurs (like a `KeyboardInterrupt`) that is not handled, and it is raised up to the top level, stopping execution.

The "should never pass silently" part of the zen aphorism discourages the use of over-zealous error trapping. Here's an example you can try *in a separate terminal* so that you can kill it more easily once you get the point:

```
>>> while True:
...     try:
...         print("nyah", end=" ")
...     except:
...         pass
```

Or don't try it. The `except` clause without any specified exception will catch every-thing, including `KeyboardInterrupt` (Ctrl+C in a POSIX terminal), and ignore it; so it swallows the dozens of interrupts you try to give it to shut the thing down. It's not just the interrupt issue—a broad `except` clause can also hide bugs, leaving them to cause some problem later on, when it will be harder to diagnose. We repeat, *don't let errors pass silently*: always explicitly identify by name the exceptions you will catch, and handle only those exceptions. If you simply want to log or otherwise acknowl-edge the exception and re-raise it, like in the following snippet, that's OK. Just don't let the error pass silently (without handling or re-raising it):

```
>>> while True:
...     try:
...         print("ni", end="-")
...     except:
...         print("An exception happened. Raising.")
...         raise
```

Function arguments should be intuitive to use

Your choices in API design will determine the downstream developer's experience when interacting with a function. Arguments can be passed to functions in four dif-ferent ways:

```
         ❶          ❷          ❸        ❹
def func(positional, keyword=value, *args, **kwargs):
    pass
```

❶ *Positional arguments* are mandatory and have no default values.

❷ *Keyword arguments* are optional and have default values.

❸ An *arbitrary argument list* is optional and has no default values.

❹ An *arbitrary keyword argument dictionary* is optional and has no default values.

Here are tips for when to use each method of argument passing:

Positional arguments

Use these when there are only a few function arguments, which are fully part of the function's meaning, with a natural order. For instance, in send(message, recipient) or point(x, y) the user of the function has no difficulty remembering that those two functions require two arguments, and in which order.

Usage antipattern: It is possible to use argument names, and switch the order of arguments when calling functions—for example, calling send(recipi ent="World", message="The answer is 42.") and point(y=2, x=1). This reduces readability and is unnecessarily verbose. Use the more straightforward calls to send("The answer is 42", "World") and point(1, 2).

Keyword arguments

When a function has more than two or three positional parameters, its signature is more difficult to remember, and using keyword arguments with default values is helpful. For instance, a more complete send function could have the signature send(message, to, cc=None, bcc=None). Here cc and bcc are optional and evaluate to None when they are not passed another value.

Usage antipattern: It is possible to follow the order of arguments in the definition without explicitly naming the arguments, like in send("42", "Frankie", "Benjy", "Trillian"), sending a blind carbon copy to Trillian. It is also possible to name arguments in another order, like in send("42", "Frankie", bcc="Trillian", cc="Benjy"). Unless there's a strong reason not to, it's better to use the form that is the closest to the function definition: send("42", "Frankie", cc="Benjy", bcc="Trillian").

Never is often better than right now

It is often harder to remove an optional argument (and its logic inside the function) that was added "just in case" and is seemingly never used, than to add a new optional argument and its logic when needed.

Arbitrary argument list

Defined with the *args construct, it denotes an extensible number of positional arguments. In the function body, args will be a tuple of all the remaining positional arguments. For example, send(message, *args) can also be called with each recipient as an argument: send("42", "Frankie", "Benjy", "Tril lian"); and in the function body, args will be equal to ("Frankie", "Benjy", "Trillian"). A good example of when this works is the print function.

Caveat: If a function receives a list of arguments of the same nature, it's often more clear to use a list or any sequence. Here, if send has multiple recipients, we can define it explicitly: send(message, recipients) and call it with send("42", ["Benjy", "Frankie", "Trillian"]).

Arbitrary keyword argument dictionary

Defined via the **kwargs construct, it passes an undetermined series of named arguments to the function. In the function body, kwargs will be a dictionary of all the passed named arguments that have not been caught by other keyword arguments in the function signature. An example of when this is useful is in logging; formatters at different levels can seamlessly take what information they need without inconveniencing the user.

Caveat: The same caution as in the case of *args is necessary, for similar reasons: these powerful techniques are to be used when there is a proven necessity to use them, and they should not be used if the simpler and clearer construct is sufficient to express the function's intention.

> The variable names *args and **kwargs can (and should) be replaced with other names, when other names make more sense.

It is up to the programmer writing the function to determine which arguments are positional arguments and which are optional keyword arguments, and to decide whether to use the advanced techniques of arbitrary argument passing. After all, there should be one—and preferably only one—obvious way to do it. Other users will appreciate your effort when your Python functions are:

- Easy to read (meaning the name and arguments need no explanation)
- Easy to change (meaning adding a new keyword argument won't break other parts of the code)

If the implementation is hard to explain, it's a bad idea

A powerful tool for hackers, Python comes with a very rich set of hooks and tools allowing you to do almost any kind of tricky tricks. For instance, it is possible to:

- Change how objects are created and instantiated
- Change how the Python interpreter imports modules
- Embed C routines in Python

All these options have drawbacks, and it is always better to use the most straightforward way to achieve your goal. The main drawback is that readability suffers when using these constructs, so whatever you gain must be more important than the loss of readability. Many code analysis tools, such as pylint or pyflakes, will be unable to parse this "magic" code.

A Python developer should know about these nearly infinite possibilities, because it instills confidence that no impassable problem will be on the way. However, knowing how and particularly when *not* to use them is very important.

Like a kung fu master, a Pythonista knows how to kill with a single finger, and never to actually do it.

We are all responsible users

As already demonstrated, Python allows many tricks, and some of them are potentially dangerous. A good example is that any client code can override an object's properties and methods: there is no "private" keyword in Python. This philosophy is very different from highly defensive languages like Java, which provide a lot of mechanisms to prevent any misuse, and is expressed by the saying: "We are all responsible users."

This doesn't mean that, for example, no properties are considered private, and that proper encapsulation is impossible in Python. Rather, instead of relying on concrete walls erected by the developers between their code and others' code, the Python community prefers to rely on a set of conventions indicating that these elements should not be accessed directly.

The main convention for private properties and implementation details is to prefix all "internals" with an underscore (e.g., `sys._getframe`). If the client code breaks this rule and accesses these marked elements, any misbehavior or problems encountered if the code is modified are the responsibility of the client code.

Using this convention generously is encouraged: any method or property that is not intended to be used by client code should be prefixed with an underscore. This will guarantee a better separation of duties and easier modification of existing code; it will always be possible to publicize a private property, but making a public property private might be a much harder operation.

Return values from one place

When a function grows in complexity, it is not uncommon to use multiple return statements inside the function's body. However, to keep a clear intent and sustain readability, it is best to return meaningful values from as few points in the body as possible.

The two ways to exit from a function are upon error, or with a return value after the function has been processed normally. In cases when the function cannot perform correctly, it can be appropriate to return a `None` or `False` value. In this case, it is better to return from the function as early as the incorrect context has been detected, to flatten the structure of the function: all the code after the return-because-of-failure statement can assume the condition is met to further compute the function's main result. Having multiple such return statements is often necessary.

Still, when possible, keep a single exit point—it's difficult to debug functions when you first have to identify which return statement is responsible for your result. Forcing the function to exit in just one place also helps to factor out some code paths, as the multiple exit points probably are a hint that such a refactoring is needed. This example is not bad code, but it could possibly be made more clear, as indicated in the comments:

```python
def select_ad(third_party_ads, user_preferences):
    if not third_party_ads:
        return None  # Raising an exception might be better
    if not user_preferences:
        return None  # Raising an exception might be better
    # Some complex code to pick the best_ad given the
    # available ads and the individual's preferences...
    # Resist the temptation to return best_ad if succeeded...
    if not best_ad:
        # Some Plan-B computation of best_ad
    return best_ad  # A single exit point for the returned value
                    # will help when maintaining the code
```

Conventions

Conventions make sense to everyone, but may not be the only way to do things. The conventions we show here are the more commonly used choices, and we recommend them as the more readable option.

Alternatives to checking for equality

When you don't need to explicitly compare a value to True, or None, or 0, you can just add it to the if statement, like in the following examples. (See "Truth Value Testing" (*http://docs.python.org/library/stdtypes.html#truth-value-testing*) for a list of what is considered false).

Bad	Good
```if attr == True: print 'True!'```	```# Just check the value if attr: print 'attr is truthy!' # or check for the opposite if not attr: print 'attr is falsey!' # but if you only want 'True' if attr is True: print 'attr is True'```
```if attr == None: print 'attr is None!'```	```# or explicitly check for None if attr is None: print 'attr is None!'```

Accessing dictionary elements

Use the `x in d` syntax instead of the `dict.has_key` method, or pass a default argument to `dict.get()`:

Bad	Good
```>>> d = {'hello': 'world'} >>> >>> if d.has_key('hello'): ... print(d['hello']) # prints 'world' ... else: ... print('default_value') ... world```	```>>> d = {'hello': 'world'} >>> >>> print d.get('hello', 'default_value') world >>> print d.get('howdy', 'default_value') default_value >>> >>> # Or: ... if 'hello' in d: ... print(d['hello']) ... world```

Manipulating lists

List comprehensions provide a powerful, concise way to work with lists (for more information, see the entry in The Python Tutorial (*http://docs.python.org/tutorial/ datastructures.html#list-comprehensions*)). Also, the `map()` and `filter()` functions can perform operations on lists using a different, more concise syntax:

Standard loop	List comprehension
```# Filter elements greater than 4 a = [3, 4, 5] b = [] for i in a: if i > 4: b.append(i)```	```# The list comprehension is clearer a = [3, 4, 5] b = [i for i in a if i > 4] # Or: b = filter(lambda x: x > 4, a)```

Standard loop	List comprehension
```# Add three to all list members.```	```# Also clearer in this case```

```
# Add three to all list members.    # Also clearer in this case
a = [3, 4, 5]                        a = [3, 4, 5]
for i in range(len(a)):              a = [i + 3 for i in a]
    a[i] += 3
                                     # Or:
                                     a = map(lambda i: i + 3, a)
```

Use `enumerate()` to keep a count of your place in the list. It is more readable than manually creating a counter, and it is better optimized for iterators:

```
>>> a = ["icky", "icky", "icky", "p-tang"]
>>> for i, item in enumerate(a):
...     print("{i}: {item}".format(i=i, item=item))
...
0: icky
1: icky
2: icky
3: p-tang
```

Continuing a long line of code

When a logical line of code is longer than the accepted limit,[4] you need to split it over multiple physical lines. The Python interpreter will join consecutive lines if the last character of the line is a backslash. This is helpful in some cases, but should usually be avoided because of its fragility: a whitespace character added to the end of the line, after the backslash, will break the code and may have unexpected results.

A better solution is to use parentheses around your elements. Left with an unclosed parenthesis on an end-of-line, the Python interpreter will join the next line until the parentheses are closed. The same behavior holds for curly and square braces:

Bad	Good

```
french_insult = \                    french_insult = (
"Your mother was a hamster, and \        "Your mother was a hamster, and "
your father smelt of elderberries!"      "your father smelt of elderberries!"
                                     )

from some.deep.module.in.a.module \  from some.deep.module.in.a.module import (
    import a_nice_function, \            a_nice_function,
        another_nice_function, \         another_nice_function,
        yet_another_nice_function        yet_another_nice_function
                                     )
```

---

4 A max of 80 characters according to PEP 8, 100 according to many others, and for you, whatever your boss says. Ha! But honestly, anyone who's ever had to use a terminal to debug code while standing up next to a rack will quickly come to appreciate the 80-character limit (at which code doesn't wrap on a terminal) and in fact prefer 75–77 characters to allow for line numbering in Vi.

However, more often than not, having to split a long logical line is a sign that you are trying to do too many things at the same time, which may hinder readability.

Idioms

Although there usually is one—and preferably only one—obvious way to do it, the way to write idiomatic (or *Pythonic*) code can be non-obvious to Python beginners at first (unless they're Dutch[5]). So, good idioms must be consciously acquired.

Unpacking

If you know the length of a list or tuple, you can assign names to its elements with unpacking. For example, because it's possible to specify the number of times to split a string in `split()` and `rsplit()`, the righthand side of an assignment can be made to split only once (e.g., into a filename and an extension), and the lefthand side can contain both destinations simultaneously, in the correct order, like this:

```
>>> filename, ext = "my_photo.orig.png".rsplit(".", 1)
>>> print(filename, "is a", ext, "file.")
my_photo.orig is a png file.
```

You can use unpacking to swap variables as well:

```
a, b = b, a
```

Nested unpacking works, too:

```
a, (b, c) = 1, (2, 3)
```

In Python 3, a new method of extended unpacking was introduced by PEP 3132 (*https://www.python.org/dev/peps/pep-3132/*):

```
a, *rest = [1, 2, 3]
# a = 1, rest = [2, 3]

a, *middle, c = [1, 2, 3, 4]
# a = 1, middle = [2, 3], c = 4
```

Ignoring a value

If you need to assign something while unpacking, but will not need that variable, use a double underscore (__):

```
filename = 'foobar.txt'
basename, __, ext = filename.rpartition('.')
```

---

5 See Zen 14. Guido, our BDFL, happens to be Dutch.

Many Python style guides recommend a single underscore (_) for throwaway variables rather than the double underscore (__) recommended here. The issue is that a single underscore is commonly used as an alias for the `gettext.gettext()` function, and is also used at the interactive prompt to hold the value of the last operation. Using a double underscore instead is just as clear and almost as convenient, and eliminates the risk of accidentally overwriting the single underscore variable, in either of these other use cases.

Creating a length-*N* list of the same thing

Use the Python list * operator to make a list of the same immutable item:

```
>>> four_nones = [None] * 4
>>> print(four_nones)
[None, None, None, None]
```

But be careful with mutable objects: because lists are mutable, the * operator will create a list of *N* references to the *same* list, which is not likely what you want. Instead, use a list comprehension:

Bad	Good

`>>> four_lists = [[]] * 4`
`>>> four_lists[0].append("Ni")`
`>>> print(four_lists)`
`[['Ni'], ['Ni'], ['Ni'], ['Ni']]`
	`>>> four_lists = [[] for __ in range(4)]`
	`>>> four_lists[0].append("Ni")`
	`>>> print(four_lists)`
	`[['Ni'], [], [], []]`

A common idiom for creating strings is to use `str.join()` on an empty string. This idiom can be applied to lists and tuples:

```
>>> letters = ['s', 'p', 'a', 'm']
>>> word = ''.join(letters)
>>> print(word)
spam
```

Sometimes we need to search through a collection of things. Let's look at two options: lists and sets.

Take the following code for example:

```
>>> x = list(('foo', 'foo', 'bar', 'baz'))
>>> y = set(('foo', 'foo', 'bar', 'baz'))
>>>
>>> print(x)
['foo', 'foo', 'bar', 'baz']
>>> print(y)
{'foo', 'bar', 'baz'}
>>>
>>> 'foo' in x
True
```

```
>>> 'foo' in y
True
```

Even though both boolean tests for list and set membership look identical, *foo* `in y` is utilizing the fact that sets (and dictionaries) in Python are hash tables,[6] the lookup performance between the two examples is different. Python will have to step through each item in the list to find a matching case, which is time-consuming (the time difference becomes significant for larger collections). But finding keys in the set can be done quickly, using the hash lookup. Also, sets and dictionaries drop duplicate entries, which is why dictionaries cannot have two identical keys. For more information, see this Stack Overflow discussion on list versus dict (*http://stackoverflow.com/questions/513882*).

Exception-safe contexts

It is common to use `try/finally` clauses to manage resources like files or thread locks when exceptions may occur. PEP 343 (*https://www.python.org/dev/peps/pep-0343/*) introduced the `with` statement and a context manager protocol into Python (in version 2.5 and beyond)—an idiom to replace these `try/finally` clauses with more readable code. The protocol consists of two methods, `__enter__()` and `__exit__()`, that when implemented for an object allow it to be used via the new `with` statement, like this:

```
>>> import threading
>>> some_lock = threading.Lock()
>>>
>>> with some_lock:
...     # Make Earth Mark One, run it for 10 million years ...
...     print(
...         "Look at me: I design coastlines.\n"
...         "I got an award for Norway."
...     )
...
```

which would previously have been:

```
>>> import threading
>>> some_lock = threading.Lock()
>>>
>>> some_lock.acquire()
>>> try:
...     # Make Earth Mark One, run it for 10 million years ...
...     print(
```

---

6 By the way, this is why only *hashable* objects can be stored in sets or used as dictionary keys. To make your own Python objects hashable, define an `object.__hash__(self)` member function that returns an integer. Objects that compare equal must have the same hash value. The Python documentation (*https://docs.python.org/3/reference/datamodel.html#object.__hash__*) has more information.

```
...         "Look at me: I design coastlines.\n"
...         "I got an award for Norway."
...     )
... finally:
...     some_lock.release()
```

The standard library module `contextlib` (*https://docs.python.org/3/library/context lib.html*) provides additional tools that help turn functions into context managers, enforce the call of an object's `close()` method, suppress exceptions (Python 3.4 and greater), and redirect standard output and error streams (Python 3.4 or 3.5 and greater). Here is an example use of `contextlib.closing()`:

```
>>> from contextlib import closing
>>> with closing(open("outfile.txt", "w")) as output:
...     output.write("Well, he's...he's, ah...probably pining for the fjords.")
...
56
```

but because `__enter__()` and `__exit__()` methods are defined for the object that handles file I/O,[7] we can use the `with` statement directly, without the `closing`:

```
>>> with open("outfile.txt", "w") as output:
    output.write(
        "PININ' for the FJORDS?!?!?!? "
        "What kind of talk is that?, look, why did he fall "
        "flat on his back the moment I got 'im home?\n"
    )
...
123
```

Common Gotchas

For the most part, Python aims to be a clean and consistent language that avoids surprises. However, there are a few cases that can be confusing to newcomers.

Some of these cases are intentional but can be potentially surprising. Some could arguably be considered language warts. In general, though, what follows is a collection of potentially tricky behaviors that might seem strange at first glance, but are generally sensible once you're aware of the underlying cause for the surprise.

Mutable default arguments

Seemingly the *most* common surprise new Python programmers encounter is Python's treatment of mutable default arguments in function definitions.

---

7 In this case, the `__exit__()` method just calls the I/O wrapper's `close()` method, to close the file descriptor. On many systems, there's a maximum allowable number of open file descriptors, and it's good practice to release them when they're done.

What you wrote:

```
def append_to(element, to=[]):
    to.append(element)
    return to
```

What you might have expected to happen:

```
my_list = append_to(12)
print(my_list)

my_other_list = append_to(42)
print(my_other_list)
```

A new list is created each time the function is called if a second argument isn't provided, so that the output is:

```
[12]
[42]
```

What actually happens:

```
[12]
[12, 42]
```

A new list is created *once* when the function is defined, and the same list is used in each successive call: Python's default arguments are evaluated *once* when the function is defined, not each time the function is called (like it is in say, Ruby). This means that if you use a mutable default argument and mutate it, you *will* have mutated that object for all future calls to the function as well.

What you should do instead:

Create a new object each time the function is called, by using a default arg to signal that no argument was provided (None is often a good choice):

```
def append_to(element, to=None):
    if to is None:
        to = []
    to.append(element)
    return to
```

When this gotcha isn't a gotcha:

Sometimes you can specifically "exploit" (i.e., use as intended) this behavior to maintain state between calls of a function. This is often done when writing a caching function (which stores results in-memory), for example:

```
def time_consuming_function(x, y, cache={}):
    args = (x, y)
    if args in cache:
        return cache[args]
    # Otherwise this is the first time with these arguments.
    # Do the time-consuming operation...
```

```
        cache[args] = result
        return result
```

Late binding closures

Another common source of confusion is the way Python binds its variables in closures (or in the surrounding global scope).

What you wrote:
```
def create_multipliers():
    return [lambda x : i * x for i in range(5)]
```

What you might have expected to happen:
```
for multiplier in create_multipliers():
    print(multiplier(2), end=" ... ")
print()
```

A list containing five functions that each have their own closed-over i variable that multiplies their argument, producing:

```
0 ... 2 ... 4 ... 6 ... 8 ...
```

What actually happens:
```
8 ... 8 ... 8 ... 8 ... 8 ...
```

Five functions are created; instead all of them just multiply x by 4. Why? Python's closures are *late binding*. This means that the values of variables used in closures are looked up at the time the inner function is called.

Here, whenever *any* of the returned functions are called, the value of i is looked up in the surrounding scope at call time. By then, the loop has completed, and i is left with its final value of 4.

What's particularly nasty about this gotcha is the seemingly prevalent misinformation that this has something to do with lambda expressions (*https:// docs.python.org/3/tutorial/controlflow.html#lambda-expressions*) in Python. Functions created with a lambda expression are in no way special, and in fact the same exact behavior is exhibited by just using an ordinary def:

```
def create_multipliers():
    multipliers = []

    for i in range(5):
        def multiplier(x):
            return i * x
        multipliers.append(multiplier)

    return multipliers
```

What you should do instead:

The most general solution is arguably a bit of a hack. Due to Python's aforementioned behavior concerning evaluating default arguments to functions (see "Mutable default arguments" on page 62), you can create a closure that binds immediately to its arguments by using a default argument:

```
def create_multipliers():
    return [lambda x, i=i : i * x for i in range(5)]
```

Alternatively, you can use the `functools.partial()` function:

```
from functools import partial
from operator import mul

def create_multipliers():
    return [partial(mul, i) for i in range(5)]
```

When this gotcha isn't a gotcha:

Sometimes you want your closures to behave this way. Late binding is good in lots of situations (e.g., in the Diamond project, "Example use of a closure (when the gotcha isn't a gotcha)" on page 115). Looping to create unique functions is unfortunately a case where it can cause hiccups.

Structuring Your Project

By *structure* we mean the decisions you make concerning how your project best meets its objective. The goal is to best leverage Python's features to create clean, effective code. In practical terms, that means the logic and dependencies in both your code and in your file and folder structure are clear.

Which functions should go into which modules? How does data flow through the project? What features and functions can be grouped together and isolated? By answering questions like these, you can begin to plan, in a broad sense, what your finished product will look like.

The *Python Cookbook* has a chapter on modules and packages (*http://bit.ly/python-cookbook-ch10*) that describes in detail how `__import__` statements and packaging works. The purpose of this section is to outline aspects of Python's module and import systems that are central to enforcing structure in your project. We then discuss various perspectives on how to build code that can be extended and tested reliably.

Thanks to the way imports and modules are handled in Python, it is relatively easy to structure a Python project: there are few constraints and the model for importing modules is easy to grasp. Therefore, you are left with the pure architectural task of crafting the different parts of your project and their interactions.

Modules

Modules are one of Python's main abstraction layers, and probably the most natural one. Abstraction layers allow a programmer to separate code into parts that hold related data and functionality.

For example, if one layer of a project handles interfacing with user actions, while another handles low-level manipulation of data, the most natural way to separate these two layers is to regroup all interfacing functionality in one file, and all low-level operations in another file. This grouping places them into two separate modules. The interface file would then import the low-level file with the `import` *module* or `from` *module* `import` *attribute* statements.

As soon as you use `import` statements, you also use modules. These can be either built-in modules (such as `os` and `sys`), third-party packages you have installed in your environment (such as Requests or NumPy), or your project's internal modules. The following code shows some example `import` statements and confirms that an imported module is a Python object with its own data type:

```
>>> import sys  # built-in module
>>> import matplotlib.pyplot as plt  # third-party module
>>>
>>> import mymodule as mod  # internal project module
>>>
>>> print(type(sys), type(plt), type(mod))
<class 'module'> <class 'module'> <class 'module'>
```

To keep in line with the style guide (*https://www.python.org/dev/peps/pep-0008/*), keep module names short and lowercase. And be sure to avoid using special symbols like the dot (.) or question mark (?), which would interfere with the way Python looks for modules. So a filename like *my.spam.py*[8] is one you should avoid; Python would expect to find a *spam.py* file in a folder named my, which is not the case. The Python documentation (*http://docs.python.org/tutorial/modules.html#packages*) gives more details about using dot notation.

Importing modules

Aside from some naming restrictions, nothing special is required to use a Python file as a module, but it helps to understand the import mechanism. First, the `import` `modu` statement will look for the definition of `modu` in a file named *modu.py* in the same directory as the caller if a file with that name exists. If it is not found, the Python interpreter will search for *modu.py* in Python's search path (*https://*

---

8 If you'd like, you could name your module *my_spam.py*, but even our friend the underscore should not be seen often in module names (underscores give the impression of a variable name).

---

docs.python.org/2/library/sys.html#sys.path) recursively and raise an `ImportError` exception if it is not found. The value of the search path is platform-dependent and includes any user- or system-defined directories in the environment's $PYTHONPATH (or %PYTHONPATH% in Windows). It can be manipulated or inspected in a Python session:

```
import sys
>>> sys.path
[ '', '/current/absolute/path', 'etc']
# The actual list contains every path that is searched
# when you import libraries into Python, in the order
# that they'll be searched.
```

Once *modu.py* is found, the Python interpreter will execute the module in an isolated scope. Any top-level statement in *modu.py* will be executed, including other imports, if any exist. Function and class definitions are stored in the module's dictionary.

Finally, the module's variables, functions, and classes will be available to the caller through the module's *namespace*, a central concept in programming that is particularly helpful and powerful in Python. Namespaces provide a scope containing named attributes that are visible to each other but not directly accessible outside of the namespace.

In many languages, an include file directive causes the preprocessor to, effectively, copy the contents of the included file into the caller's code. It's different in Python: the included code is isolated in a module namespace. The result of the `import modu` statement will be a module object named `modu` in the global namespace, with the attributes defined in the module accessible via dot notation: `modu.sqrt` would be the `sqrt` object defined inside of *modu.py*, for example. This means you generally don't have to worry that the included code could have unwanted effects—for example, overriding an existing function with the same name.

Namespace Tools

The functions `dir()`, `globals()`, and `locals()` help with quick namespace introspection:

- `dir(object)` returns a list of attributes that are accessible via the object
- `globals()` returns a dictionary of the attributes currently in the global namespace, along with their values.
- `locals()` returns a dictionary of the attributes in the current local namespace (e.g., within a function), along with their values.

> For more information, see "Data model" (*https://docs.python.org/3/reference/datamo del.html*) in Python's official documentation.

It is possible to simulate the more standard behavior by using a special syntax of the `import` statement: `from modu import *`. However, this is generally considered bad practice: using `import *` makes code harder to read, makes dependencies less compartmentalized, and can clobber (overwrite) existing defined objects with the new definitions inside the imported module.

Using `from modu import func` is a way to import only the attribute you want into the global namespace. While much less harmful than `from modu import *` because it shows explicitly what is imported in the global namespace. Its only advantage over a simpler `import modu` is that it will save you a little typing.

Table 4-1 compares the different ways to import definitions from other modules.

Table 4-1. Different ways to import definitions from modules

Very bad (confusing for a reader)	Better (obvious which new names are in the global namespace)	Best (immediately obvious where the attribute comes from)
`from modu import *`	`from modu import sqrt`	`import modu`
`x = sqrt(4)`	`x = sqrt(4)`	`x = modu.sqrt(4)`
Is sqrt part of modu? Or a built-in? Or defined above?	Has sqrt been modified or redefined in between, or is it the one in modu?	Now sqrt is visibly part of modu's namespace.

As mentioned in "Code Style" on page 47, readability is one of the main features of Python. Readable code avoids useless boilerplate text and clutter. But terseness and obscurity are the limits where brevity should stop. Explicitly stating where a class or function comes from, as in the `modu.func()` idiom, greatly improves code readability and understandability in all but the simplest single-file projects.

Structure Is Key

Though you can structure a project however you like, some pitfalls to avoid are:

Multiple and messy circular dependencies
> If your classes `Table` and `Chair` in *furn.py* need to import `Carpenter` from *workers.py* to answer a question such as `table.is_done_by()`, and if the class `Carpenter` needs to import `Table` and `Chair`, to answer `carpenter.what_do()`, then you have a circular dependency—*furn.py* depends on *workers.py*, which depends on *furn.py*. In this case, you will have to resort to fragile hacks such as using `import` statements inside methods to avoid causing an `ImportError`.

Hidden coupling

Each and every change in `Table`'s implementation breaks 20 tests in unrelated test cases because it breaks `Carpenter`'s code, which requires very careful surgery to adapt the change. This means you have too many assumptions about `Table` in `Carpenter`'s code.

Heavy use of global state or context

Instead of explicitly passing (height, width, type, wood) to each other, `Table` and `Carpenter` rely on global variables that can be modified and are modified on the fly by different agents. You need to scrutinize all access to these global variables to understand why a rectangular table became a square, and discover that remote template code is also modifying this context, messing with table dimensions.

Spaghetti code

Multiple pages of nested `if` clauses and `for` loops with a lot of copy-pasted procedural code and no proper segmentation are known as *spaghetti code*. Python's meaningful indentation (one of its most controversial features) makes it hard to maintain this kind of code, so you may not see too much of it.

Ravioli code

This is more likely in Python than spaghetti code. *Ravioli code* consists of hundreds of similar little pieces of logic, often classes or objects, without proper structure. If you never can remember whether you have to use `FurnitureTable`, `AssetTable` or `Table`, or even `TableNew` for your task at hand, you might be swimming in ravioli code. Diamond, Requests, and Werkzeug (in the next chapter) avoid ravioli code by collecting their useful but unrelated pieces of logic into a *utils.py* module or a *utils* package to reuse across the project.

Packages

Python provides a very straightforward packaging system, which extends the module mechanism to a directory.

Any directory with an *__init__.py* file is considered a Python package. The top-level directory with an *__init__.py* is the *root package*.[9] The different modules in the package are imported in a similar manner as plain modules, but with a special behavior for the *__init__.py* file, which is used to gather all package-wide definitions.

---

9 Thanks to PEP 420 (*https://www.python.org/dev/peps/pep-0420/*), which was implemented in Python 3.3, there is now an alternative to the root package, called the *namespace package*. Namespace packages must not have an *__init__.py* and can be dispersed across multiple directories in `sys.path`. Python will gather all of the pieces together and present them together to the user as a single package.

A file *modu.py* in the directory *pack/* is imported with the statement `import pack.modu`. The interpreter will look for an *__init__.py* file in `pack` and execute all of its top-level statements. Then it will look for a file named *pack/modu.py* and execute all of its top-level statements. After these operations, any variable, function, or class defined in *modu.py* is available in the `pack.modu` namespace.

A commonly seen issue is too much code in *__init__.py* files. When the project's complexity grows, there may be subpackages and sub-subpackages in a deep directory structure. In this case, importing a single item from a sub-sub-package will require executing all *__init__.py* files met while traversing the tree.

It is normal, even good practice, to leave an *__init__.py* empty when the package's modules and subpackages do not need to share any code—the HowDoI and Diamond projects that are used as examples in the next section both have no code except version numbers in their *__init__.py* files. The Tablib, Requests, and Flask projects contain a top-level documentation string and `import` statements that expose the intended API for each project, and the Werkzeug project also exposes its top-level API but does it using lazy loading (extra code that only adds content to the namespace as it is used, which speeds up the initial `import` statement).

Lastly, a convenient syntax is available for importing deeply nested packages: `import very.deep.module as mod`. This allows you to use `mod` in place of the verbose repetition of `very.deep.module`.

Object-Oriented Programming

Python is sometimes described as an object-oriented programming language. This can be somewhat misleading and needs to be clarified.

In Python, everything is an object, and can be handled as such. This is what is meant when we say that functions are first-class objects. Functions, classes, strings, and even types are objects in Python: they all have a type, can be passed as function arguments, and may have methods and properties. In this understanding, Python is an object-oriented language.

However, unlike Java, Python does not impose object-oriented programming as the main programming paradigm. It is perfectly viable for a Python project to not be object oriented—that is, to use no (or very few) class definitions, class inheritance, or any other mechanisms that are specific to object-oriented programming. These features are *available*, but not *obligatory*, for us Pythonistas. Moreover, as seen in "Modules" on page 66, the way Python handles modules and namespaces gives the developer a natural way to ensure the encapsulation and separation of abstraction layers—the most common reasons to use object orientation—*without* classes.

Proponents of functional programming (a paradigm that, in its purest form, has no assignment operator, no side effects, and basically chains functions to accomplish tasks), say that bugs and confusion occur when a function does different things depending on the external state of the system—for example, a global variable that indicates whether or not a person is logged in. Python, although not a purely functional language, has tools that make functional programming possible, (*http://bit.ly/functional-programming-python*) and then we can restrict our use of custom classes to situations where we want to glue together a state and a functionality.

In some architectures, typically web applications, multiple instances of Python processes are spawned to respond to external requests that can happen at the same time. In this case, holding some state into instantiated objects, which means keeping some static information about the world, is prone to *race conditions*, a term used to describe the situation where, at some point between the initialization of the state of an object (usually done with the `Class.__init__()` method in Python) and the actual use of the object state through one of its methods, the state of the world has changed.

For example, a request may load an item in memory and later mark it as added to a user's shopping cart. If another request sells the item to another person at the same time, it may happen that the sale actually occurs after the first session loaded the item, and then we are trying to sell inventory already flagged as sold. This and other issues led to a preference for stateless functions.

Our recommendation is as follows: when working with code that relies on some persistent context or global state (like most web applications), use functions and procedures with as few implicit contexts and side effects as possible. A function's implicit context is made up of any of the global variables or items in the persistence layer that are accessed from within the function. *Side effects* are the changes that a function makes to its implicit context. If a function saves or deletes data in a global variable or in the persistence layer, it is said to have a side effect.

Custom classes in Python should be used to carefully isolate functions with context and side effects from functions with logic (called *pure functions*). Pure functions are deterministic: given a fixed input, the output will always be the same. This is because they do not depend on context, and do not have side effects. The `print()` function, for example, is impure because it returns nothing but writes to standard output as a side effect. Here are some benefits of having pure, separate functions:

- Pure functions are much easier to change or replace if they need to be refactored or optimized.
- Pure functions are easier to test with unit-tests there is less need for complex context setup and data cleaning afterward.

- Pure functions are easier to manipulate, decorate (more on decorators in a moment), and pass around.

In summary, for some architectures, pure functions are more efficient building blocks than classes and objects because they have no context or side effects. As an example, the I/O functions related to each of the file formats in the Tablib library (*tablib/formats/*.py*—we'll look at Tablib in the next chapter) are pure functions, and not part of a class, because all they do is read data into a separate `Dataset` object that persists the data, or write the `Dataset` to a file. But the `Session` object in the Requests library (also coming up in the next chapter) is a class, because it has to persist the cookie and authentication information that may be exchanged in an HTTP session.

 Object orientation is useful and even necessary in many cases—for example, when developing graphical desktop applications or games, where the things that are manipulated (windows, buttons, avatars, vehicles) have a relatively long life of their own in the computer's memory. This is also one motive behind object-relational mapping, which maps rows in databases to objects in code, discussed further in "Database Libraries" on page 284.

Decorators

Decorators were added to Python in version 2.4 and are defined and discussed in PEP 318 (*https://www.python.org/dev/peps/pep-0318/*). A decorator is a function or a class method that wraps (or decorates) another function or method. The decorated function or method will replace the original function or method. Because functions are first-class objects in Python, this can be done manually, but using the `@decorator` syntax is clearer and preferred. Here is an example of how to use a decorator:

```
>>> def foo():
...     print("I am inside foo.")
...
...
...
>>> import logging
>>> logging.basicConfig()
>>>
>>> def logged(func, *args, **kwargs):
...     logger = logging.getLogger()
...     def new_func(*args, **kwargs):
...         logger.debug("calling {} with args {} and kwargs {}".format(
...                     func.__name__, args, kwargs))
...         return func(*args, **kwargs)
...     return new_func
...
>>>
>>>
```

```
... @logged
... def bar():
...     print("I am inside bar.")
...
>>> logging.getLogger().setLevel(logging.DEBUG)
>>> bar()
DEBUG:root:calling bar with args () and kwargs {}
I am inside bar.
>>> foo()
I am inside foo.
```

This mechanism is useful for isolating the core logic of the function or method. A good example of a task that is better handled with decoration is memoization or caching: you want to store the results of an expensive function in a table and use them directly instead of recomputing them when they have already been computed. This is clearly not part of the function logic. As of PEP 3129 (*https://www.python.org/dev/peps/pep-3129/*), starting in Python 3, decorators can also be applied to classes.

Dynamic Typing

Python is dynamically typed (as opposed to statically typed), meaning variables do not have a fixed type. Variables are implemented as pointers to an object, making it possible for the variable a to be set to the value 42, then to the value "thanks for all the fish", then to a function.

The dynamic typing used in Python is often considered to be a weakness, because it can lead to complexities and hard-to-debug code: if something named a can be set to many different things, the developer or the maintainer must track this name in the code to make sure it has not been set to a completely unrelated object. Table 4-2 illustrates good and bad practice when using names.

Table 4-2. Avoid using the same variable name for different things

Advice	Bad	Good

Use short functions or methods to reduce the risk of using the same name for two unrelated things.	`a = 1`
	`a = 'answer is {}'.format(a)`
		`def get_answer(a):`
		`    return 'answer is {}'.format(a)`
		
		`a = get_answer(1)`

Use different names for related items when they have a different type.	`# A string ...`
	`items = 'a b c d'`
	`# No, a list ...`
	`items = items.split(' ')`
	`# No, a set ...`
	`items = set(items)`
		`items_string = 'a b c d'`
		`items_list = items.split(' ')`
		`items = set(items_list)`

There is no efficiency gain when reusing names: the assignment will still create a new object. And when the complexity grows and each assignment is separated by other lines of code, including branches and loops, it becomes harder to determine a given variable's type.

Some coding practices, like functional programming, recommend against reassigning variables. In Java, a variable can be forced to always contain the same value after assignment by using the final keyword. Python does not have a final keyword, and it would be against its philosophy. But assigning a varible only once may be a good discipline; it helps reinforce the concept of mutable versus immutable types.

 Pylint (*https://www.pylint.org/*) will warn you if you reassign a variable to two different types.

Mutable and Immutable Types

Python has two kinds of built-in or user-defined[10] types:

```
# Lists are mutable
my_list = [1, 2, 3]
my_list[0] = 4
print my_list  # [4, 2, 3] <- The same list, changed.

# Integers are immutable
x = 6
x = x + 1  # The new x occupies a different location in memory.
```

Mutable types

These allow in-place modification of the object's content. Examples are lists and dictionaries, which have mutating methods like list.append() or dict.pop() and can be modified in place.

Immutable types

These types provide no method for changing their content. For instance, the variable x set to the integer 6 has no "increment" method. To compute x + 1, you have to create another integer and give it a name.

One consequence of this difference in behavior is that mutable types cannot be used as dictionary keys, because if the value ever changes, it will not hash to the same value, and dictionaries use hashing[11] for key storage. The immutable equivalent of a

---

10 Instructions to define your own types in C are provided in the Python extension documentation. (*https://docs.python.org/3/extending/newtypes.html*)

11 An example of a simple hashing algorithm is to convert the bytes of an item to an integer, and take its value modulo some number. This is how memcached (*http://www.memcached.org*) distributes keys across multiple computers.

---

list is the tuple, created with parentheses—for example, (1, 2). It cannot be changed in place and so can be used as a dictionary key.

Using properly mutable types for objects that are intended to be mutable (e.g., my_list = [1, 2, 3]) and immutable types for objects that are intended to have a fixed value (e.g., islington_phone = ("220", "7946", "0347")) clarifies the intent of the code for other developers.

One peculiarity of Python that can surprise newcomers is that strings are immutable; attempting to change one will yield a type error:

```
>>> s = "I'm not mutable"
>>> s[1:7] = " am"
Traceback (most recent call last):
  File "<stdin>", line 1, in <module>
TypeError: 'str' object does not support item assignment
```

This means that when constructing a string from its parts, it is much more efficient to accumulate the parts in a list, because it is mutable, and then join the parts together to make the full string. Also, a Python *list comprehension*, which is a shorthand syntax to iterate over an input to create a list, is better and faster than constructing a list from calls to append() within a loop. Table 4-3 shows different ways to create a string from an iterable.

Table 4-3. Example ways to concatenate a string

Bad	Good	Best
`>>> s = ""`	`>>> s = []`	`>>> r = (97, 98, 99)`
`>>> for c in (97, 98, 98):`	`>>> for c in (97, 98, 99):`	`>>> s = [unichr(c) for c in r]`
`...     s += unichr(c)`	`...     s.append(unichr(c))`	`>>> print("".join(s))`
`...`	`...`	`abc`
`>>> print(s)`	`>>> print("".join(s))`	
`abc`	`abc`	

The main Python page has a good discussion on this kind of optimization (*https://www.python.org/doc/essays/list2str/*).

Finally, if the number of elements in a concatenation is known, pure string addition is faster (and more straightforward) than creating a list of items just to do a "".join(). All of the following formatting options to define cheese do the same thing:[12]

```
>>> adj = "Red"
>>> noun = "Leicester"
```

---

12 We should admit that even though, according to PEP 3101 (*https://www.python.org/dev/peps/pep-3101/*), the percent-style formatting (*%s, %d, %f*) has been deprecated now for over a decade, most old hats still use it, and PEP 460 (*https://www.python.org/dev/peps/pep-0460/*) just introduced this same method to format bytes or bytearray objects.

```
>>>
>>> cheese = "%s %s" % (adj, noun)  # This style was deprecated (PEP 3101)
>>> cheese = "{} {}".format(adj, noun)  # Possible since Python 3.1
>>> cheese = "{0} {1}".format(adj, noun)  # Numbers can also be reused
>>> cheese = "{adj} {noun}".format(adj=adj, noun=noun)  # This style is best
>>> print(cheese)
Red Leicester
```

Vendorizing Dependencies

A package that *vendorizes dependencies* includes external dependencies (third-party libraries) within its source, often inside of a folder named *vendor*, or *packages*. There is a very good blog post (*http://bit.ly/on-vendorizing*) on the subject that lists the main reasons a package owner might do this (basically, to avoid various dependency issues), and discusses alternatives.

Consensus is that in almost all cases, it is better to keep the dependency separate, as it adds unnecessary content (often megabytes of extra code) to the repository; virtual environments used in combination with *setup.py* (preferred, especially when your package is a library) or a *requirements.txt* (which, when used, will override dependencies in *setup.py* in the case of conflicts) can restrict dependencies to a known set of working versions.

If those options are not enough, it might be helpful to contact the owner of the dependency to maybe resolve the issue by updating their package (e.g., your library many depend on an upcoming release of their package, or may need a specific new feature added), as those changes would likely benefit the entire community. The caveat is, if you submit pull requests for big changes, you may be expected to maintain those changes when further suggestions and requests come in; for this reason, both Tablib and Requests vendorize at least some dependencies. As the community moves into complete adoption of Python 3, hopefully fewer of the most pressing issues will remain.

Testing Your Code

Testing your code is very important. People are much more likely to use a project that actually works.

Python first included doctest and unittest in Python 2.1, released in 2001, embracing *test-driven development (TDD)*, where the developer first writes tests that define the main operation and edge cases for a function, and then writes the function to pass those tests. Since then, TDD has become accepted and widely adopted in business and in open source projects—it's a good idea to practice writing the testing code and the running code in parallel. Used wisely, this method helps you precisely define your code's intent and have a more modular architecture.

Tips for testing

A test is about the most massively useful code a hitchhiker can write. We've summarized some of our tips here.

Just one thing per test. A testing unit should focus on one tiny bit of functionality and prove it correct.

Independence is imperative. Each test unit must be fully independent: able to run alone, and also within the test suite, regardless of the order they are called. The implication of this rule is that each test must be loaded with a fresh dataset and may have to do some cleanup afterward. This is usually handled by `setUp()` and `tearDown()` methods.

Precision is better than parsimony. Use long and descriptive names for testing functions. This guideline is slightly different than for running code, where short names are often preferred. The reason is testing functions are never called explicitly. `square()` or even `sqr()` is OK in running code, but in testing code, you should have names such as `test_square_of_number_2()` or `test_square_negative_number()`. These function names are displayed when a test fails and should be as descriptive as possible.

Speed counts. Try hard to make tests that are fast. If one test needs more than a few milliseconds to run, development will be slowed down, or the tests will not be run as often as is desirable. In some cases, tests can't be fast because they need a complex data structure to work on, and this data structure must be loaded every time the test runs. Keep these heavier tests in a separate test suite that is run by some scheduled task, and run all other tests as often as needed.

RTMF (Read the manual, friend!). Learn your tools and learn how to run a single test or a test case. Then, when developing a function inside a module, run this function's tests often, ideally automatically when you save the code.

Test everything when you start—and again when you finish. Always run the full test suite before a coding session, and run it again after. This will give you more confidence that you did not break anything in the rest of the code.

Version control automation hooks are fantastic. It is a good idea to implement a hook that runs all tests before pushing code to a shared repository. You can directly add hooks to your version control system, and some IDEs provide ways to do this more simply in their own environments. Here are the links to the popular systems' documentation, which will step you through how to do this:

- GitHub (*https://developer.github.com/webhooks/*)
- Mercurial (*http://bit.ly/mercurial-handling-repo*)

- Subversion (*http://bit.ly/svn-repo-hook*)

Write a breaking test if you want to take a break.   If you are in the middle of a development session and have to interrupt your work, it is a good idea to write a broken unit test about what you want to develop next. When coming back to work, you will have a pointer to where you were and get back on track faster.

In the face of ambiguity, debug using a test.   The first step when you are debugging your code is to write a new test pinpointing the bug. While it is not always possible to do, those bug catching tests are among the most valuable pieces of code in your project.

If the test is hard to explain, good luck finding collaborators.   When something goes wrong or has to be changed, if your code has a good set of tests, you or other maintainers will rely largely on the testing suite to fix the problem or modify a given behavior. Therefore, the testing code will be read as much as—or even *more* than—the running code. A unit test whose purpose is unclear is not very helpful in this case.

If the test is easy to explain, it is almost always a good idea.   Another use of the testing code is as an introduction to new developers. When other people will have to work on the code base, running and reading the related testing code is often the best thing they can do. They will (or should) discover the hot spots, where most difficulties arise, and the corner cases. If they have to add some functionality, the first step should be to add a test and, by this means, ensure the new functionality is not already a working path that has not been plugged into the interface.

Above all, don't panic.   It's open source! The whole world's got your back.

Testing Basics

This section lists the basics of testing—for an idea about what options are available—and gives a few examples taken from the Python projects we dive into next, in Chapter 5. There is an entire book on TDD in Python, and we don't want to rewrite it. Check out *Test-Driven Development with Python* (O'Reilly) (obey the testing goat!).

unittest

unittest is the batteries-included test module in the Python standard library. Its API will be familiar to anyone who has used any of the JUnit (Java)/nUnit (.NET)/CppUnit (C/C++) series of tools.

Creating test cases is accomplished by subclassing unittest.TestCase. In this example code, the test function is just defined as a new method in MyTest:

```
# test_example.py
import unittest

def fun(x):
```

```
        return x + 1

class MyTest(unittest.TestCase):
    def test_that_fun_adds_one(self):
        self.assertEqual(fun(3), 4)

class MySecondTest(unittest.TestCase):
    def test_that_fun_fails_when_not_adding_number(self):
        self.assertRaises(TypeError, fun, "multiply six by nine")
```

 Test methods must start with the string `test` or they will not run. Test modules (files) are expected to match the pattern `test*.py` by default but can match any pattern given to the `--pattern` keyword argument on the command line.

To run all tests in that `TestClass`, open a terminal shell; and in the same directory as the file, invoke Python's `unittest` module on the command line, like this:

```
$ python -m unittest test_example.MyTest
.
----------------------------------------------------------------------
Ran 1 test in 0.000s

OK
```

Or to run all tests in a file, name the file:

```
$ python -m unittest test_example
.
----------------------------------------------------------------------
Ran 2 tests in 0.000s

OK
```

Mock (in unittest)

As of Python 3.3, `unittest.mock` (*https://docs.python.org/dev/library/unittest.mock*) is available in the standard library. It allows you to replace parts of your system under test with mock objects and make assertions about how they have been used.

For example, you can *monkey patch* a method like in the following example (a monkey patch is code that modifies or replaces other existing code at runtime.) In this code, the existing method named `ProductionClass.method`, for the instance we create named `instance`, is replaced with a new object, `MagicMock`, which will always return the value 3 when called, and which counts the number of method calls it receives, records the signature it was called with, and contains assertion methods for testing purposes:

```
from unittest.mock import MagicMock

instance = ProductionClass()
instance.method = MagicMock(return_value=3)
instance.method(3, 4, 5, key='value')

instance.method.assert_called_with(3, 4, 5, key='value')
```

To mock classes or objects in a module under test, use the `patch` decorator. In the following example, an external search system is replaced with a mock that always returns the same result (as used in this example, the patch is only for the duration of the test):

```
import unittest.mock as mock

def mock_search(self):
    class MockSearchQuerySet(SearchQuerySet):
        def __iter__(self):
            return iter(["foo", "bar", "baz"])
    return MockSearchQuerySet()

# SearchForm here refers to the imported class reference
# myapp.SearchForm, and modifies this instance, not the
# code where the SearchForm class itself is initially
# defined.
@mock.patch('myapp.SearchForm.search', mock_search)
def test_new_watchlist_activities(self):
    # get_search_results runs a search and iterates over the result
    self.assertEqual(len(myapp.get_search_results(q="fish")), 3)
```

Mock has many other ways you can configure it and control its behavior. These are detailed in the Python documentation for `unittest.mock`. (*http://docs.python.org/3/library/unittest.mock.html*)

doctest

The doctest module searches for pieces of text that look like interactive Python sessions in docstrings, and then executes those sessions to verify that they work exactly as shown.

Doctests serve a different purpose than proper unit tests. They are usually less detailed and don't catch special cases or obscure regression bugs. Instead, they are useful as an expressive documentation of the main use cases of a module and its components (an example of a happy path (*https://en.wikipedia.org/wiki/Happy_path*)). However, doctests should run automatically each time the full test suite runs.

Here's a simple doctest in a function:

```
def square(x):
    """Squares x.
```

```
    >>> square(2)
    4
    >>> square(-2)
    4
    """

    return x * x

if __name__ == '__main__':
    import doctest
    doctest.testmod()
```

When you run this module from the command line (i.e., python module.py), the doctests will run and complain if anything is not behaving as described in the doc-strings.

Examples

In this section, we'll take excerpts from our favorite packages to highlight good testing practice using real code. The test suites require additional libraries not included in the packages (e.g., Requests uses Flask to mock up an HTTP server) which are included in their projects' *requirements.txt* file.

For all of these examples, the expected first steps are to open a terminal shell, change directories to a place where you work on open source projects, clone the source repository, and set up a virtual environment, like this:

```
$ git clone https://github.com/username/projectname.git
$ cd projectname
$ virtualenv -p python3 venv
$ source venv/bin/activate
(venv)$ pip install -r requirements.txt
```

Example: Testing in Tablib

Tablib uses the unittest module in Python's standard library for its testing. The test suite does not come with the package; you must clone the GitHub repository for the files. Here is an excerpt, with important parts annotated:

```
#!/usr/bin/env python
# -*- coding: utf-8 -*-
"""Tests for Tablib."""

import json
import unittest
import sys
import os
import tablib
from tablib.compat import markup, unicode, is_py3
from tablib.core import Row
```

```
class TablibTestCase(unittest.TestCase):   ❶
    """Tablib test cases."""

    def setUp(self):   ❷
        """Create simple data set with headers."""

        global data, book

        data = tablib.Dataset()
        book = tablib.Databook()

        #
        #  ... skip additional setup not used here ...
        #


    def tearDown(self):   ❸
        """Teardown."""
        pass


    def test_empty_append(self):   ❹
        """Verify append() correctly adds tuple with no headers."""
        new_row = (1, 2, 3)
        data.append(new_row)

        # Verify width/data
        self.assertTrue(data.width == len(new_row))
        self.assertTrue(data[0] == new_row)


    def test_empty_append_with_headers(self):   ❺
        """Verify append() correctly detects mismatch of number of
        headers and data.
        """
        data.headers = ['first', 'second']
        new_row = (1, 2, 3, 4)

        self.assertRaises(tablib.InvalidDimensions, data.append, new_row)
```

❶ To use unittest, subclass unittest.TestCase, and write test methods whose names begin with test. The TestCase provides assert methods that check for equality, truth, data type, set membership, and whether exceptions are raised— see the documentation (*http://bit.ly/unittest-testcase*) for more details.

❷ TestCase.setUp() is run before every single test method in the TestCase.

❸ `TestCase.tearDown()` is run after every single test method in the `TestCase`.[13]

❹ All test methods must begin with `test`, or they will not be run.

❺ There can be multiple tests within a single `TestCase`, but each one should test just one thing.

If you were contributing to Tablib, the first thing you'd do after cloning it is run the test suite and confirm that nothing breaks. Like this:

```
(venv)$ ### inside the top-level directory, tablib/
(venv)$ python -m unittest  test_tablib.py
..........................................................
----------------------------------------------------------------------
Ran 62 tests in 0.289s

OK
```

As of Python 2.7, `unittest` also includes its own test discovery mechanisms, using the `discover` option on the command line:

```
(venv)$ ### *above* the top-level directory, tablib/
(venv)$ python -m unittest discover tablib/
..........................................................
----------------------------------------------------------------------
Ran 62 tests in 0.234s

OK
```

After confirming all of the tests pass, you'd (a) find the test case related to the part you're changing and run it often while you're modifying the code, or (b) write a new test case for the feature you're adding or the bug you're tracking down and run *that* often while modifying the code. The following snippet is an example:

```
(venv)$ ### inside the top-level directory, tablib/
(venv)$ python -m unittest test_tablib.TablibTestCase.test_empty_append
.
----------------------------------------------------------------------
Ran 1 test in 0.001s

OK
```

---

13 Note that `unittest.TestCase.tearDown` will not be run if the code errors out. This may be a surprise if you've used features in `unittest.mock` to alter the code's actual behavior. In Python 3.1, the method `unittest.TestCase.addCleanup()` was added; it pushes a cleanup function and its arguments to a stack that will be called one by one after `unittest.TestCase.tearDown()` or else called anyway regardless of whether `tearDown()` was called. For more information, see the documentation on `unittest.TestCase.addCleanup()`. (*http://docs.python.org/3/library/unittest.html#unittest.TestCase.addCleanup*)

Once your code works, you'd run the entire test suite again before pushing it to the repository. Because you're running these tests so often, it makes sense that they should be as fast as possible. There are a lot more details about using unittest in the standard library unittest documentation (*http://bit.ly/unittest-library*).

Example: Testing in Requests

Requests uses `py.test`. To see it in action, open a terminal shell, change into a temporary directory, clone Requests, install the dependencies, and run `py.test`, as shown here:

```
$ git clone -q https://github.com/kennethreitz/requests.git
$
$ virtualenv venv -q -p python3  # dash -q for 'quiet'
$ source venv/bin/activate
(venv)$
(venv)$ pip install -q -r requests/requirements.txt   # 'quiet' again...
(venv)$ cd requests
(venv)$ py.test
========================== test session starts ===========================
platform darwin -- Python 3.4.3, pytest-2.8.1, py-1.4.30, pluggy-0.3.1
rootdir: /tmp/requests, inifile:
plugins: cov-2.1.0, httpbin-0.0.7
collected 219 items

tests/test_requests.py ......................................................
X........................................
tests/test_utils.py ..s...........................................

========= 217 passed, 1 skipped, 1 xpassed in 25.75 seconds ==================
```

Other Popular Tools

The testing tools listed here are less frequently used, but still popular enough to mention.

pytest

pytest (*http://pytest.org/latest/*) is a no-boilerplate alternative to Python's standard unittest module, meaning it doesn't require the scaffolding of test classes, and maybe not even setup and teardown methods. To install it, use `pip` like usual:

```
$ pip install pytest
```

Despite being a fully featured and extensible test tool, it boasts a simple syntax. Creating a test suite is as easy as writing a module with a couple of functions:

```
# content of test_sample.py
def func(x):
    return x + 1
```

```
def test_answer():
    assert func(3) == 5
```

and then running the py.test command is far less work than would be required for the equivalent functionality with the unittest module:

```
$ py.test
=========================== test session starts ============================
platform darwin -- Python 2.7.1 -- pytest-2.2.1
collecting ... collected 1 items

test_sample.py F

================================= FAILURES =================================
_____ test_answer _____

    def test_answer():
>       assert func(3) == 5
E       assert 4 == 5
E        + where 4 = func(3)

test_sample.py:5: AssertionError
========================= 1 failed in 0.02 seconds =========================
```

Nose

Nose (*http://readthedocs.org/docs/nose/en/latest/*) extends unittest to make testing easier:

```
$ pip install nose
```

Nose provides automatic test discovery to save you the hassle of manually creating test suites. It also provides numerous plug-ins for features such as xUnit-compatible test output, coverage reporting, and test selection.

tox

tox (*http://testrun.org/tox/latest/*) is a tool for automating test environment management and testing against multiple interpreter configurations:

```
$ pip install tox
```

tox allows you to configure complicated multiparameter test matrices via a simple ini-style configuration file.

Options for older versions of Python

If you aren't in control of your Python version but still want to use these testing tools, here are a few options.

unittest2. unittest2 (*http://pypi.python.org/pypi/unittest2*) is a backport of Python 2.7's unittest module which has an improved API and better assertions than the ones available in previous versions of Python.

If you're using Python 2.6 or below (meaning you probably work at a large bank or Fortune 500 company), you can install it with `pip`:

```
$ pip install unittest2
```

You may want to import the module under the name unittest to make to make it easier to port code to newer versions of the module in the future:

```
import unittest2 as unittest

class MyTest(unittest.TestCase):
    ...
```

This way if you ever switch to a newer Python version and no longer need the unittest2 module, you can simply change the import in your test module without the need to change any other code.

Mock. If you liked "Mock (in unittest)" on page 79 but use a Python version below 3.3, you can still use `unittest.mock` by importing it as a separate library:

```
$ pip install mock
```

fixture. fixture (*http://farmdev.com/projects/fixture/*) can provide tools that make it easier to set up and tear down database backends for testing. It can load mock datasets for use with SQLAlchemy, SQLObject, Google Datastore, Django ORM, and Storm. There are still new releases, but it has only been tested on Python 2.4 through Python 2.6.

Lettuce and Behave

Lettuce and Behave are packages for doing *behavior-driven development* (BDD) in Python. BDD is a process that sprung out of TDD (obey the testing goat!) in the early 2000s, wishing to substitute the word "test" in test-driven development with "behavior" to overcome newbies' initial trouble grasping TDD. The name was first coined by Dan North in 2003 and introduced to the world along with the Java tool JBehave in a 2006 article for *Better Software* magazine that is reproduced in Dan North's blog post, "Introducing BDD." (*http://dannorth.net/introducing-bdd/*)

BDD grew very popular after the 2011 release of *The Cucumber Book* (Pragmatic Bookshelf), which documents a Behave package for Ruby. This inspired Gabriel Falco's Lettuce (*http://lettuce.it/*), and Peter Parente's Behave (*http://pythonhosted.org/behave/*) in our community.

Behaviors are described in plain text using a syntax named Gherkin that is human-readable *and* machine-processable. The following tutorials may be of use:

- Gherkin tutorial (*https://github.com/cucumber/cucumber/wiki/Gherkin*)
- Lettuce tutorial (*http://lettuce.it/tutorial/simple.html*)
- Behave tutorial (*http://tott-meetup.readthedocs.org/en/latest/sessions/behave.html*)

Documentation

Readability is a primary focus for Python developers, in both project and code documentation. The best practices described in this section can save both you and others a lot of time.

Project Documentation

There is API documentation for project users, and then there is additional project documentation for those who want to contribute to to the project. This section is about the additional project documentation.

A *README* file at the root directory should give general information to both users and maintainers of a project. It should be raw text or written in some very easy to read markup, such as reStructured Text (recommended because right now it's the only format that can be understood by PyPI[14]) or Markdown. (*https://help.github.com/articles/basic-writing-and-formatting-syntax/*) It should contain a few lines explaining the purpose of the project or library (without assuming the user knows anything about the project), the URL of the main source for the software, and some basic credit information. This file is the main entry point for readers of the code.

An *INSTALL* file is less necessary with Python (but may be helpful to comply with licence requirements such as the GPL). The installation instructions are often reduced to one command, such as `pip install module` or `python setup.py install` and added to the *README* file.

A *LICENSE* file should *always* be present and specify the license under which the software is made available to the public. (See "Choosing a License" on page 93 for more information.)

A *TODO* file or a TODO section in *README* should list the planned development for the code.

---

14 For those interested, there's some discussion about adding Markdown support (*https://bitbucket.org/pypa/pypi/issues/148/support-markdown-for-readmes*) for the README files on PyPI.

A *CHANGELOG* file or section in *README* should compile a short overview of the changes in the code base for the latest versions.

Project Publication

Depending on the project, your documentation might include some or all of the following components:

- An *introduction* should provide a very short overview of what can be done with the product, using one or two extremely simplified use cases. This is the 30-second pitch for your project.
- A *tutorial* should show some primary use cases in more detail. The reader will follow a step-by-step procedure to set up a working prototype.
- An *API reference* is typically generated from the code (see "Docstring Versus Block Comments" on page 89). It will list all publicly available interfaces, parameters, and return values.
- *Developer documentation* is intended for potential contributors. This can include code conventions and the general design strategy of the project.

Sphinx

Sphinx (*http://sphinx.pocoo.org*) is far and away the most popular[15] Python documentation tool. *Use it.* It converts the reStructured Text markup language into a range of output formats, including HTML, LaTeX (for printable PDF versions), manual pages, and plain text.

There is also *great, free* hosting for your Sphinx documentation: Read the Docs (*http://readthedocs.org*). Use that, too. You can configure it with commit hooks to your source repository so that rebuilding your documentation will happen automatically.

Sphinx is famous for its API generation, but it also works well for general project documentation. The online Hitchhiker's Guide to Python (*http://docs.python-guide.org/*) is built with Sphinx and is hosted on Read the Docs.

---

15 Other tools that you might see are Pycco, Ronn, Epydoc (now discontinued), and MkDocs. Pretty much everyone uses Sphinx and we recommend you do, too.

reStructured Text

Sphinx uses reStructured Text (*http://docutils.sourceforge.net/rst.html*), and nearly all Python documentation is written using it. If the content of your `long_description` argument to `setuptools.setup()` is written in reStructured Text, it will be rendered as HTML on PyPI—other formats will just be presented as text. It's like Markdown with all the optional extensions built in. Good resources for the syntax are:

- The reStructuredText Primer (*http://sphinx.pocoo.org/rest.html*)
- reStructuredText Quick Reference (*http://bit.ly/restructured-text*)

Or just start contributing to your favorite package's documentation and learn by reading.

Docstring Versus Block Comments

Docstrings and block comments aren't interchangeable. Both can be used for a function or class. Here's an example using both:

```
# This function slows down program execution for some reason. ❶
def square_and_rooter(x):
    """Return the square root of self times self.""" ❷
    ...
```

❶ The leading comment block is a programmer's note.

❷ The docstring describes the *operation* of the function or class and will be shown in an interactive Python session when the user types `help(square_and_rooter)`.

Docstrings placed at the beginning of a module or at the top of an *__init__.py* file will also appear in `help()`. Sphinx's autodoc feature can also automatically generate documentation using appropriately formatted docstrings. Instructions for how to do this, and how to format your docstrings for autodoc, are in the Sphinx tutorial (*http://www.sphinx-doc.org/en/stable/tutorial.html#autodoc*). For further details on docstrings, see PEP 257 (*https://www.python.org/dev/peps/pep-0257/*).

Logging

The logging module has been a part of Python's Standard Library since version 2.3. It is succinctly described in PEP 282 (*https://www.python.org/dev/peps/pep-0282/*). The documentation is notoriously hard to read, except for the basic logging tutorial (*http://docs.python.org/howto/logging.html#logging-basic-tutorial*).

Logging serves two purposes:

Diagnostic logging
> Diagnostic logging records events related to the application's operation. If a user calls in to report an error, for example, the logs can be searched for context.

Audit logging
> Audit logging records events for business analysis. A user's transactions (such as a clickstream) can be extracted and combined with other user details (such as eventual purchases) for reports or to optimize a business goal.

Logging Versus Print

The only time that `print` is a better option than logging is when the goal is to display a help statement for a command-line application. Other reasons why logging is better than `print`:

- The log record (*https://docs.python.org/library/logging.html#logrecord-attributes*), which is created with every logging event, contains readily available diagnostic information such as the filename, full path, function, and line number of the logging event.

- Events logged in included modules are automatically accessible via the root logger to your application's logging stream, unless you filter them out.

- Logging can be selectively silenced by using the method `logging.Logger.setLevel()` or disabled by setting the attribute `logging.Logger.disabled` to `True`.

Logging in a Library

Notes for configuring logging for a library are in the logging tutorial (*http://bit.ly/configuring-logging*). Another good resource for example uses of logging is the libraries we mention in the next chapter. Because the *user*, not the library, should dictate what happens when a logging event occurs, one admonition bears repeating:

> It is strongly advised that you do not add any handlers other than `NullHandler` to your library's loggers.

The `NullHandler` does what its name says—nothing. The user will otherwise have to expressly turn off your logging if they don't want it.

Best practice when instantiating loggers in a library is to only create them using the `__name__` global variable: the `logging` module creates a hierarchy of loggers using dot notation, so using `__name__` ensures no name collisions.

Here is an example of best practice from the Requests source (*https://github.com/kennethreitz/requests*)—place this in your project's top-level *__init__.py*:

```
# Set default logging handler to avoid "No handler found" warnings.
import logging
try:  # Python 2.7+
    from logging import NullHandler
except ImportError:
    class NullHandler(logging.Handler):
        def emit(self, record):
            pass

logging.getLogger(__name__).addHandler(NullHandler())
```

Logging in an Application

The Twelve-Factor App (*http://12factor.net*), an authoritative reference for good practice in application development, contains a section on logging best practice (*http://12factor.net/logs*). It emphatically advocates for treating log events as an event stream, and for sending that event stream to standard output to be handled by the application environment.

There are at least three ways to configure a logger:

	Pros	Cons
Using an INI-formatted file	It's possible to update configuration while running using the function `logging.config.listen()` to listen for changes on a socket.	You have less control (e.g., custom subclassed filters or loggers) than possible when configuring a logger in code.
Using a dictionary or a JSON-formatted file	In addition to updating while running, it is also possible to load from a file using the json module, in the standard library since Python 2.6.	You have less control than when configuring a logger in code.
Using code	You have complete control over the configuration.	Any modifications require a change to source code.

Example configuration via an INI file

More details about the INI file format are in the logging configuration section of the logging tutorial (*https://docs.python.org/howto/logging.html#configuring-logging*). A minimal configuration file would look like this:

```
[loggers]
keys=root

[handlers]
keys=stream_handler

[formatters]
keys=formatter
```

```
[logger_root]
level=DEBUG
handlers=stream_handler

[handler_stream_handler]
class=StreamHandler
level=DEBUG
formatter=formatter
args=(sys.stderr,)

[formatter_formatter]
format=%(asctime)s %(name)-12s %(levelname)-8s %(message)s
```

The `asctime`, `name`, `levelname`, and `message` are all optional attributes available from the logging library. The full list of options and their definitions is available in the Python documentation (*http://bit.ly/logrecord-attributes*). Let us say that our logging configuration file is named *logging_config.ini*. Then to set up the logger using this configuration in the code, we'd use `logging.config.fileConfig()`:

```
import logging
from logging.config import fileConfig

fileConfig('logging_config.ini')
logger = logging.getLogger()
logger.debug('often makes a very good meal of %s', 'visiting tourists')
```

Example configuration via a dictionary

As of Python 2.7, you can use a dictionary with configuration details. PEP 391 (*https://www.python.org/dev/peps/pep-0391*) contains a list of the mandatory and optional elements in the configuration dictionary. Here's a minimal implementation:

```
import logging
from logging.config import dictConfig

logging_config = dict(
    version = 1,
    formatters = {
        'f': {'format':
              '%(asctime)s %(name)-12s %(levelname)-8s %(message)s'}
    },
    handlers = {
        'h': {'class': 'logging.StreamHandler',
              'formatter': 'f',
              'level': logging.DEBUG}
    },
    loggers = {
        'root': {'handlers': ['h'],
                 'level': logging.DEBUG}
    }
)
```

```
dictConfig(logging_config)

logger = logging.getLogger()
logger.debug('often makes a very good meal of %s', 'visiting tourists')
```

Example configuration directly in code

And last, here is a minimal logging configuration directly in code:

```
import logging

logger = logging.getLogger()
handler = logging.StreamHandler()
formatter = logging.Formatter(
        '%(asctime)s %(name)-12s %(levelname)-8s %(message)s')
handler.setFormatter(formatter)
logger.addHandler(handler)
logger.setLevel(logging.DEBUG)

logger.debug('often makes a very good meal of %s', 'visiting tourists')
```

Choosing a License

In the United States, when no license is specified with your source publication, users have no legal right to download, modify, or distribute it. Furthermore, people can't contribute to your project unless you tell them what rules to play by. You *need* a license.

Upstream Licenses

If you are deriving from another project, your choice may be determined by upstream licenses. For example, the Python Software Foundation (PSF) asks all contributors to Python source code to sign a contributor agreement that formally licenses their code to the PSF (retaining their own copyright) under one of two licenses.[16]

Because both of those licenses allow users to sublicense under different terms, the PSF is then free to distribute Python under its own license, the Python Software Foundation License. A FAQ for the PSF License (*https://wiki.python.org/moin/Python SoftwareFoundationLicenseFaq*) goes into detail about what users can and cannot do in plain (not legal) language. It is not intended for further use beyond licensing the PSF's distribution of Python.

---

16 As of this writing, they were the Academic Free License v. 2.1 or the Apache License, Version 2.0. The full description of how this works is on the PSF's contributions page (*https://www.python.org/psf/contrib/*).

Options

There are plenty of licenses available to choose from. The PSF recommends using one of the Open Source Institute (OSI)–approved licenses (*http://opensource.org/licenses*). If you wish to eventually contribute your code to the PSF, the process will be much easier if you start with one of the licenses specified on the contributions page (*https://www.python.org/psf/contrib/*).

 Remember to change the placeholder text in the template licenses to actually reflect your information. For example, the MIT license template contains `Copyright (c) <year> <copyright holders>` on its second line. Apache License, Version 2.0 requires no modification.

Open source licenses tend to fall into one of two categories:[17]

Permissive licenses

Permissive licenses, often also called Berkeley Software Distribution (BSD)–style licenses, focus more on the user's freedom to do with the software as they please. Some examples:

- The Apache licenses—version 2.0 (*https://opensource.org/licenses/Apache-2.0*) is the current one, modified so that people can include it without modification in any project, can include the license by reference instead of listing it in every file, and can use Apache 2.0–licensed code with the GNU General Public License version 3.0 (GPLv3).

- Both the BSD 2-clause and 3-clause licenses—the three-clause license (*https://opensource.org/licenses/BSD-3-Clause*) is the two-clause license plus an additional restriction on use of the issuer's trademarks.

- The Massachusetts Institute of Technology (MIT) licenses (*https://opensource.org/licenses/MIT*)—both the Expat and the X11 versions are named after popular products that use the respective licenses.

- The Internet Software Consortium (ISC) license (*https://opensource.org/licenses/ISC*)—it's almost identical to the MIT license except for a few lines now deemed to be extraneous.

---

17 All of the licenses described here are OSI-approved, and you can learn more about them from the main OSI license page (*https://opensource.org/licenses*).

Copyleft licenses

Copyleft licenses, or less permissive licenses, focus more on making sure that the source code itself—including any changes made to it—is made available. The GPL family is the most well known of these. The current version is GPLv3 (*https://opensource.org/licenses/GPL-3.0*).

 The GPLv2 license is not compatible with Apache 2.0; so code licensed with GPLv2 cannot be mixed with Apache 2.0–licensed projects. But Apache 2.0–licensed projects *can* be used in GPLv3 projects (which must subsequently all be GPLv3).

Licenses meeting the OSI criteria all allow commercial use, modification of the software, and distribution downstream—with different restrictions and requirements. All of the ones listed in Table 4-4 also limit the issuer's liability and require the user to retain the original copyright and license in any downstream distribution.

Table 4-4. Topics discussed in popular licenses

License family	Restrictions	Allowances	Requirements
BSD	Protects issuer's trademark (BSD 3-clause)	Allows a warranty (BSD 2-clause and 3-clause)	—
MIT (X11 or Expat), ISC	Protects issuer's trademark (ISC and MIT/X11)	Allows sublicensing with a different license	—
Apache version 2.0	Protects issuer's trademark	Allows sublicensing, use in patents	Must state changes made to the source
GPL	Prohibits sublicensing with a different license	Allows a warranty, and (GPLv3 only) use in patents	Must state changes to the source and include source code

Licensing Resources

Van Lindberg's book *Intellectual Property and Open Source* (O'Reilly) is a great resource on the legal aspects of open source software. It will help you understand not only licenses, but also the legal aspects of other intellectual property topics like trademarks, patents, and copyrights as they relate to open source. If you're not that concerned about legal matters and just want to choose something quickly, these sites can help:

- GitHub offers a handy guide (*http://choosealicense.com/*) that summarizes and compares licenses in a few sentences.

- TLDRLegal (*http://tldrlegal.com/*)[18] lists what can, cannot, and must be done under the terms of each license in quick bullets.
- The OSI list of approved licenses (*http://opensource.org/licenses*) contains the full text of all licenses that have passed their license review process for compliance with the Open Source Definition (allowing software to be freely used, modified, and shared).

---

18 *tl;dr* means "Too long; didn't read," and apparently existed as editor shorthand before popularization on the Internet.

## CHAPTER 5

Reading Great Code

Programmers read a *lot* of code. One of the core tenets behind Python's design is readability, and one secret to becoming a great programmer is to read, understand, and comprehend excellent code. Such code typically follows the guidelines outlined in "Code Style" on page 47 and does its best to express a clear and concise intent to the reader.

This chapter shows excerpts from some very readable Python projects that illustrate topics covered in Chapter 4. As we describe them, we'll also share techniques for reading code.[1]

Here's a list of projects highlighted in this chapter in the order they will appear:

- HowDoI (*https://github.com/gleitz/howdoi*) is a console application that searches the Internet for answers to coding questions, written in Python.

- Diamond (*https://github.com/python-diamond/Diamond*) is a Python daemon[2] that collects metrics and publishes them to Graphite or other backends. It is capable of collecting CPU, memory, network, I/O, load and disk metrics. Additionally, it features an API for implementing custom collectors to gather metrics from almost any source.

- Tablib (*https://github.com/kennethreitz/tablib*) is a format-agnostic tabular dataset library.

---

1 For a book that contains decades of experience about reading and refactoring code, we recommend *Object-Oriented Reengineering Patterns* (*http://scg.unibe.ch/download/oorp/index.html*) (Square Bracket Associates) by Serge Demeyer, Stéphane Ducasse, and Oscar Nierstrasz.

2 A *daemon* is a computer program that runs as a background process.

- Requests (*https://github.com/kennethreitz/requests*) is a HyperText Transfer Protocol (HTTP) library for human beings (the 90% of us who just want an HTTP client that automatically handles password authentication and complies with the half-dozen standards (*https://www.w3.org/Protocols/*) to perform things like a multipart file upload with one function call).

- Werkzeug (*https://github.com/mitsuhiko/werkzeug*) started as a simple collection of various utilities for Web Service Gateway Interface (WSGI) applications and has become one of the most advanced WSGI utility modules.

- Flask (*https://github.com/mitsuhiko/flask*) is a web microframework for Python based on Werkzeug and Jinja2. It's good for getting simple web pages up quickly.

There is a lot more to all of these projects than what we're mentioning, and we really, really hope that after this chapter you'll be motivated to download and read at least one or two of them in depth yourself (and maybe even present what you learn to a local user group).

Common Features

Some features are common across all of the projects: details from a snapshot of each one show very few (fewer than 20, excluding whitespace and comments) lines of code on average per function, and a lot of blank lines. The larger, more complex projects use docstrings and/or comments; usually more than a fifth of the content of the code base is some sort of documentation. But we can see from HowDoI, which has no docstrings because it is not for interactive use, that comments are not necessary when the code is straightforward. Table 5-1 shows common practices in these projects.

Table 5-1. Common features in the example projects

Package	License	Line count	Docstrings (% of lines)	Comments (% of lines)	Blank lines (% of lines)	Average function length
HowDoI	MIT	262	0%	6%	20%	13 lines of code
Diamond	MIT	6,021	21%	9%	16%	11 lines of code
Tablib	MIT	1,802	19%	4%	27%	8 lines of code
Requests	Apache 2.0	4,072	23%	8%	19%	10 lines of code
Flask	BSD 3-clause	10,163	7%	12%	11%	13 lines of code
Werkzeug	BSD 3-clause	25,822	25%	3%	13%	9 lines of code

In each section, we use a different code-reading technique to figure out what the project is about. Next, we single out code excerpts that demonstrate ideas mentioned elsewhere in this guide. (Just because we don't highlight things in one project doesn't mean they don't exist; we just want to provide good coverage of concepts across these examples.) You should finish this chapter more confident about reading code, with examples that reinforce what makes good code, and with some ideas you'd like to incorporate in your own code later.

HowDoI

With fewer than 300 lines of code, The HowDoI project, by Benjamin Gleitzman, is a great choice to start our reading odyssey.

Reading a Single-File Script

A script usually has a clear starting point, clear options, and a clear ending point. This makes it easier to follow than libraries that present an API or provide a framework.

Get the HowDoI module from GitHub:[3]

```
$ git clone https://github.com/gleitz/howdoi.git
$ virtualenv -p python3 venv  # or use mkvirtualenv, your choice...
$ source venv/bin/activate
(venv)$ cd howdoi/
(venv)$ pip install --editable .
(venv)$ python test_howdoi.py  # Run the unit tests.
```

You should now have the howdoi executable installed in *venv/bin*. (You can look at it if you want by typing cat `which howdoi` on the command line.) It was auto-generated when you ran pip install.

Read HowDoI's documentation

HowDoI's documentation is in the *README.rst* file in the HowDoI repository on GitHub (*https://github.com/gleitz/howdoi*): it's a small command-line application that allows users to search the Internet for answers to programming questions.

From the command line in a terminal shell, we can type howdoi --help for the usage statement:

```
(venv)$ howdoi --help
usage: howdoi [-h] [-p POS] [-a] [-l] [-c] [-n NUM_ANSWERS] [-C] [-v]
              [QUERY [QUERY ...]]

instant coding answers via the command line

positional arguments:
  QUERY                  the question to answer

optional arguments:
```

---

3 If you run into trouble with lxml requiring a more recent libxml2 shared library, just install an earlier version of lxml by typing: pip uninstall lxml;pip install lxml==3.5.0. It will work fine.

```
-h, --help              show this help message and exit
-p POS, --pos POS       select answer in specified position (default: 1)
-a, --all               display the full text of the answer
-l, --link              display only the answer link
-c, --color             enable colorized output
-n NUM_ANSWERS, --num-answers NUM_ANSWERS
                        number of answers to return
-C, --clear-cache       clear the cache
-v, --version           displays the current version of howdoi
```

That's it—from the documentation we know that HowDoI gets answers to coding questions from the Internet, and from the usage statement we know we can choose the answer in a specific position, can colorize the output, get multiple answers, and that it keeps a cache that can be cleared.

Use HowDoI

We can confirm we understand what HowDoI does by actually using it. Here's an example:

```
(venv)$ howdoi --num-answers 2 python lambda function list comprehension
--- Answer 1 ---
[(lambda x: x*x)(x) for x in range(10)]

--- Answer 2 ---
[x() for x in [lambda m=m: m for m in [1,2,3]]]
# [1, 2, 3]
```

We've installed HowDoI, read its documentation, and can use it. On to reading actual code!

Read HowDoI's code

If you look inside the *howdoi/* directory, you'll see it contains two files: an *__init__.py*, which contains a single line that defines the version number, and *howdoi.py*, which we'll open and read.

Skimming *howdoi.py*, we see each new function definition is used in the next function, making it is easy to follow. And each function does just one thing—the thing its name says. The main function, `command_line_runner()`, is near the bottom of *howdoi.py*.

Rather than reprint HowDoI's source here, we can illustrate its call structure using the call graph in Figure 5-1. It was created by Python Call Graph (*https://pycall graph.readthedocs.io*), which provides a visualization of the functions called when running a Python script. This works well with command-line applications thanks to a single start point and the relatively few paths through their code. (Note that we manually deleted functions not in the HowDoI project from the rendered image to legibly fit it on the page, and slightly recolored and reformatted it.)

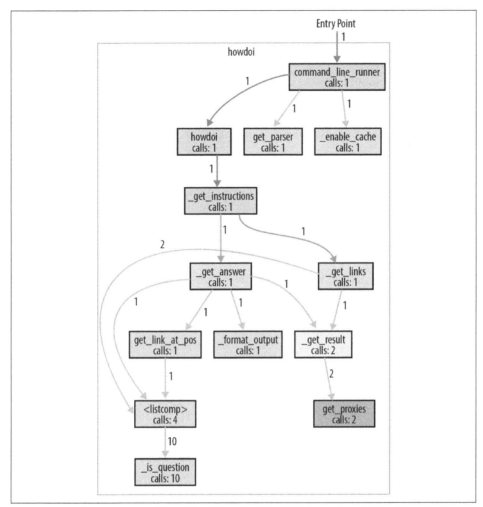

Figure 5-1. Clean paths and clear function names in this howdoi call graph

The code could have been all one large, incomprehensible spaghetti function. Instead, intentional choices structure the code into compartmentalized functions with straightforward names. Here's a brief description of the execution depicted in Figure 5-1: command_line_runner() parses the input and passes the user flags and the query to howdoi(). Then, howdoi() wraps _get_instructions() in a try/except statement so that it can catch connection errors and print a reasonable error message (because application code should not terminate on exceptions).

The primary functionality is in _get_instructions(): it calls _get_links() to do a Google search of Stack Overflow for links that match the query, then calls _get_answer() once for each resulting link (up to the number of links that the user specified on the command line—the default is just one link).

The _get_answer() function follows a link to Stack Overflow, extracts code from the answer, colorizes it, and returns it to _get_instructions(), which will combine all of the answers into one string, and return it. Both _get_links() and _get_answer() call _get_result() to actually do the HTTP request: _get_links() for the Google query, and _get_answer() for the resulting links from the Google query.

All _get_result() does is wrap requests.get() with a try/except statement so that it can catch SSL errors, print an error message, and re-raise the exception so that the top-level try/except can catch it and exit. Catching all exceptions before exiting is best practice for application programs.

HowDoI's Packaging

HowDoI's *setup.py*, above the *howdoi/* directory, is a good example setup module because in addition to normal package installation, it also installs an executable (which you can refer to when packaging your own command-line utility). The setup tools.setup() function uses keyword arguments to define all of the configuration options. The part that identifies the executable is associated with the keyword argument entry_points:

```
setup(
    name='howdoi',
    ##~~ ... Skip the other typical entries ...
    entry_points={
        'console_scripts': [  ❶
            'howdoi = howdoi.howdoi:command_line_runner',  ❷
        ]
    },
    ## ~~  ... Skip the list of dependencies ...
)
```

❶ The keyword to list console scripts is console_scripts.

❷ This declares the executable named howdoi will have as its target the function howdoi.howdoi.command_line_runner(). So later when reading, we will know command_line_runner() is the starting point for running the whole application.

Structure Examples from HowDoI

HowDoI is a small library, and we'll be highlighting structure much more elsewhere, so there are only a few notes here.

Let each function do just one thing

We can't reiterate enough how beneficial it is for readers to separate out HowDoI's internal functions to each do just one thing. Also, there are functions whose sole purpose is to wrap other functions with a try/except statement. (The only function with a try/except that doesn't follow this practice is _format_output(), which leverages try/except clauses to identify the correct coding language for syntax highlighting, not for exception handling.)

Leverage data available from the system

HowDoI checks and uses relevant system values, such as urllib.request.getprox ies(), to handle the use of proxy servers (this can be the case in organizations like schools that have an intermediary server filtering the connection to the Internet), or in this snippet:

```
XDG_CACHE_DIR = os.environ.get(
    'XDG_CACHE_HOME',
    os.path.join(os.path.expanduser('~'), '.cache')
)
```

How do you know that these variables exist? The need for urllib.request.getprox ies() is evident from the optional arguments in requests.get()—so part of this information comes from understanding the API of libraries you call. Environment variables are often utility-specific, so if a library is intended for use with a particular database or other sister application, those applications' documentation list relevant environment variables. For plain POSIX systems, a good place to start is Ubuntu's list of default environment variables, (*https://help.ubuntu.com/community/Environment Variables*) or else the base list of environment variables in the POSIX specification (*http://bit.ly/posix-env-variables*), which links to various relevant other lists.

Style Examples from HowDoI

HowDoI mostly follows PEP 8, but not pedantically, and not when it restricts readability. For example, import statements are at the top of the file, but standard library and external modules are intermixed. And although the string constants in USER_AGENTS are much longer than 80 characters, there is no natural place to break the strings, so they are left intact.

These next excerpts highlight other style choices we've previously advocated for in Chapter 4.

Underscore-prefixed function names (we are all responsible users)

Almost every function in HowDoI is prefixed with an underscore. This identifies them as for internal use only. For most of them, this is because if called, there is the possibility of an uncaught exception—anything that calls _get_result() risks this—until the howdoi() function, which handles the possible exceptions.

The rest of the internal functions (_format_output(), _is_question(), _enable_cache(), and _clear_cache()) are identified as such because they're simply not intended for use outside of the package. The testing script, *howdoi/test_howdoi.py*, only calls the nonprefixed functions, checking that the formatter works by feeding a command-line argument for colorization to the top-level howdoi.howdoi() function, rather than by feeding code to howdoi._format_output().

Handle compatibility in just one place (readability counts)

Differences between versions of possible dependencies are handled before the main code body so the reader knows there won't be dependency issues, and version checking doesn't litter the code elsewhere. This is nice because HowDoI is shipped as a command-line tool, and the extra effort means users won't be forced to change their Python environment just to accommodate the tool. Here is the snippet with the workarounds:

```
try:
    from urllib.parse import quote as url_quote
except ImportError:
    from urllib import quote as url_quote

try:
    from urllib import getproxies
except ImportError:
    from urllib.request import getproxies
```

And the following snippet resolves the difference between Python 2 and Python 3's Unicode handling in seven lines, by creating the function u(x) to either do nothing or emulate Python 3. Plus it follows Stack Overflow's new citation guideline (*http://meta.stackexchange.com/questions/271080*), by citing the original source:

```
# Handle Unicode between Python 2 and 3
# http://stackoverflow.com/a/6633040/305414
if sys.version < '3':
    import codecs
    def u(x):
        return codecs.unicode_escape_decode(x)[0]
else:
    def u(x):
        return x
```

Pythonic choices (beautiful is better than ugly)

The following snippet from *howdoi.py* shows thoughtful, Pythonic choices. The function get_link_at_pos() returns False if there are no results, or else identifies the links that are to Stack Overflow questions, and returns the one at the desired position (or the last one if there aren't enough links):

```python
def _is_question(link):  ❶
    return re.search('questions/\d+/', link)

# [ ... skip a function ... ]

def get_link_at_pos(links, position):
    links = [link for link in links if _is_question(link)]  ❷
    if not links:
        return False  ❸

    if len(links) >= position:
        link = links[position-1]  ❹
    else:
        link = links[-1]  ❺
    return link  ❻
```

❶ The first function, _is_question(), is defined as a separate one liner, giving clear meaning to an otherwise opaque regular expression search.

❷ The list comprehension reads like a sentence, thanks to the separate definition of _is_question() and meaningful variable names.

❸ The early return statement flattens the code.

❹ The additional step of assigning to the variable link here…

❺ …and here, rather than two separate return statements with no named variable at all, reinforces the purpose of get_link_at_pos() with clear variable names. The code is self-documenting.

❻ The single return statement at the highest indentation level explicitly shows that all paths through the code exit either right away—because there are no links—or at the end of the function, returning a link. Our quick rule of thumb works: we can read the first and last line of this function and understand what it does. (Given multiple links and a position, get_link_at_pos() returns one single link: the one at the given position.)

Diamond

Diamond is a daemon (an application that runs continuously as a background process) that collects system metrics and publishes them to downstream programs like MySQL, Graphite (*http://graphite.readthedocs.org/*) (a platform open sourced by Orbitz in 2008 that stores, retrieves, and optionally graphs numeric time-series data), and others. We'll get to explore good package structure, as Diamond is a multifile application, much larger than HowDoI.

Reading a Larger Application

Diamond is still a command-line application, so like with HowDoI, there's still a clear starting point and clear paths of execution, although the supporting code now spans multiple files.

Get Diamond from GitHub (the documentation says it only runs on CentOS or Ubuntu, but code in its *setup.py* makes it appear to support all platforms; however, some of the commands that default collectors use to monitor memory, disk space, and other system metrics are not on Windows). As of this writing, it still uses Python 2.7:

```
$ git clone https://github.com/python-diamond/Diamond.git
$ virtualenv -p python2 venv  # It's not Python 3 compatible yet...
$ source venv/bin/activate
(venv)$ cd Diamond/
(venv)$ pip install --editable .
(venv)$ pip install mock docker-py  # These are dependencies for testing.
(venv)$ pip install mock  # This is also a dependency for testing.
(venv)$ python test.py  # Run the unit tests.
```

Like with the HowDoI library, Diamond's setup script installs executables in *venv/ bin/*: diamond and diamond-setup. This time they're not automatically generated— they're prewritten scripts in the project's *Diamond/bin/* directory. The documentation says that diamond starts the server, and diamond-setup is an optional tool to walk users through interactive modification of the collector settings in the configuration file.

There are a lot of additional directories, and the diamond package is underneath *Diamond/src* in this project directory. We are going to look at files in *Diamond/src* (which contains the main code), *Diamond/bin* (which contains the executable diamond), and *Diamond/conf* (which contains the sample configuration file). The rest of the directories and files may be of interest to people distributing similar applications but is not what we want to cover right now.

Read Diamond's documentation

First, we can get a sense of what the project is and what it does by scanning the online documentation (*http://diamond.readthedocs.io/*). Diamond's goal is to make it easy to gather system metrics on clusters of machines. Originally open sourced by Bright-Cove, Inc., in 2011, it now has over 200 contributors.

After describing its history and purpose, the documentation tells you how to install it, and then says how to run it: just modify the example configuration file (in our download it's in *conf/diamond.conf.example*), put it in the default location (*/etc/diamond/ diamond.conf*) or a path you'll specify on the command line, and you're set. There's also a helpful section on configuration in the Diamond wiki page (*https://github.com/ BrightcoveOS/Diamond/wiki/Configuration*).

From the command line, we can get the usage statement via `diamond --help`:

```
(venv)$ diamond --help
Usage: diamond [options]

Options:
  -h, --help             show this help message and exit
  -c CONFIGFILE, --configfile=CONFIGFILE
                         config file
  -f, --foreground       run in foreground
  -l, --log-stdout       log to stdout
  -p PIDFILE, --pidfile=PIDFILE
                         pid file
  -r COLLECTOR, --run=COLLECTOR
                         run a given collector once and exit
  -v, --version          display the version and exit
  --skip-pidfile         Skip creating PID file
  -u USER, --user=USER   Change to specified unprivileged user
  -g GROUP, --group=GROUP
                         Change to specified unprivileged group
  --skip-change-user     Skip changing to an unprivileged user
  --skip-fork            Skip forking (damonizing) process
```

From this, we know it uses a configuration file; by default, it runs in the background; it has logging; you can specifiy a PID (process ID) file; you can test collectors; you can change the process's user and group; and it by default will daemonize (fork) the process.[4]

Use Diamond

To understand it even better, we can run Diamond. We need a modified configuration file, which we can put in a directory we make called *Diamond/tmp*. From inside the *Diamond* directory, type:

```
(venv)$ mkdir tmp
(venv)$ cp conf/diamond.conf.example tmp/diamond.conf
```

Then edit *tmp/diamond.conf* to look like this:

---

4 When you daemonize a process, you fork it, detach its session ID, and fork it again, so that the process is totally disconnected from the terminal you're running it in. (Nondaemonized programs exit when the terminal is closed—you may have seen the warning message "Are you sure you want to close this terminal? Closing it will kill the following processes:" before listing all of the currently running processes.) A daemonized process will run even after the terminal window closes. It's named daemon after Maxwell's daemon (*https:// en.wikipedia.org/wiki/Daemon_(computing)#Terminology*) (a clever daemon, not a nefarious one).

```
### Options for the server
[server]
# Handlers for published metrics.  ❶
handlers = diamond.handler.archive.ArchiveHandler
user =  ❷
group =
# Directory to load collector modules from  ❸
collectors_path = src/collectors/

### Options for handlers  ❹
[handlers]
[[default]]

[[ArchiveHandler]]
log_file = /dev/stdout

### Options for collectors
[collectors]
[[default]]
# Default Poll Interval (seconds)
interval = 20

### Default enabled collectors
[[CPUCollector]]
enabled = True

[[MemoryCollector]]
enabled = True
```

We can tell from the example configuration file that:

❶   There are multiple handlers, which we can select by class name.

❷   We have control over the user and group that the daemon runs as (empty means
to use the current user and group).

❸   We can specify a path to look for collector modules. This is how Diamond will
know where the custom `Collector` subclasses are: we directly state it in the configuration file.

❹   We can also store configure handlers individually.

Next, run Diamond with options that set logging to */dev/stdout* (with default formatting configurations), that keep the application in the foreground, that skip writing the
PID file, and that use our new configuration file:

```
(venv)$ diamond -l -f --skip-pidfile --configfile=tmp/diamond.conf
```

To end the process, type Ctrl+C until the command prompt reappears. The log output demonstrates what collectors and handlers do: collectors collect different metrics

(such as the MemoryCollector's total, available, free, and swap memory sizes), which the handlers format and send to various destinations, such as Graphite, MySQL, or in our test case, as log messages to */dev/stdout*.

Reading Diamond's code

IDEs can be useful when reading larger projects—they can quickly locate the original definitions of functions and classes in the source code. Or, given a definition, they can find all places in the project where it is used. For this functionality, set the IDE's Python interpreter to the one in your virtual environment.[5]

Instead of following each function as we did with HowDoI, Figure 5-2 follows the import statements; the diagram just shows which modules in Diamond import which other modules. Drawing sketches like these helps by providing a very high-level look for larger projects: you hide the trees so you can see the forest. We can start with the diamond executable file on the top left and follow the imports through the Diamond project. Aside from the diamond executable, every square outline denotes a file (module) or directory (package) in the *src/diamond* directory.

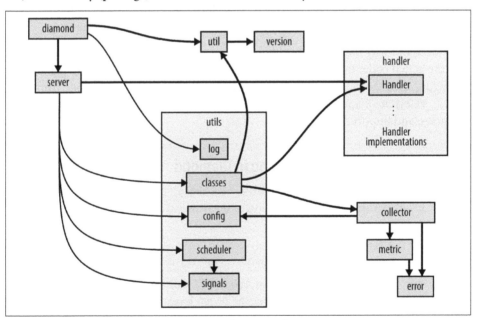

Figure 5-2. The module import structure of Diamond

---

5 In PyCharm, do this by navigating in the menu bar to PyCharm → Preferences → Project:Diamond → Project Interpreter, and then selecting the path to the Python interpreter in the current virtual environment.

Diamond's well-organized and appropriately named modules make it possible to get an idea of what the code is doing solely from our diagram: diamond gets the version from util, then sets up logging using utils.log and starts a Server instance using server. The Server imports from almost all of the modules in the utils package, using utils.classes to acess both the Handlers in handler and the collectors, config to read the configuration file and obtain settings for the collectors (and the extra paths to the user-defined collectors), and scheduler and signals to set the polling interval for the collectors to calculate their metrics, and to set up and start the handlers processing the queue of metrics to send them to their various destinations.

The diagram doesn't include the helper modules *convertor.py* and *gmetric.py*, which are used by specific collectors, or the over 20 handler implementations defined in the handler subpackage, or the over 100 collector implementations defined in the project's *Diamond/src/collectors/* directory (which is installed elsewhere when not installed the way we did for reading—that is, using PyPI or Linux package distributions, instead of source). These are imported using diamond.classes.load_dynamic_class(), which then calls the function dia mond.util.load_class_from_name() to load the classes from the string names given in the configuration file, so the import statements do not explicitly name them.

To understand why there is both a utils package and a util module, you have to dig into the actual code: the util module provides functions related more to Diamond's packaging than to its operation—a function to get the version number from ver sion.__VERSION__, and two functions that parse strings that identify either modules or classes, and import them.

Logging in Diamond

The function diamond.utils.log.setup_logging(), found in *src/diamond/utils/log.py*, is called from the main() function in the diamond executable when starting the daemon:

```
# Initialize logging
log = setup_logging(options.configfile, options.log_stdout)
```

If options.log_stdout is True, setup_logging() will set up a logger with default formatting to log to standard output at the DEBUG level. Here's the excerpt that does that:

```
##~~ ... Skip everything else ...

def setup_logging(configfile, stdout=False):
    log = logging.getLogger('diamond')

    if stdout:
        log.setLevel(logging.DEBUG)
```

```
                streamHandler = logging.StreamHandler(sys.stdout)
                streamHandler.setFormatter(DebugFormatter())
                streamHandler.setLevel(logging.DEBUG)
                log.addHandler(streamHandler)
        else:
            ##~~ ... Skip this ...
```

Otherwise, it parses the configuration file using `logging.config.file.fileCon` `fig()` from the Python Standard Library. Here is the function call—it's indented because it's inside the preceding `if`/`else` statement, and a `try`/`except` block:

```
            logging.config.fileConfig(configfile,
                                        disable_existing_loggers=False)
```

The logging configuration ignores keywords in the configuration file that aren't related to logging. This is how Diamond can use the same configuration file for both its own and the logging configuration. The sample configuration file, located in *Diamond/conf/diamond.conf.example*, identifies the logging handler among the other Diamond handlers:

```
    ### Options for handlers
    [handlers]

    # daemon logging handler(s)
    keys = rotated_file
```

It defines example loggers later in the configuration file, under the header "Options for logging," recommending the logging config file documentation (*http://bit.ly/ config-file-format*) for details.

Structure Examples from Diamond

Diamond is more than an executable application—it's also a library that provides a way for users to create and use custom collectors.

We'll highlight more things we like about the overall package structure, and then dig into how exactly Diamond makes it possible for the application to import and use externally defined collectors.

Separate different functionality into namespaces (they are one honking great idea)

The diagram in Figure 5-2 shows the server module interacting with three other modules in the project: `diamond.handler`, `diamond.collector`, and `diamond.utils`. The *utils* subpackage could realistically have contained all of its classes and functions in a single, large *util.py* module, but there was an opportunity to use namespaces to separate code into related groups, and the development team took it. Honking great!

All of the implementations of Handlers are contained in *diamond/handler* (which makes sense), but the structure for the Collectors is different. There's not a directory, only a module *diamond/collector.py* that defines the `Collector` and `ProcessCollec` `tor` base classes. All implementations of the Collectors are defined instead in *Diamond/src/collectors/* and would be installed in the virtual environment under *venv/share/diamond/collectors* when installing from PyPI (as recommended) rather than from GitHub (like we did to read it). This helps the user to create new implementations of Collectors: placing all of the collectors in the same location makes it easier for the application to find them and easier for library users to follow their example.

Finally, each Collector implementation in *Diamond/src/collectors* is in its own directory (rather than in a single file), which makes it possible to keep each Collector implementation's tests separate. Also honking great.

User-extensible custom classes (complex is better than complicated)

It's easy to add new Collector implementations: just subclass the `diamond.collec` `tor.Collector` *abstract base class*,[6] implement a `Collector.collect()` method, and place the implementation in its own directory in *venv/src/collectors/*.

Underneath, the implementation is complex, but the user doesn't see it. This section shows both the simple user-facing part of Diamond's Collector API and the complex code that makes this user interface possible.

Complex versus complicated. We can boil down the user experience of working with *complex* code to be something like experiencing a Swiss watch—it just works, but inside there are a ton of precisely made little pieces, all interfacing with remarkable precision, in order to create the effortless user experience. Using *complicated* code, on the other hand, is like piloting an airplane—you really have to know what you're doing to not crash and burn.[7] We don't want to live in a world without airplanes, but we *do* want our watches to work without us having to be rocket scientists. Wherever it's possible, less complicated user interfaces are a good thing.

The simple user interface. To create a custom data collector, the user must subclass the abstract class, `Collector`, and then provide, via the configuration file, the path to that new collector. Here is an example of a new Collector definition from *Diamond/src/collectors/cpu/cpu.py*. When Python searches for the `collect()` method, it will look

---

6 In Python, an abstract base class is a class that has left certain methods undefined, with the expectation that the developer will define them in the subclass. In the abstract base class, this function raises a `NotImplemente` `dError`. A more modern alternative is to use Python's module for abstract base classes, abc (*https://docs.python.org/3/library/abc.html*), first implemented in Python 2.6, which will error when constructing an incomplete class rather than when trying to access that class's unimplemented method. The full specification is defined in PEP 3119 (*https://www.python.org/dev/peps/pep-3119*).

7 This is a paraphrase of a great blog post on the subject by Larry Cuban, a professor emeritus of education at Stanford, titled "The Difference Between Complicated and Complex Matters." (*http://bit.ly/complicated-vs-complex*)

---

in the CPUCollector for a definition first, and then if it doesn't find the definition, it will use diamond.collector.Collector.collect(), which raises the NotImplementedError.

Minimal collector code would look like this:

```
# coding=utf-8
import diamond.collector
import psutil

class CPUCollector(diamond.collector.Collector):

    def collect(self):
        #  In Collector, this just contains raise(NotImplementedError)
        metric_name = "cpu.percent"
        metric_value = psutil.cpu_percent()
        self.publish(metric_name, metric_value)
```

The default place to store the collector definitions is in the directory *venv/share/diamond/collectors/*; but you can store it wherever you define in the collectors_path value in the configuration file. The class name, CPUCollector, is already listed in the example configuration file. Except for adding a hostname or a hostname_method specification either in the overall defaults (under the text in the configuration file) or in the individual collector's overrides, as shown in the following example, there need not be any other changes (the documentation lists all of the optional collector settings (*http://bit.ly/optional-collector-settings*)):

```
[[CPUCollector]]
enabled = True
hostname_method = smart
```

The more complex internal code.   Behind   the   scenes,   the   Server   will   call utils.load_collectors() using the path specified in collectors_path. Here is most of that function, truncated for brevity:

```
def load_collectors(paths=None, filter=None):
    """Scan for collectors to load from path"""
    # Initialize return value
    collectors = {}
    log = logging.getLogger('diamond')

    if paths is None:
        return

    if isinstance(paths, basestring):   ❶
        paths = paths.split(',')
        paths = map(str.strip, paths)

    load_include_path(paths)   ❷
```

```
for path in paths:
    ##~~ Skip lines that confirm 'path' exists.

    for f in os.listdir(path):

        # Are we a directory? If so, process down the tree
        fpath = os.path.join(path, f)
        if os.path.isdir(fpath):
            subcollectors = load_collectors([fpath])   ❸
            for key in subcollectors:   ❹
                collectors[key] = subcollectors[key]

        # Ignore anything that isn't a .py file
        elif (os.path.isfile(fpath)
              ##~~ ... Skip tests confirming fpath is a Python module ...
              ):

            ##~~ ... Skip the part that ignores filtered paths ...
            modname = f[:-3]

            try:
                # Import the module
                mod = __import__(modname, globals(), locals(), ['*'])   ❺
            except (KeyboardInterrupt, SystemExit), err:
                ##~~ ... Log the exception and quit ...
            except:
                ##~~ ... Log the exception and continue ...

            # Find all classes defined in the module
            for attrname in dir(mod):
                attr = getattr(mod, attrname)   ❻
                # Only attempt to load classes that are subclasses
                # of Collectors but are not the base Collector class
                if (inspect.isclass(attr)
                        and issubclass(attr, Collector)
                        and attr != Collector):
                    if attrname.startswith('parent_'):
                        continue
                    # Get class name
                    fqcn = '.'.join([modname, attrname])
                    try:
                        # Load Collector class
                        cls = load_dynamic_class(fqcn, Collector)   ❼
                        # Add Collector class
                        collectors[cls.__name__] = cls   ❽
                    except Exception:
                        ##~~ log the exception and continue ...

# Return Collector classes
return collectors
```

❶ Break up the string (first function call); otherwise, the paths are lists of string paths to where the user-defined custom `Collector` subclasses are defined.

❷ This recursively descends the paths given, inserting every directory into `sys.path` so that later the Collectors can be imported.

❸ Here's the recursion—`load_collectors()` is calling itself.[8]

❹ After loading the subdirectories' collectors, update the original dictionary of custom collectors with the new ones from those subdirectories.

❺ Since the introduction of Python 3.1, the `importlib` module in Python's standard library provides a preferred way to do this (via the module `impor tlib.import_module`; parts of `importlib.import_module` have also been backported to Python 2.7). This demonstrates how to programmatically import a module given the string module name.

❻ Here's how to programmatically access attributes in a module given just the string attribute name.

❼ Actually, `load_dynamic_class` may not be necessary here. It re-imports the module, checks that the named class is actually a class, checks that it's actually a Collector, and if so returns the newly loaded class. Redundancies sometimes occur in open source code written by large groups.

❽ Here's how they get the class name to use later when applying the configuration file options given only the string class name.

Style Examples from Diamond

There's a great example use of a closure in Diamond that demonstrates what was said in "Late binding closures" on page 64 about this behavior often being desirable.

Example use of a closure (when the gotcha isn't a gotcha)

A *closure* is a function that makes use of variables available in the local scope that would otherwise not be available when the function is called. They can be difficult to implement and understand in other languages, but are not hard to implement in

---

8 Python has a recursion limit (a maximum number of times a function is allowed to call itself) that's relatively restrictive by default, to discourage excessive use of recursion. Get your recursion limit by typing `import sys; sys.getrecursionlimit()`.

Python, because Python treats functions just like any other object.[9] For example, functions can be passed around as arguments, or returned from other functions. Here's an example excerpt from the `diamond` executable that shows how to implement a closure in Python:

```
##~~ ... Skip the import statements ...   ❶

def main():
    try:
        ##~~  ... Skip code that creates the command-line parser ...

        # Parse command-line Args
        (options, args) = parser.parse_args()

        ##~~  ... Skip code that parses the configuration file ...
        ##~~  ... Skip code that sets up the logger ...

    # Pass the exit upstream rather then handle it as an general exception
    except SystemExit, e:
        raise SystemExit

    ##~~  ... Skip code that handles other exceptions related to setup ...

    try:
        # PID MANAGEMENT   ❷
        if not options.skip_pidfile:
            # Initialize PID file
            if not options.pidfile:
                options.pidfile = str(config['server']['pid_file'])

            ##~~ ... Skip code to open and read the PID file if it exists, ...
            ##~~ ... and then delete the file if there is no such PID ...
            ##~~ ... or exits if there is already a running process. ...


            ##~~  ... Skip the code that sets the group and user ID ...
            ##~~  ... and the code that changes the PID file permissions. ...

            ##~~  ... Skip the code that checks whether to run as a daemon, ...
            ##~~  ... and if so detaches the process. ...


        # PID MANAGEMENT   ❸
        if not options.skip_pidfile:
            # Finish initializing PID file
            if not options.foreground and not options.collector:
                # Write PID file
```

---

9 Programming languages that can do this are said to have *first-class functions*—functions are treated as first-class citizens, like any other object.

```
        pid = str(os.getpid())
        try:
            pf = file(options.pidfile, 'w+')
        except IOError, e:
            log.error("Failed to write child PID file: %s" % (e))
            sys.exit(1)
        pf.write("%s\n" % pid)
        pf.close()
        # Log
        log.debug("Wrote child PID file: %s" % (options.pidfile))

    # Initialize server
    server = Server(configfile=options.configfile)

    def sigint_handler(signum, frame):  ❹
        log.info("Signal Received: %d" % (signum))
        # Delete PID file
        if not options.skip_pidfile and os.path.exists(options.pidfile):  ❺
            os.remove(options.pidfile)
            # Log
            log.debug("Removed PID file: %s" % (options.pidfile))
        sys.exit(0)

    # Set the signal handlers
    signal.signal(signal.SIGINT, sigint_handler)  ❻
    signal.signal(signal.SIGTERM, sigint_handler)

    server.run()

# Pass the exit upstream rather then handle it as a general exception
except SystemExit, e:
    raise SystemExit

##~~  ... Skip code that handles any other exceptions ...
##~~  ... and all of the rest of the script.
```

❶   When we skip code, the missing parts will be summarized by a comment preceded by two tildes (##~~ like this).

❷   The reason for the PID[10] file is to make sure the daemon is unique (i.e., not accidentally started twice), to communicate the associated process ID quickly to other scripts, and to make it evident that an abnormal termination has occurred (because in this script, the PID file is deleted upon normal termination).

---

10 *PID* stands for "process identifier." Every process has a unique identifier that is available in Python using the os module in the standard library: os.getpid().

❸ All of this code is just to provide context leading up to the closure. At this point, either the process is running as a daemon (and now has a different process ID than before) or it will skip this part because it's already written its correct PID to the PID file.

❹ This (`sigint_handler()`) is the closure. It is defined inside of `main()`, rather than at the top level, outside of any functions, because it needs to know whether to look for a PID file, and if so where to look.

❺ It gets this information from the command-line options, which it can't obtain until after the call to `main()`. That means all of the options related to the PID file are local variables in `main`'s namespace.

❻ The closure (the function `sigint_handler()`) is sent to the signal handler and will be used to handle `SIGINT` and `SIGTERM`.

Tablib

Tablib is a Python library that converts between different data formats, storing data in a `Dataset` object, or multiple Datasets in a `Databook`. Datasets stored in the JSON, YAML, DBF, and CSV file formats can be imported, and datasets can be exported to XLSX, XLS, ODS, JSON, YAML, DBF, CSV, TSV, and HTML. Tablib was first released by Kenneth Reitz in 2010. It has the intuitive API design typical of Reitz's projects.

Reading a Small Library

Tablib is a library, not an application, so there isn't a single obvious entry point like there is with HowDoI and Diamond.

Get Tablib from GitHub:

```
$ git clone https://github.com/kennethreitz/tablib.git
$ virtualenv -p python3 venv
$ source venv/bin/activate
(venv)$ cd tablib
(venv)$ pip install --editable .
(venv)$ python test_tablib.py  # Run the unit tests.
```

Read Tablib's documentation

Tablib's documentation (*http://docs.python-tablib.org/*) starts off immediately with a use case, and then goes into describing its capabilities in more detail: it provides a `Dataset` object that has rows, headers, and columns. You can do I/O from various formats to the `Dataset` object. And the advanced usage section says you can add tags to rows, and create derived columns that are functions of other columns.

Use Tablib

Tablib is a library, not an executable like HowDoI or Diamond, so you can open a
Python interactive session and have the expectation that you can use use the help()
function to explore the API. Here's our example of the tablib.Dataset class, the different data formats, and how I/O works:

```
>>> import tablib
>>> data = tablib.Dataset()
>>> names = ('Black Knight', 'Killer Rabbit')
>>>
>>> for name in names:
...     fname, lname = name.split()
...     data.append((fname, lname))
...
>>> data.dict
[['Black', 'Knight'], ['Killer', 'Rabbit']]
>>>
>>> print(data.csv)
Black,Knight
Killer,Rabbit

>>> data.headers=('First name', 'Last name')
>>> print(data.yaml)
- {First name: Black, Last name: Knight}
- {First name: Killer, Last name: Rabbit}

>>> with open('tmp.csv', 'w') as outfile:
...     outfile.write(data.csv)
...
64
>>> newdata = tablib.Dataset()
>>> newdata.csv = open('tmp.csv').read()
>>> print(newdata.yaml)
- {First name: Black, Last name: Knight}
- {First name: Killer, Last name: Rabbit}
```

Read Tablib's code

The file structure under *tablib/* looks like this:

```
tablib
|--- __init__.py
|--- compat.py
|--- core.py
|--- formats/
|--- packages/
```

The two directories, *tablib/formats/* and *tablib/packages/*, will be discussed in a few
sections.

Python supports module-level docstrings as well as the docstrings we've already described—a string literal that is the first statement in a function, class, or class method. Stack Overflow has good advice on how to document a module (*http://stack overflow.com/a/2557196*). For us, this means another way to explore source code is by typing head *.py in a terminal shell while in the directory at the top level of the package—to show all of the module docstrings at once. Here's what we get:

```
(venv)$ cd tablib
(venv)$ head *.py
==> __init__.py <==   ❶
""" Tablib. """

from tablib.core import (
    Databook, Dataset, detect, import_set, import_book,
    InvalidDatasetType, InvalidDimensions, UnsupportedFormat,
    __version__
)


==> compat.py <==   ❷
# -*- coding: utf-8 -*-

"""

tablib.compat
~~~~~~~~~~~~~~

Tablib compatiblity module.

"""


==> core.py <==   ❸
# -*- coding: utf-8 -*-
"""
    tablib.core
    ~~~~~~~~~~~

    This module implements the central Tablib objects.

    :copyright: (c) 2014 by Kenneth Reitz.
    :license: MIT, see LICENSE for more details.
"""
```

We learn that:

❶ The top-level API (the contents of *__init__.py* are accessible from tablib after an import tablib statement) has just nine entry points: the Databook and Dataset classes are mentioned in the documentation, detect could be for identifying formatting, import_set and import_book must import data, and the last three classes—`InvalidDatasetType`, `InvalidDimensions`, and `UnsupportedFormat`—look like exceptions. (When code follows PEP 8, we can tell which objects are custom classes from their capitalization.)

❷ *tablib/compat.py* is a compatibility module. A quick look inside will show that it handles Python 2/Python 3 compatibility issues in a similar way to HowDoI, by resolving different locations and names to the same symbol for use in *tablib/core.py*.

❸ *tablib/core.py*, like it says, implements the central Tablib objects like `Dataset` and `Databook`.

Tablib's Sphinx Documentation

Tablib's documentation (*http://docs.python-tablib.org/*) provides a good example use of Sphinx (*http://www.sphinx-doc.org/en/stable/tutorial.html*) because it's a small library, and it makes use of a lot of Sphinx extensions (*http://www.sphinx-doc.org/en/stable/extensions.html*).

The documenation's current Sphinx build is at Tablib's documentation page (*http://docs.python-tablib.org/*). If you want to build the documentation yourself (Windows users will need a `make` command (*http://gnuwin32.sourceforge.net/packages/make.htm*) —it's old but works fine), do this:

```
(venv)$ pip install sphinx
(venv)$ cd docs
(venv)$ make html
(venv)$ open _build/html/index.html  # To view the result.
```

Sphinx provides a number of theme options (*http://www.sphinx-doc.org/en/stable/theming.html*) with default layout templates and CSS themes. Tablib's templates for two of the notes on the left sidebar are in *docs/_templates/*. Their names are not arbitrary; they're in *basic/layout.html*. You can find that file in the Sphinx themes directory, which can be located by typing this on the command line:

```
(venv)$ python -c 'import sphinx.themes;print(sphinx.themes.__path__)'
```

Advanced users can also look in in *docs/_themes/kr/*, a custom theme that extends the basic layout. It is selected by adding the *_themes/* directory to the system path, setting `html_theme_path = ['_themes']` and setting `html_theme = 'kr'` in *docs/conf.py*.

To include API documentation that's automatically generated from the docstrings in your code, use `autoclass::`. You have to copy the docstring formatting in Tablib for this to work:

```
.. autoclass:: Dataset
   :inherited-members:
```

To get this functionality, you have to answer "yes" to the question about including the "autodoc" Sphinx extension when you run `sphinx-quickstart` to create a new Sphinx project. The `:inherited-members:` directive also adds documentation for the attributes inherited from parent classes.

Structure Examples from Tablib

The primary thing we want to highlight form Tablib is the absence of the use of classes in the modules in *tablib/formats/*—it's a perfect example of the statement we made earlier about not overusing classes. Next, we show excerpts of how Tablib uses the decorator syntax and the `property` class (*https://docs.python.org/library/functions.html#property*) to create derived attributes like the dataset's height and width, and how it dynamically registers file formats to avoid duplicating what would be boilerplate code for each of the different format types (CSV, YAML, etc.).

The last two subsections are a little obscure—we look at how Tablib vendorizes dependencies, and then discuss the `__slots__` property of new class objects. You can skip these sections and still lead a happy, Pythonic life.

No needless object-oriented code in formats (use namespaces for grouping functions)

The *formats* directory contains all of the defined file formats for I/O. The module names, *_csv.py*, *_tsv.py*, *_json.py*, *_yaml.py*, *_xls.py*, *_xlsx.py*, *_ods.py*, and *_xls.py* are prefixed with an underscore—this indicates to the library user that they are not intended for direct use. We can change directories into *formats*, and search for classes and functions. Using `grep ^class formats/*.py` reveals there are no class definitions, and using `grep ^def formats/*.py` shows that each module contains some or all of the following functions:

- `detect(stream)` infers the file format based on the stream content.
- `dset_sheet(dataset, ws)` formats the Excel spreadsheet cells.
- `export_set(dataset)` exports the Dataset to the given format, returning a formatted string with the new format. (Or, for Excel, returning a `bytes` object—or a binary-formatted string in Python 2.)
- `import_set(dset, in_stream, headers=True)` replaces the contents of the dataset with the contents of the input stream.
- `export_book(databook)` exports the Datasheets in the Databook to the given format, returning a string or `bytes` object.
- `import_book(dbook, in_stream, headers=True)` replaces the contents of the databook with the contents of the input stream.

This is an example of using modules as namespaces (after all, they *are* one honking great idea) to separate functions, rather than using unnecessary classes. We know each function's purpose from its name: for example, `formats._csv.import_set()`, `formats._tsv.import_set()`, and `formats._json.import_set()` import datasets from CSV, TSV, and JSON-formatted files, respectively. The other functions do data exporting and file format detection, when possible, for each of Tablib's available formats.

Descriptors and the property decorator (engineer immutability when the API would benefit)

Tablib is our first library that uses Python's decorator syntax, described in "Decorators" on page 72. The syntax uses the @ symbol in front of a function name, placed directly above another function. It modifies (or "decorates") the function directly below. In the following excerpt, `property` changes the functions `Dataset.height` and `Dataset.width` into descriptors—classes with at least one of the `__get__()`, `__set__()`, or `__delete__()` ("getter", "setter", or "delete") methods defined. For example, the attribute lookup `Dataset.height` will trigger the getter, setter, or delete function depending on the context in which that attribute is used. This behavior is only possible for new-style classes, discussed momentarily. See this useful Python tutorial on descriptors (*https://docs.python.org/3/howto/descriptor.html*) for more information.

```
class Dataset(object):
    #
    # ... omit the rest of the class definition for clarity
    #

    @property   ❶
    def height(self):
        """The number of rows currently in the :class:`Dataset`.
           Cannot be directly modified.   ❷
        """
        return len(self._data)


    @property
    def width(self):
        """The number of columns currently in the :class:`Dataset`.
           Cannot be directly modified.
        """
        try:
            return len(self._data[0])
        except IndexError:
            try:
                return len(self.headers)
            except TypeError:
                return 0
```

❶ This is how to use a decorator. In this case, `property` modifies `Dataset.height` to behave as a property rather than as a bound method. It can only operate on class methods.

❷ When `property` is applied as a decorator, the `height` attribute will return the height of the `Dataset` but it is not possible to assign a height to the `Dataset` by invoking `Dataset.height`.

Here is what the `height` and `width` attributes look like when used:

```
>>> import tablib
>>> data = tablib.Dataset()
>>> data.header = ("amount", "ingredient")
>>> data.append(("2 cubes", "Arcturan Mega-gin"))
>>> data.width
2
>>> data.height
1
>>>
>>> data.height = 3
Traceback (most recent call last):
  File "<stdin>", line 1, in <module>
AttributeError: can't set attribute
```

So, `data.height` can be accessed like an attribute, but it's not settable—it's calculated from the data and so is always current. This is ergonomic API design: `data.height` is easier to type than `data.get_height()`; it's clear what the meaning of `data.height` is; and because it is calculated from the data (and the property is not settable—only the "getter" function is defined), there isn't a danger that it will be out of sync from the correct number.

The `property` decorator can only be applied to attributes of classes, and only to classes that derive from the base object `object` (e.g., `class MyClass(object)` not `class MyClass()`—inheritance from `object` is always the case in Python 3).

This same tool is used to create Tablib's data import and export API in the various formats: Tablib does not store the string value for each of the CSV, JSON, and YAML outputs. Rather, the `Dataset` attributes `csv`, `json`, and `yaml` are properties, like `Data set.height` and `Dataset.width` in the preceding example—they call a function that generates the result from the stored data or parses the input format and then replaces the core data. But there's only one dataset.

When `data.csv` is on the left of an equals sign, the property's "setter" function is called, to parse the dataset from the CSV format. And when `data.yaml` is on the right of an equals sign, or alone, the "getter" is called, to create a string with the given format from the internal dataset. Here is an example:

```
>>> import tablib
>>> data = tablib.Dataset()
>>>
>>> data.csv = "\n".join((   ❶
...      "amount,ingredient",
...      "1 bottle,Ol' Janx Spirit",
...      "1 measure,Santraginus V seawater",
...      "2 cubes,Arcturan Mega-gin",
...      "4 litres,Fallian marsh gas",
...      "1 measure,Qalactin Hypermint extract",
...      "1 tooth,Algolian Suntiger",
...      "a sprinkle,Zamphuor",
...      "1 whole,olive"))
>>>
>>> data[2:4]
[('2 cubes', 'Arcturan Mega-gin'), ('4 litres', 'Fallian marsh gas')]
>>>
>>> print(data.yaml)   ❷
- {amount: 1 bottle, ingredient: Ol Janx Spirit}
- {amount: 1 measure, ingredient: Santraginus V seawater}
- {amount: 2 cubes, ingredient: Arcturan Mega-gin}
- {amount: 4 litres, ingredient: Fallian marsh gas}
- {amount: 1 measure, ingredient: Qalactin Hypermint extract}
- {amount: 1 tooth, ingredient: Algolian Suntiger}
- {amount: a sprinkle, ingredient: Zamphuor}
- {amount: 1 whole, ingredient: olive}
```

❶ data.csv on the lefthand side of the equals sign (assignment operator) invokes formats.csv.import_set(), with data as the first argument, and the string of Gargle Blaster ingredients as its second argument.

❷ data.yaml alone invokes formats.yaml.export_set(), with data as its argument, outputting the formatted YAML string for the print() function.

The "getter", "setter", and also a "deleter" function can be bound to a single attribute using property. Its signature is property(fget=None, fset=None, fdel=None, doc=None), in which fget identifies the "getter" function (formats.csv.import_set()), fset identifies the "setter" function (formats.csv.export_set()), and fdel identifies the "deleter" function, which is left as None. We will see the code where the formatting properties are set, programmatically, next.

Programmatically registered file formats (don't repeat yourself)

Tablib places all of the file formatting routines in the *formats* subpackage. This structure choice makes the main *core.py* module cleaner and the entire package modular; it's easy to add new file formats. Although it would have been possible to paste chunks of nearly identical code and import each file format's import and export behaviors separately, all of the formats are *programmatically* loaded into the `Dataset` class to properties named after each format.

We're printing the entire contents of *formats/__init__.py* in the following code example because it's not too large a file, and we want to show where `formats.available` is defined:

```
# -*- coding: utf-8 -*-  ❶

""" Tablib - formats
"""

from . import _csv as csv
from . import _json as json
from . import _xls as xls
from . import _yaml as yaml
from . import _tsv as tsv
from . import _html as html
from . import _xlsx as xlsx
from . import _ods as ods

available = (json, xls, yaml, csv, tsv, html, xlsx, ods)  ❷
```

❶ This line explicitly tells the Python interpreter that the file encoding is UTF-8.[11]

❷ Here's the definition of `formats.available`, right in *formats/__init__.py*. It's also available via `dir(tablib.formats)`, but this explicit list is easier to understand.

In *core.py*, rather than about 20 (ugly, hard to maintain) repeated function definitions for each format option, the code imports each format programmatically by calling `self._register_formats()` at the end of the `Dataset`'s `__init__()` method. We've excerpted just `Dataset._register_formats()` here:

```
class Dataset(object):
    #
    #  ... skip documentation and some definitions  ...
    #

    @classmethod  ❶
    def _register_formats(cls):
        """Adds format properties."""
        for fmt in formats.available:  ❷
            try:
                try:
                    setattr(cls, fmt.title,
```

---

11 ASCII is default in Python 2, and UTF-8 is default in Python 3. There are multiple allowed ways to communicate encoding, all listed in PEP 263 (*https://www.python.org/dev/peps/pep-0263/*). You can use the one that works best with your favorite text editor.

```
                    property(fmt.export_set, fmt.import_set))   ❸
                except AttributeError:   ❹
                    setattr(cls, fmt.title, property(fmt.export_set))   ❺

        except AttributeError:
            pass   ❻

    #
    # ... skip more definitions ...
    #

    @property   ❼
    def tsv():
        """A TSV representation of the :class:`Dataset` object. The top
        row will contain headers, if they have been set. Otherwise, the
        top row will contain the first row of the dataset.

        A dataset object can also be imported by setting
        the :class:`Dataset.tsv` attribute. ::

            data = tablib.Dataset()
            data.tsv = 'age\tfirst_name\tlast_name\n90\tJohn\tAdams'   ❽

        Import assumes (for now) that headers exist.
        """
        pass
```

❶ The @classmethod symbol is a *decorator*, described more extensively in "Decorators" on page 72, that modifies the method _register_formats() so that it passes the object's class (Dataset) rather than the object instance (self) as its first argument.

❷ The formats.available is defined in *formats/__init__.py* and contains all of the available formatting options.

❸ In this line, setattr assigns a value to the attribute named fmt.title (i.e., Data set.csv or Dataset.xls). The value it assigns is a special one; prop erty(fmt.export_set, fmt.import_set) turns Dataset.csv into a *property*.

❹ There will be an AttributeError if fmt.import_set is not defined.

❺ If there is no import function, try to assign just the export behavior.

❻ If there is neither an export nor an import function to assign, just don't assign anything.

❼ Each of the file formats is defined as a property here, with a descriptive docstring. The docstring will be retained when `property()` is called at tag ❸ or ❺ to assign the extra behaviors.

❽ The `\t` and `\n` are string escape sequences that represent the Tab character and a newline, respectively. They're all listed in Python's string literals documentation (*https://docs.python.org/3/reference/lexical_analysis.html#index-18*).

But We Are All Responsible Users

These uses of the `@property` decorator are *not* like the uses of similar tools in Java, where the goal is to control the user's access to data. That goes against the Python philosophy that *we are all responsible users*. Instead, the purpose of `@property` is to separate the data from view functions related to the data (in this case, the height, width, and various storage formats). When there doesn't need to be a preprocessing or postprocessing "getter" or "setter" function, the more Pythonic option is to just assign the data to a regular attribute and let the user interact with it.

Vendorized dependencies in packages (an example of how to vendorize)

Tablib's dependencies are currently vendorized (meaning they are shipped bundled with the code—in this case, in the directory *packages*) but may be moved to a plug-in system in the future. The *packages* directory contains third-party packages included inside Tablib to ensure compatibility, rather than the other option, which is to specify versions in the *setup.py* file that will be downloaded and installed when Tablib is installed. This technique is discussed in "Vendorizing Dependencies" on page 76; the choice for Tablib was made both to reduce the number of dependencies the user would have to download, and because sometimes there are different packages for Python 2 and Python 3, which are both included. (The appropriate one is imported, and their functions set to a common name, in *tablib/compat.py*). That way, Tablib can have one single code base instead of two—one for each version of Python. Because each of these dependencies has its own license, a *NOTICE* document was added to the top level of the project directory that lists each dependency's license.

Saving memory with __slots__ (optimize judiciously)

Python prefers readability over speed. Its entire design, its Zen aphorisms, and its early influence from educational languages like ABC (*http://bit.ly/abc-to-python*) are all about placing user-friendliness above performance (although we'll talk about more optimization options in "Speed" on page 233).

The use of `__slots__` in tablib is a case where optimization matters. This is a slightly obscure reference, and it's only available for new-style classes (described in a few

---

pages), but we want to show that it's possible to optimize Python when necessary. This optimization is only useful when you have tons of very small objects by reducing the footprint of each class instance by the size of one dictionary (large objects would make this small savings irrelevant, and fewer objects make the savings not worth it). Here is an excerpt from the __slots__ documentation (*http://bit.ly/__slots__-doc*):

> By default, instances of classes have a dictionary for attribute storage. This wastes space for objects having very few instance variables. The space consumption can become acute when creating large numbers of instances.

> The default can be overridden by defining __slots__ in a class definition. The __slots__ declaration takes a sequence of instance variables and reserves just enough space in each instance to hold a value for each variable. Space is saved because __dict__ is not created for each instance.

Normally, this isn't something to care about—notice that __slots__ doesn't appear in the Dataset or Databook classes, just the Row class—but because there can be thousands of rows of data, __slots__ is a good idea. The Row class is not exposed in *tablib/__init__.py* because it is a helper class to Dataset, instantiated once for every row. This is how its definition looks in the beginning part of the definition of the Row class:

```
class Row(object):
    """Internal Row object. Mainly used for filtering."""

    __slots__ = ['_row', 'tags']

    def __init__(self, row=list(), tags=list()):
        self._row = list(row)
        self.tags = list(tags)

    #
    #   ... etc. ...
    #
```

The problem now is that there is no longer a __dict__ attribute in the Row instances, but the pickle.dump() function (used for object serialization) by default uses __dict__ to serialize the object unless the method __getstate__() is defined. Likewise, during unpickling (the process that reads the serialized bytes and reconstructs the object in memory), if __setstate__() is not defined, pickle.load() will load to the object's __dict__ attribute. Here is how to get around that:

```
class Row(object):
    #
    #   ... skip the other definitions ...
    #

    def __getstate__(self):

        slots = dict()
```

```
            for slot in self.__slots__:
                attribute = getattr(self, slot)
                slots[slot] = attribute
            return slots

        def __setstate__(self, state):
            for (k, v) in list(state.items()):
                setattr(self, k, v)
```

For more information about __getstate__() and __setstate__() and pickling, see the __getstate__ documentation (*http://bit.ly/__getstate__-doc*).

Style Examples from Tablib

We have one single style example from Tablib—operator overloading—which gets into the details of Python's data model. Customizing the behavior of your classes makes it easier for those who use your API to write beautiful code.

Operator overloading (beautiful is better than ugly)

This code section uses Python's operator overloading to enable operations on either the Dataset's rows or columns. The following first sample code shows interactive use of the bracket operator ([ ]) for both numerical indices and column names, and the second one shows the code that uses this behavior:

```
>>> data[-1]   ❶
('1 whole', 'olive')
>>>
>>> data[-1] = ['2 whole', 'olives']   ❷
>>>
>>> data[-1]
('2 whole', 'olives')   ❸
>>>
>>> del data[2:7]   ❹
>>>
>>> print(data.csv)
amount,ingredient   ❺
1 bottle,Ol' Janx Spirit
1 measure,Santraginus V seawater
2 whole,olives

>>> data['ingredient']   ❻
["Ol' Janx Spirit", 'Santraginus V seawater', 'olives']
```

❶   When using numbers, accessing data via the bracket operator ([]) gives the row at the specified location.

❷   This is assignment using the bracket operator …

❸   ... it becomes 2 olives instead of the original one.

❹   This is deletion using a *slice*—2:7 denotes all of the numbers 2,3,4,5,6 but not
    7.

❺   See how the recipe afterward is much smaller.

❻   It is also possible to access columns by name.

The part of the Dataset code that defines the behavior of the bracket operator shows
how to handle access both by column name and by row number:

```python
class Dataset(object):
    #
    #  ... skip  the rest of the definitions for brevity ...
    #

    def __getitem__(self, key):
        if isinstance(key, str) or isinstance(key, unicode):  ❶
            if key in self.headers:  ❷
                pos = self.headers.index(key) # get 'key' index from each data
                return [row[pos] for row in self._data]
            else:  ❸
                raise KeyError
        else:
            _results = self._data[key]
            if isinstance(_results, Row):  ❹
                return _results.tuple
            else:
                return [result.tuple for result in _results]  ❺


    def __setitem__(self, key, value):  ❻
        self._validate(value)
        self._data[key] = Row(value)


    def __delitem__(self, key):
        if isinstance(key, str) or isinstance(key, unicode):  ❼
            if key in self.headers:
                pos = self.headers.index(key)
                del self.headers[pos]

                for row in self._data:
                    del row[pos]
            else:
                raise KeyError
        else:
            del self._data[key]
```

❶ First, check whether we are seeking a column (`True` if key is a string) or a row (`True` if the `key` is an integer or slice).

❷ Here the code checks for the key to be in `self.headers`, and then...

❸ ...explicitly raises a `KeyError` so that access by column name behaves as one would expect a dictionary to. The whole `if/else` pair is not necessary for the operation of the function—if it were omitted, a `ValueError` would still be raised by `self.headers.index(key)` if key were not in `self.headers`. The only purpose for this check is to provide a more informative error for the library user.

❹ This is how the code determines whether `key` was a number or a slice (like `2:7`). If a slice, the `_results` would be a list, not a Row.

❺ Here is where the slice is processed. Because the rows are returned as tuples, the values are an immutable copy of the acual data, and the dataset's values (actually stored as lists) won't accidentally be corrupted by an assignment.

❻ The `__setitem__()` method can change a single row but not a column. This is intentional; there is no way provided to change the content of an entire column; and for data integrity, this is probably not a bad choice. The user can always transform the column and insert it at any position using one of the methods `insert_col()`, `lpush_col()`, or `rpush_col()`.

❼ The `__delitem__()` method can either delete a column or a row, using the same logic as `__getitem__()`.

For more information about additional operator overloading and other special methods, see the Python documentation on Special method names (*http://bit.ly/special-method-names*).

Requests

On Valentine's day in 2011, Kenneth Reitz released a love letter to the Python community: the Requests library. Its enthusiastic adoption emphatically makes the case for intuitive API design (meaning the API is so straightforward you almost don't need documentation).

Reading a Larger Library

Requests is a larger library than Tablib, with many more modules, but we'll still approach reading it the same way—by looking at the documentation and following the API through the code.

Get Requests from GitHub:

```
$ git clone https://github.com/kennethreitz/requests.git
$ virtualenv -p python3 venv
$ source venv/bin/activate
(venv)$ cd requests
(venv)$ pip install --editable .
(venv)$ pip install -r requirements.txt  # Required for unit tests
(venv)$ py.test tests  # Run the unit tests.
```

Some tests may fail—for example, if your service provider intercepts 404 errors to give some advertising page, you won't get the ConnectionError.

Read Requests's documentation

Requests is a bigger package, so first just scan the section titles from the Requests documentation (*http://docs.python-requests.org/*). Requests extends urrlib and httplib from Python's standard library to provide methods that perform HTTP requests. The library includes support for international domains and URLs, automatic decompression, automatic content decoding, browser style SSL verification, HTTP(S) proxy support, and other features, which are all defined by the Internet Engineering Task Force (IETF) standards for HTTP in their requests for comment (RFCs) 7230 through 7235.[12]

Requests strives to cover *all* of the IETF's HTTP specifications, using only a handful of functions, a bunch of keyword arguments, and a few featureful classes.

Use Requests

Like with Tablib, there is enough information in the docstrings to use Requests without actually reading the online documentation. Here's a brief interaction:

```
>>> import requests
>>> help(requests)  # Shows a usage statement and says to see `requests.api`
>>> help(requests.api)  # Shows a detailed API description
>>>
>>> result = requests.get('https://pypi.python.org/pypi/requests/json')
>>> result.status_code
200
>>> result.ok
True
>>> result.text[:42]
'{\n    "info": {\n        "maintainer": null'
>>>
>>> result.json().keys()
```

---

12 If you need a vocabulary refresh, RFC 7231 is the HTTP semantics document. (*http://bit.ly/http-semantics*) If you scan the table of contents and read the introduction, you'll know enough about the scope to tell whether the definition you want is covered, and where to find it.

```
dict_keys(['info', 'releases', 'urls'])
>>>
>>> result.json()['info']['summary']
'Python HTTP for Humans.'
```

Read Requests's code

Here are the contents of the Requests package:

```
$ ls
__init__.py     cacert.pem  ❶     exceptions.py     sessions.py
adapters.py     certs.py          hooks.py          status_codes.py
api.py          compat.py         models.py         structures.py
auth.py         cookies.py        packages/ ❷       utils.py
```

❶ *cacert.pem* is a default certificate bundle to use when checking SSL certificates.

❷ Requests has a flat structure, except for a *packages* directory that vendorizes (contains the external libraries) `chardet` and `urllib3`. These dependencies are imported as `requests.packages.chardet` and `requests.packages.urllib3`, so programmers can still access `chardet` and `urllib3` from the standard library.

We can mostly figure out what's happening thanks to well-chosen module names, but if we want a little more imformation, we can again peek at the module docstrings by typing `head *.py` in the top-level directory. The following lists displays these module docstrings, slightly truncated. (It doesn't show *compat.py*. We can tell from its name, especially because it's named the same as in Reitz's Tablib library, that it takes care of Python 2 to Python 3 compatibility.)

api.py
> Implements the Requests API

hooks.py
> Provides the capabilities for the Requests hooks system

models.py
> Contains the primary objects that power Requests

sessions.py
> Provides a Session object to manage and persist settings across requests (cookies, auth, proxies)

auth.py
> Contains the authentication handlers for Requests

status_codes.py
> A lookup table mapping status titles to status codes

cookies.py
> Compatibility code to be able to use `cookielib.CookieJar` with requests

adapters.py
> Contains the transport adapters Requests uses to define and maintain connections

exceptions.py
> All of Requests' exceptions

structures.py
> Data structures that power Requests

certs.py
> Returns the preferred default CA certificate bundle listing trusted SSL certificates

utils.py
> Provides utility functions that are used within Requests that are also useful for external consumption

Insights from reading all of the headers:

- There is a hook system (*hooks.py*), implying the user can modify how Requests works. We won't discuss it in depth because it will take us too far off topic.

- The main module is *models.py*, as it contains "the primary objects that power Requests."

- The reason `sessions.Session` exists is to persist cookies across multiple requests (that might occur during authentication, for example).

- The actual HTTP connection is made by objects from *adapters.py*.

- The rest is kind of obvious: *auth.py* is for authentication, *status_codes.py* has the status codes, *cookies.py* is for adding and removing cookies, *exceptions.py* is for exceptions, *structures.py* contains data structures (e.g., a case-insensitive dictionary), and *utils.py* contains utility functions.

The idea to put communication separately in *adapters.py* is innovative (at least to this writer). It means `models.Request`, `models.PreparedRequest`, and `models.Response` don't actually *do* anything—they *just store data*, possibly manipulating it a bit for presentation, pickling, or encoding purposes. Actions are handled by separate classes that exist specifically to perform an action, like authentication or communication. Every class does *just one thing*, and each module contains classes that do similar things—a Pythonic approach most of us already adhere to with our function definitions.

Requests's Sphinx-Compatible Docstrings

If you are starting a new project and using Sphinx and its `autodoc` extension, you will need to format your docstrings so that Sphinx can parse them.

The Sphinx documentation is not always easy to search for what keywords to place where. Many people actually recommend copying the docstrings in Requests if you want to get the format right, rather than find the instructions in the Sphinx docs. For example, here is the definition of `delete()` in *requests/api.py*:

```
def delete(url, **kwargs):
    """Sends a DELETE request.

    :param url: URL for the new :class:`Request` object.
    :param \*\*kwargs: Optional arguments that ``request`` takes.
    :return: :class:`Response <Response>` object
    :rtype: requests.Response
    """

    return request('delete', url, **kwargs)
```

The Sphinx autodoc rendering of this definition is in the online API documentation (*http://docs.python-requests.org/en/master/api/#requests.delete*).

Structure Examples from Requests

Everyone loves the Requests API—it is easy to remember and helps its users to write simple, beautiful code. This section first discusses the design preference for more comprehensible error messages and an easy-to-memorize API that we think went into creation of the `requests.api` module, and then explores the differences between the `requests.Request` and `urllib.request.Request` object, offering an opinion on why `requests.Request` exists.

Top-level API (preferably only one obvious way to do it)

The functions defined in *api.py* (except `request()`) are named after HTTP request methods.[13] Each request method is the same except for its method name and the choice of exposed keyword parameters, so we're truncating this exerpt from *requests/api.py* after the `get()` function:

```
# -*- coding: utf-8 -*-

"""
```

---

13 These are defined in section 4.3 of the current Hypertext Transfer Protocol request for comments (*http://bit.ly/http-method-def*).

```
requests.api
~~~~~~~~~~~~

This module implements the Requests API.

:copyright: (c) 2012 by Kenneth Reitz.
:license: Apache2, see LICENSE for more details.

"""

from . import sessions


def request(method, url, **kwargs):   ❶
    """Constructs and sends a :class:`Request <Request>`.

    :param method: method for the new :class:`Request` object.
    :param url: URL for the new :class:`Request` object.
    :param params: (optional) Dictionary or bytes to be sent in the query string
                   for the :class:`Request`.

    ... skip the documentation for the remaining keyword arguments ...   ❷

    :return: :class:`Response <Response>` object
    :rtype: requests.Response

    Usage::

      >>> import requests
      >>> req = requests.request('GET', 'http://httpbin.org/get')
      <Response [200]>
    """

    # By using the 'with' statement, we are sure the session is closed, thus we
    # avoid leaving sockets open which can trigger a ResourceWarning in some
    # cases, and look like a memory leak in others.
    with sessions.Session() as session:   ❸
        return session.request(method=method, url=url, **kwargs)


def get(url, params=None, **kwargs):   ❹
    """Sends a GET request.

    :param url: URL for the new :class:`Request` object.
    :param params: (optional) Dictionary or bytes to be sent in the query string
                   for the :class:`Request`.
    :param \*\*kwargs: Optional arguments that ``request`` takes.
    :return: :class:`Response <Response>` object
    :rtype: requests.Response
    """
```

```
    kwargs.setdefault('allow_redirects', True) ❺
    return request('get', url, params=params, **kwargs) ❻
```

❶ The request() function contains a **kwargs in its signature. This means extraneous keyword arguments will not cause an exception, and it hides options from
the user.

❷ The documentation omitted here for brevity describes every keyword argument
that has an associated action. If you use **kwargs in your function signature, this
is the only way the user can tell what the contents of **kwargs should be, short of
looking at the code themselves.

❸ The with statement is how Python supports a runtime context. It can be used
with any object that has an __enter__() and an __exit__() method defined.
__enter()__ will be called upon entering the with statement, and __exit__()
will be called upon exit, regardless of whether that exit is normal or due to an
exception.

❹ The get() function specifically pulls out the params=None keyword, applying a
default value of None. The params keyword argument relevant for get because it's
for terms to be used in an HTTP query string. Exposing selected keyword arguments gives flexibility to the advanced user (via the remaining **kwargs) while
making usage obvious for the 99% of people who don't need advanced options.

❺ The default for the request() function is to not allow redirects, so this step sets it
to True unless the user set it already.

❻ The get() function then simply calls request() with its first parameter set to
"get". Making get a function has two advantages over just using a string argument like request("get", ...). First, it becomes obvious, even without documentation, which HTTP methods are available with this API. Second, if the user
makes a typographical error in the method name, a NameError will be raised earlier, and probably with a less confusing traceback, than would happen with error
checking deeper in the code.

No new functionality is added in *requests/api.py*; it exists to present a simple API for
the user. Plus, putting the string HTTP methods directly into the API as function
names means any typographical error with the method name will be caught and identified early, for example:

```
>>> requests.foo('http://www.python.org')
Traceback (most recent call last):
  File "<stdin>", line 1, in <module>
AttributeError: 'module' object has no attribute 'foo'
>>>
```

```
>>> requests.request('foo', 'http://www.python.org')
<Response [403]>
```

The Request and PreparedRequest objects (we're all responsible users)

_init__.py_ exposes Request, PreparedRequest, and Response from *models.py* as part of the main API. Why does models.Request even exist? There's already a url lib.requests.Request in the standard library, and in *cookies.py* there is specifically a MockRequest object that wraps models.Request so that it works like url lib.requests.Request for http.cookiejar.[14] That means whatever methods are needed for the Request object to interface with the cookies library are intentionally excluded from requests.Request. What is the point of all this extra work?

The extra methods in MockRequest (which exists to emulate url lib.request.Request for the cookie library) are used by the cookie library to manage cookies. Except for the get_type() function (which usually returns "http" or "https" when using Requests) and the unverifiable property (True for our case), they're all related to the URL or the request headers:

Related to the header

add_unredirected_header()
    Add a new key, value pair to the header.

get_header()
    Get a specific name in the header dictionary.

get_new_headers()
    Get the dictionary containing new headers (added by cookielib).

has_header()
    Check whether a name exists in the header dictionary.

Related to the URL

get_full_url()
    Does just what it says.

host *and* origin_req_host
    Properties that are set by calling the methods get_host() and get_ori gin_req_host(), respectively.

---

14 The module http.cookiejar was previously cookielib in Python 2, and urllib.requests.Request was previously urllib2.Request in Python 2.

```
get_host()
```
Extract the host from the URL (e.g., *www.python.org* from *https://www.python.org/dev/peps/pep-0008/*).

```
get_origin_req_host()
```
Call `get_host()`.[15]

They're all access functions, except for `MockRequest.add_unredirected_header()`. The `MockRequest` docstring notes that "the original request object is read-only."

In `requests.Request`, data attributes are instead directly exposed. This makes all of the accessor functions unnecessary: to get or set the headers, access *request-instance*.`headers`. It's just a dictionary. Likewise, the user can just get or change the string URL: *request-instance*.`url`.

The `PreparedRequest` object is initialized empty, and is populated with a call to *prepared-request-instance*.`prepare()`, filled with the relevant data (usually from the calling the `Request` object). It's at this point that things like correct capitalization and encoding are applied. The object's contents will, once prepared, be ready to send to the server, but every attribute is still directly exposed. Even `PreparedRequest._cookies` is exposed, although its prepended underscore is a gentle reminder that the attribute is not intended for use outside of the class, without forbidding such access (we are all responsible users).

This choice exposes the objects to user modification, but they are much more readable, and a little bit of extra work inside of `PreparedRequest` corrects capitalization issues and allows use of a dictionary in place of a `CookieJar` (look for the `if isinstance()/else` statement):

```python
#
#  ... from models.py ...
#

class PreparedRequest():
    #
    #  ... skip everything else ...
    #

    def prepare_cookies(self, cookies):
        """Prepares the given HTTP cookie data.

        This function eventually generates a ``Cookie`` header from the
        given cookies using cookielib. Due to cookielib's design, the header
```

---

15 This method makes it possible to handle cross-origin requests (like getting a JavaScript library hosted on a third-party site). It is supposed to return the origin host of the request, defined in IETF RFC 2965. (*http://bit.ly/http-state-management*)

```
    will not be regenerated if it already exists, meaning this function
    can only be called once for the life of the
    :class:`PreparedRequest <PreparedRequest>` object. Any subsequent calls
    to ``prepare_cookies`` will have no actual effect, unless the "Cookie"
    header is removed beforehand."""

    if isinstance(cookies, cookielib.CookieJar):
        self._cookies = cookies
    else:
        self._cookies = cookiejar_from_dict(cookies)

    cookie_header = get_cookie_header(self._cookies, self)
    if cookie_header is not None:
        self.headers['Cookie'] = cookie_header
```

These things may not seem like a big deal, but it's small choices like these that make
an API intuitive to use.

Style Examples from Requests

The style examples from Requests are a good example use for sets (which we think
aren't used often enough!) and a look at the `requests.status_codes` module, which
exists to make the style of the rest of the code simpler by avoiding hardcoded HTTP
status codes everywhere else in the code.

Sets and set arithmetic (a nice, Pythonic idiom)

We haven't yet shown an example use of Python sets in action. Python sets behave
like sets in math—you can do subtraction, unions (the *or* operator), and intersections
(the *and* operator):

```
>>> s1 = set((7,6))
>>> s2 = set((8,7))
>>> s1
{6, 7}
>>> s2
{8, 7}
>>> s1 - s2   # set subtraction
{6}
>>> s1 | s2   # set union
{8, 6, 7}
>>> s1 & s2   # set intersection
{7}
```

Here's one, down toward the end of this function from *cookies.py* (with the label ❷):

```
#
# ... from cookies.py ...
#

def create_cookie(name, value, **kwargs):   ❶
```

```
    """Make a cookie from underspecified parameters.

    By default, the pair of `name` and `value` will be set for the domain ''
    and sent on every request (this is sometimes called a "supercookie").
    """
    result = dict(
        version=0,
        name=name,
        value=value,
        port=None,
        domain='',
        path='/',
        secure=False,
        expires=None,
        discard=True,
        comment=None,
        comment_url=None,
        rest={'HttpOnly': None},
        rfc2109=False,)

    badargs = set(kwargs) - set(result)    ❷
    if badargs:
        err = 'create_cookie() got unexpected keyword arguments: %s'    ❸
        raise TypeError(err % list(badargs))    ❸

    result.update(kwargs)    ❹
    result['port_specified'] = bool(result['port'])    ❺
    result['domain_specified'] = bool(result['domain'])
    result['domain_initial_dot'] = result['domain'].startswith('.')
    result['path_specified'] = bool(result['path'])

    return cookielib.Cookie(**result)    ❻
```

❶ The **kwargs specification allows the user to provide any or none of the key-
    word options for a cookie.

❷ Set arithmetic! Pythonic. Simple. And in the standard library. On a dictionary,
    set() forms a set of the keys.

❸ This is a great example of spliting a long line into two shorter lines that make
    much better sense. No harm done from the extra err variable.

❹ The result.update(kwargs) updates the result dictionary with the key/value
    pairs in the kwargs dictionary, replacing existing pairs or creating ones that didn't
    exist.

❺ Here the call to bool() coerces the value to True if the object is truthy (meaning
    it evaluates to True—in this case, bool(result['port']) evaluates to True if it's
    not None and it's not an empty container).

❻ The signature to initialize `cookielib.Cookie` is actually 18 positional arguments and one keyword argument (`rfc2109` defaults to `False`). It's impossible for us average humans to memorize which position has which value, so here Requests takes advantage of being able to assign positional arguments by name as keyword arguments, sending the whole dictionary.

Status codes (readability counts)

The entire *status_codes.py* exists to create an object that can look up status codes by attribute. We're showing the definition of the lookup dictionary in *status_codes.py* first, and then an excerpt of code that uses it from *sessions.py*:

```
#
#  ... excerpted from requests/status_codes.py ...
#

_codes = {

    # Informational.
    100: ('continue',),
    101: ('switching_protocols',),
    102: ('processing',),
    103: ('checkpoint',),
    122: ('uri_too_long', 'request_uri_too_long'),
    200: ('ok', 'okay', 'all_ok', 'all_okay', 'all_good', '\\o/', '✓'),   ❶
    201: ('created',),
    202: ('accepted',),
    #
    #  ... skipping ...
    #

    # Redirection.
    300: ('multiple_choices',),
    301: ('moved_permanently', 'moved', '\\o-'),
    302: ('found',),
    303: ('see_other', 'other'),
    304: ('not_modified',),
    305: ('use_proxy',),
    306: ('switch_proxy',),
    307: ('temporary_redirect', 'temporary_moved', 'temporary'),
    308: ('permanent_redirect',
          'resume_incomplete', 'resume',),   # These 2 to be removed in 3.0   ❷

    #
    #  ... skipping the rest ...
    #
}

codes = LookupDict(name='status_codes')   ❸
```

```
for code, titles in _codes.items():
    for title in titles:
        setattr(codes, title, code)   ❹
        if not title.startswith('\\'):
            setattr(codes, title.upper(), code)   ❺
```

❶ All of these options for an OK status will become keys in the lookup dictionary.
Except for the happy person (\\o/) and the check mark (✔).

❷ The deprecated values are on a separate line so that the future delete will be clean
and obvious in version control.

❸ The LookupDict allows dot-access of its elements like in the next line.

❹ codes.ok == 200 and codes.okay == 200.

❺ And also codes.OK == 200 and codes.OKAY == 200.

All of this work for the status codes was to make the lookup dictionary codes. Why?
Instead of very typo-prone hardcoded integers all over the code, this is easy to read,
with all of the code numbers localized in a single file. Because it starts as a dictionary
keyed on the status codes, each status code integer only exists once. The possibility of
typos is much, much lower than if this were just a bunch of global variables manually
embedded into a namespace.

And converting the keys into attributes instead of using them as strings in a dictionary again reduces the risk of typographical errors. Here's the example in *sessions.py*
that's so much easier to read with words than numbers:

```
#
#  ... from sessions.py ...
#      Truncated to only show relevant content.
#
from .status_codes import codes   ❶


class SessionRedirectMixin(object):   ❷
    def resolve_redirects(self, resp, req, stream=False, timeout=None,
                          verify=True, cert=None, proxies=None,
                          **adapter_kwargs):
        """Receives a Response. Returns a generator of Responses."""

        i = 0
        hist = [] # keep track of history

        while resp.is_redirect:   ❸
            prepared_request = req.copy()

            if i > 0:
```

```
        # Update history and keep track of redirects.
        hist.append(resp)
        new_hist = list(hist)
        resp.history = new_hist

    try:
        resp.content  # Consume socket so it can be released
    except (ChunkedEncodingError, ContentDecodingError, RuntimeError):
        resp.raw.read(decode_content=False)

    if i >= self.max_redirects:
        raise TooManyRedirects(
                'Exceeded %s redirects.' % self.max_redirects
        )

    # Release the connection back into the pool.
    resp.close()

    #
    #  ... skipping content ...
    #

    # http://tools.ietf.org/html/rfc7231#section-6.4.4
    if (resp.status_code == codes.see_other and  ❹
            method != 'HEAD'):
        method = 'GET'

    # Do what the browsers do, despite standards...
    # First, turn 302s into GETs.
    if resp.status_code == codes.found and method != 'HEAD':  ❺
        method = 'GET'

    # Second, if a POST is responded to with a 301, turn it into a GET.
    # This bizarre behavior is explained in Issue 1704.
    if resp.status_code == codes.moved and method == 'POST':  ❺
        method = 'GET'

    #
    #  ... etc. ...
    #
```

❶ Here's where the status code lookup codes is imported.

❷ We describe mixin classes later in "Mixins (also one honking great idea)" on page 159. This mixin provides redirect methods for the main Session class, which is defined in this same file but not shown in our excerpt.

❸ We're entering a loop that's following the redirects for us to get at the content we want. The entire loop logic is deleted from this excerpt for brevity.

❹ Status codes as text are so much more readable than unmemorizable integers: `codes.see_other` would otherwise be 303 here.

❺ And `codes.found` would be 302, and `codes.moved` would be 301. So the code is self-documenting; we can tell meaning from the variable names; and we've avoided the possibility of littering the code with typographical errors by using dot-notation instead of a dictionary to look up strings (e.g., `codes.found` instead of `codes["found"]`).

Werkzeug

To read Werkzeug, we need to know a little about how web servers communicate with applications. The next paragraphs try to give as short an overview as possible.

Python's interface for web application-to-server interaction, WSGI, is defined in PEP 333, which was written by Phillip J. Eby in 2003.[16] It specifies how a web server (like Apache) communicates with a Python application or framework:

1. The server will call the application once per HTTP request (e.g., "GET" or "POST") it receives.

2. That application will return an iterable of bytestrings that the server will use to respond to the HTTP request.

3. The specification also says the application will take two parameters—for example, *webapp*(`environ, start_response`). The `environ` parameter will contain all of the data associated with the request, and the `start_response` parameter will be a function or other callable object that will be used to send back header (e.g., (`'Content-type', 'text/plain'`)) and status (e.g., `200 OK`) information to the server.

That summary glosses over about a half-dozen pages of additional detail. In the middle of PEP 333 is this aspirational statement about the new standard making modular web frameworks possible:

> If middleware can be both simple and robust, and WSGI is widely available in servers and frameworks, it allows for the possibility of an entirely new kind of Python web application framework: one consisting of loosely-coupled WSGI middleware components. Indeed, existing framework authors may even choose to refactor their frameworks' existing services to be provided in this way, becoming more like libraries used with WSGI, and less like monolithic frameworks. This would then allow application

---

16 Since then, PEP 333 has been superseded by a specification updated to include some Python 3–specific details, PEP 3333 (*https://www.python.org/dev/peps/pep-3333/*). For a digestible but very thorough introduction, we recommend Ian Bicking's WSGI tutorial (*http://pythonpaste.org/do-it-yourself-framework.html*).

---

developers to choose "best-of-breed" components for specific functionality, rather than having to commit to all the pros and cons of a single framework.

Of course, as of this writing, that day is doubtless quite far off. In the meantime, it is a sufficient short-term goal for WSGI to enable the use of any framework with any server.

About four years after, in 2007, Armin Ronacher released Werkzeug, with the intent of filling that hopeful need for a WSGI library that can be used to make WSGI applications and middleware components.

Werkzeug is the largest package we are reading, so we'll highlight just a few of its design choices.

Reading Code in a Toolkit

A software toolkit is a collection of compatible utilities. In Werkzeug's case, they're all related to WSGI applications. A good way to understand the distinct utilities and what they're for is to look at the unit tests, and that's how we'll approach reading Werkzeug's code.

Get Werkzeug from GitHub:

```
$ git clone https://github.com/pallets/werkzeug.git
$ virtualenv -p python3 venv
$ source venv/bin/activate
(venv)$ cd werkzeug
(venv)$ pip install --editable .
(venv)$ py.test tests  # Run the unit tests
```

Read Werkzeug's documentation

Werkzeug's documentation (*http://werkzeug.pocoo.org/*) lists the main things it provides—an implementation of the WSGI 1.0 (PEP 333 (*https://www.python.org/dev/peps/pep-0333/*)) specification, a URL routing system, the capability to parse and dump HTTP headers, objects that represent HTTP requests and HTTP responses, session and cookie support, file uploads, and other utilities and community add-ons. Plus, a full-featured debugger.

The tutorials are good, but we're using the API documentation instead to see more of the library's components. The next section takes from Werkzeug's wrappers (*http://werkzeug.pocoo.org/docs/0.11/wrappers/*) and routing documentation (*http://werkzeug.pocoo.org/docs/0.11/routing/*).

Use Werkzeug

Werkzeug provides utilities for WSGI applications, so to learn what Werkzeug provides, we can start with a WSGI application, and then use a few of Werkzeug's utilities. This first application is a slightly changed version of what's in PEP 333, and doesn't use Werkzeug yet. The second one does the same thing as the first, but using Werkzeug:

```
def wsgi_app(environ, start_response):
    headers = [('Content-type', 'text/plain'), ('charset', 'utf-8')]
    start_response('200 OK', headers)
    yield 'Hello world.'

# This app does the same thing as the one above:
response_app = werkzeug.Response('Hello world!')
```

Werkzeug implements a `werkzeug.Client` class to stand in for a real web sever when doing one-off testing like this. The client response will have the type of the `response_wrapper` argument. In this code, we create clients and use them to call the WSGI applications we made earlier. First, the plain WSGI app (but with the response parsed into a `werkzeug.Response`):

```
>>> import werkzeug
>>> client = werkzeug.Client(wsgi_app, response_wrapper=werkzeug.Response)
>>> resp=client.get("?answer=42")
>>> type(resp)
<class 'werkzeug.wrappers.Response'>
>>> resp.status
'200 OK'
>>> resp.content_type
'text/plain'
>>> print(resp.data.decode())
Hello world.
```

Next, using the `werkzeug.Response` WSGI app:

```
>>> client = werkzeug.Client(response_app, response_wrapper=werkzeug.Response)
>>> resp=client.get("?answer=42")
>>> print(resp.data.decode())
Hello world!
```

The `werkzeug.Request` class provides the contents of the environment dictionary (the `environ` argument above to `wsgi_app()`) in a form that's easier to use. It also provides a decorator to convert a function that takes a a `werkzeug.Request` and returns a `werkzeug.Response` into a WSGI app:

```
>>> @werkzeug.Request.application
... def wsgi_app_using_request(request):
...     msg = "A WSGI app with:\n    method: {}\n    path: {}\n    query: {}\n"
...     return werkzeug.Response(
...         msg.format(request.method, request.path, request.query_string))
...
```

which, when used, gives:

```
>>> client = werkzeug.Client(
...     wsgi_app_using_request, response_wrapper=werkzeug.Response)
>>> resp=client.get("?answer=42")
```

```
>>> print(resp.data.decode())
A WSGI app with:
   method: GET
   path: /
   query: b'answer=42'
```

So, we know how to use the `werkzeug.Request` and `werkzeug.Response` objects. The other thing that was featured in the documentation was the routing. Here's an excerpt that uses it—callout numbers identify both the pattern and its match:

```
>>> import werkzeug
>>> from werkzeug.routing import Map, Rule
>>>
>>> url_map = Map([      ❶
...      Rule('/', endpoint='index'),      ❷
...      Rule('/<any("Robin","Galahad","Arthur"):person>', endpoint='ask'),      ❸
...      Rule('/<other>', endpoint='other')      ❹
... ])

>>> env = werkzeug.create_environ(path='/shouldnt/match')      ❺
>>> urls = url_map.bind_to_environ(env)
>>> urls.match()
Traceback (most recent call last):
  File "<stdin>", line 1, in <module>
  File "[...path...]/werkzeug/werkzeug/routing.py", line 1569, in match
    raise NotFound()
werkzeug.exceptions.NotFound: 404: Not Found
```

❶ The `werkzeug.Routing.Map` provides the main routing functions. The rule matching is done in order; the first rule to match is the one selected.

❷ When there are no angle-bracket terms in the rule's placeholder string, it only matches on an exact match, and the second result from `urls.match()` is an empty dictionary:

```
>>> env = werkzeug.create_environ(path='/')
>>> urls = url_map.bind_to_environ(env)
>>> urls.match()
('index', {})
```

❸ Otherwise, the second entry is a dictionary mapping the named terms in the rule to their value—for example, mapping `'person'` to the value `'Galahad'`:

```
>>> env = werkzeug.create_environ(path='/Galahad?favorite+color')
>>> urls = url_map.bind_to_environ(env)
>>> urls.match()
('ask', {'person': 'Galahad'})
```

❹ Note that `'Galahad'` could have mached the route named `'other'`, but it did not —but `'Lancelot'` did—because the first rule to match the pattern is chosen:

```
>>> env = werkzeug.create_environ(path='/Lancelot')
>>> urls = url_map.bind_to_environ(env)
>>> urls.match()
('other', {'other': 'Lancelot'})
```

❺   And an exception is raised if there are no matches at all in the list of rules:

```
>>> env = werkzeug.test.create_environ(path='/shouldnt/match')
>>> urls = url_map.bind_to_environ(env)
>>> urls.match()
Traceback (most recent call last):
File "<stdin>", line 1, in <module>
File "[...path...]/werkzeug/werkzeug/routing.py", line 1569, in match
raise NotFound()
werkzeug.exceptions.NotFound: 404: Not Found
```

You'd use the map to route a request to an appropriate endpoint. The following code continues on from the predceding example to do this:

```
@werkzeug.Request.application
def send_to_endpoint(request):
    urls = url_map.bind_to_environ(request)
    try:
        endpoint, kwargs = urls.match()
        if endpoint == 'index':
            response = werkzeug.Response("You got the index.")
        elif endpoint == 'ask':
            questions = dict(
                Galahad='What is your favorite color?',
                Robin='What is the capital of Assyria?',
                Arthur='What is the air-speed velocity of an unladen swallow?')
            response = werkzeug.Response(questions[kwargs['person']])
        else:
            response = werkzeug.Response("Other: {other}".format(**kwargs))
    except (KeyboardInterrupt, SystemExit):
        raise
    except:
        response = werkzeug.Response(
            'You may not have gone where you intended to go,\n'
            'but I think you have ended up where you needed to be.',
            status=404
        )
    return response
```

To test it, use the werkzeug.Client again:

```
>>> client = werkzeug.Client(send_to_endpoint, response_wrapper=werkzeug.Response)
>>> print(client.get("/").data.decode())
You got the index.
>>>
>>> print(client.get("Arthur").data.decode())
What is the air-speed velocity of an unladen swallow?
>>>
```

```
>>> print(client.get("42").data.decode())
Other: 42
>>>
>>> print(client.get("time/lunchtime").data.decode())  # no match
You may not have gone where you intended to go,
but I think you have ended up where you needed to be.
```

Read Werkzeug's code

When test coverage is good, you can learn what a library does by looking at the unit tests. The caveat is that with unit tests, you're intentionally looking at the "trees" and not the "forest"—exploring obscure use cases intended to ensure the code doesn't break, rather than looking for interconnections between modules. This should be OK for a toolkit like Werkzeug, which we expect to have modular, loosely coupled components.

Because we familiarized ourselves with how the routing and the request and response wrappers work, *werkzeug/test_routing.py* and *werkzeug/test_wrappers.py* are good choices to read for now.

When we first open *werkzeug/test_routing.py*, we can quickly look for interconnection between the modules by searching through the entire file for the imported objects. Here are all of the import statements:

```
import pytest  ❶

import uuid  ❷

from tests import strict_eq  ❸

from werkzeug import routing as r  ❹
from werkzeug.wrappers import Response  ❺
from werkzeug.datastructures import ImmutableDict, MultiDict  ❻
from werkzeug.test import create_environ  ❼
```

❶ Of course, pytest is used here for testing.

❷ The uuid module is used in just one function, test_uuid_converter(), to confirm that the conversion from string to a uuid.UUID object (the Universal Unique Identifier string uniquely identifying objects on the Internet) works.

❸ The strict_eq() function is used often, and defined in *werkzeug/tests/__init__.py*. It's for testing, and is only necessary because in Python 2 there used to be implicit type conversion between Unicode and byte strings, but relying on this breaks things in Python 3.

❹ The werkzeug.routing module is the one that's being tested.

❺ The `Reponse` object is used in just one function, `test_dispatch()`, to confirm that `werkzeug.routing.MapAdapter.dispatch()` passes the correct information through to the dispatched WSGI application.

❻ These dictionary objects are used only once each, `ImmutableDict` to confirm that an immutable dictionary in `werkzeug.routing.Map` is indeed immutable, and `MultiDict` to provide multiple keyed values to the URL builder and confirm that it still builds the correct URL.

❼ The `create_environ()` function is for testing—it creates a WSGI environment without having to use an actual HTTP request.

The point of doing the quick searching was to quickly see the interconnection between modules. What we found out was that `werkzeug.routing` imports some special data structures, and that's all. The rest of the unit tests show the scope of the routing module. For example, non-ASCII characters can be used:

```
def test_environ_nonascii_pathinfo():
    environ = create_environ(u'/лошадь')
    m = r.Map([
        r.Rule(u'/', endpoint='index'),
        r.Rule(u'/лошадь', endpoint='horse')
    ])
    a = m.bind_to_environ(environ)
    strict_eq(a.match(u'/'), ('index', {}))
    strict_eq(a.match(u'/лошадь'), ('horse', {}))
    pytest.raises(r.NotFound, a.match, u'/барсук')
```

There are tests to build and parse URLs, and even utilities to find the closest available match, when there wasn't an actual match. You can even do all kinds of crazy custom processing when handling the type conversions/parsing from the path and the URL string:

```
def test_converter_with_tuples():
    '''
    Regression test for https://github.com/pallets/werkzeug/issues/709
    '''
    class TwoValueConverter(r.BaseConverter):

        def __init__(self, *args, **kwargs):
            super(TwoValueConverter, self).__init__(*args, **kwargs)
            self.regex = r'(\w\w+)/(\w\w+)'

        def to_python(self, two_values):
            one, two = two_values.split('/')
            return one, two

        def to_url(self, values):
            return "%s/%s" % (values[0], values[1])
```

```
map = r.Map([
    r.Rule('/<two:foo>/', endpoint='handler')
], converters={'two': TwoValueConverter})
a = map.bind('example.org', '/')
route, kwargs = a.match('/qwert/yuiop/')
assert kwargs['foo'] == ('qwert', 'yuiop')
```

Similarly, *werkzeug/test_wrappers.py* does not import much. Reading through the
tests gives an example of the scope of available functionality for the Request object—
cookies, encoding, authentication, security, cache timeouts, and even multilanguage
encoding:

```
def test_modified_url_encoding():
    class ModifiedRequest(wrappers.Request):
        url_charset = 'euc-kr'

    req = ModifiedRequest.from_values(u'/?foo=정상처리'.encode('euc-kr'))
    strict_eq(req.args['foo'], u'정상처리')
```

In general, reading the tests provides a way to see the details of what the library provides. Once satisfied that we have an idea of what Werkzeug is, we can move on.

Tox in Werkzeug

Tox (*https://tox.readthedocs.io*) is a Python command-line tool that uses virtual environments to run tests. You can run it on your own computer (tox on the command
line), so long as the Python interpreters you're using are already installed. It's integrated with GitHub, so if you have a *tox.ini* file in the top level of your repository, like
Werkzeug does, it will automatically run tests on every commit.

Here is Werkzeug's entire *tox.ini* configuration file:

```
[tox]
envlist = py{26,27,py,33,34,35}-normal, py{26,27,33,34,35}-uwsgi

[testenv]
passenv = LANG
deps=
# General
    pyopenssl
    greenlet
    pytest
    pytest-xprocess
    redis
    requests
    watchdog
    uwsgi: uwsgi

# Python 2
    py26: python-memcached
```

```
        py27: python-memcached
        pypy: python-memcached

    # Python 3
        py33: python3-memcached
        py34: python3-memcached
        py35: python3-memcached

    whitelist_externals=
        redis-server
        memcached
        uwsgi

    commands=
        normal: py.test []
        uwsgi: uwsgi
                --pyrun {envbindir}/py.test
                --pyargv -kUWSGI --cache2=name=werkzeugtest,items=20 --master
```

Style Examples from Werkzeug

Most of the major style points we made in Chapter 4 have already been covered. The first style example we chose shows an elegant way to guess types from a string, and the second one makes a case for using the VERBOSE option when defining long regular expressions—so that other people can tell what the expression does without having to spend time thinking through it.

Elegant way to guess type (if the implementation is easy to explain, it may be a good idea)

If you're like most of us, you've had to parse text files and convert content to various types. This solution is particularly Pythonic, so we wanted to include it:

```
_PYTHON_CONSTANTS = {
    'None':     None,
    'True':     True,
    'False':    False
}


def _pythonize(value):
    if value in _PYTHON_CONSTANTS:          ❶
        return _PYTHON_CONSTANTS[value]
    for convert in int, float:              ❷
        try:                                ❸
            return convert(value)
        except ValueError:
            pass
    if value[:1] == value[-1:] and value[0] in '"\'':   ❹
        value = value[1:-1]
    return text_type(value)                 ❺
```

❶ Key lookup for Python dictionaries uses hash mapping, just like set lookup. Python doesn't have switch case statements. (They were proposed and rejected for lack of popularity in PEP 3103 (*https://www.python.org/dev/peps/pep-3103/*).) Instead, Python users use if/elif/else, or as shown here, the very Pythonic option of a dictionary lookup.

❷ Note that the first conversion attempt is to the more restrictive type, int, before attempting the conversion to float.

❸ It is also Pythonic to use try/except statements to infer type.

❹ This part is necessary because the code is in *werkzeug/routing.py*, and the string being parsed is part of a URL. It's checking for quotes and unquoting the value.

❺ text_type converts strings to Unicode in a way that's both Python 2 and Python 3 compatible. It's basically the same thing as the u() function highlighted in "HowDoI" on page 99.

Regular expressions (readability counts)

If you use lengthy regular expressions in your code, please use the re.VERBOSE[17] option and make it comprehensible to the rest of us humans, like this snippet from *werkzeug/routing.py*:

```
import re

_rule_re = re.compile(r'''
    (?P<static>[^<]*)                           # static rule data
    <
    (?:
        (?P<converter>[a-zA-Z_][a-zA-Z0-9_]*)   # converter name
        (?:\((?P<args>.*?)\))?                   # converter arguments
        \:                                       # variable delimiter
    )?
    (?P<variable>[a-zA-Z_][a-zA-Z0-9_]*)        # variable name
    >
''', re.VERBOSE)
```

Structure Examples from Werkzeug

The first two examples related to structure demonstrate Pythonic ways to leverage dynamic typing. We cautioned against reassigning a variable to different values in

---

17 re.VERBOSE allows you to write more readable regular expressions by changing the way whitespace is treated, and by allowing comments. Read more in the re documentation (*https://docs.python.org/3/library/re.html*).

"Dynamic Typing" on page 73 but didn't mention any benefits. One of them is the ability to use any type of object that behaves in the expected way—*duck typing*. Duck typing approaches types with the philosophy: "If it looks like a duck[18] and quacks like a duck, then it's a duck".

They both play in different ways on ways that objects can be callable without being functions: `cached_property.__init__()` allows initialization of a class instance to be used like an ordinary function call, and `Response.__call__()` allows a `Response` instance to itself be called like a function.

The last excerpt uses Werkzeug's implementation of some mixin classes (that each define a subset of the functionality in Werkzeug's `Request` object) to discuss why they're a honking great idea.

Class-based decorators (a Pythonic use of dynamic typing)

Werkzeug makes use of duck typing to make the `@cached_property` decorator. When we talked about `property` when describing the Tablib project, we talked about it like it's a function. Usually decorators *are* functions, but because there is no enforcement of type, they can be any callable: `property` is actually a class. (You can tell it's intended to be used like a function because it is not capitalized, like PEP 8 says class names should be.) When written like a function call (`property()`), `property.__init__()` will be called to initialize and return a `property` instance—a class, with an appropriately defined `__init__()` method, works as a callable. Quack.

The following excerpt contains the entire definition of `cached_property`, which subclasses the `property` class. The documentation within `cached_property` speaks for itself. When it is used to decorate `BaseRequest.form` in the code we just saw, the *instance*.`form` will have the type `cached_property` and will behave like a dictionary as far as the user is concerned, because both the `__get__()` and `__set__()` methods are defined. The first time `BaseRequest.form` is accessed, it will read its form data (if it exists) once, and then store the data in *instance*.`form.__dict__` to be accessed in the future:

```
class cached_property(property):

    """A decorator that converts a function into a lazy property.  The
    function wrapped is called the first time to retrieve the result,
    and then that calculated result is used the next time you access
    the value::

        class Foo(object):
```

---

18 That is, if it's callable, or iterable, or has the correct method defined …

```python
    @cached_property
    def foo(self):
        # calculate something important here
        return 42
```

The class has to have a `__dict__` in order for this property to work.
"""

```python
# implementation detail: A subclass of Python's built-in property
# decorator, we override __get__ to check for a cached value. If one
# choses to invoke __get__ by hand, the property will still work as
# expected because the lookup logic is replicated in __get__ for
# manual invocation.

def __init__(self, func, name=None, doc=None):
    self.__name__ = name or func.__name__
    self.__module__ = func.__module__
    self.__doc__ = doc or func.__doc__
    self.func = func

def __set__(self, obj, value):
    obj.__dict__[self.__name__] = value

def __get__(self, obj, type=None):
    if obj is None:
        return self
    value = obj.__dict__.get(self.__name__, _missing)
    if value is _missing:
        value = self.func(obj)
        obj.__dict__[self.__name__] = value
    return value
```

Here it is in action:

```python
>>> from werkzeug.utils import cached_property
>>>
>>> class Foo(object):
...     @cached_property
...     def foo(self):
...         print("You have just called Foo.foo()!")
...         return 42
...
>>> bar = Foo()
>>>
>>> bar.foo
You have just called Foo.foo()!
42
>>> bar.foo
42
>>> bar.foo  # Notice it doesn't print again...
42
```

Response.__call__

The Response class is built using features mixed into the BaseResponse class, just like Request. We will highlight its user interface and won't show the actual code, just the docstring for BaseResponse, to show the usage details:

```
class BaseResponse(object):

    """Base response class.  The most important fact about a response object
    is that it's a regular WSGI application.  It's initialized with a couple
    of response parameters (headers, body, status code, etc.) and will start a
    valid WSGI response when called with the environ and start response
    callable.

    Because it's a WSGI application itself, processing usually ends before the
    actual response is sent to the server.  This helps debugging systems
    because they can catch all the exceptions before responses are started.

    Here is a small example WSGI application that takes advantage of the
    response objects::

        from werkzeug.wrappers import BaseResponse as Response

        def index():   ❶
            return Response('Index page')

        def application(environ, start_response):   ❷
            path = environ.get('PATH_INFO') or '/'
            if path == '/':
                response = index()   ❸
            else:
                response = Response('Not Found', status=404)   ❹
            return response(environ, start_response)   ❺
    """
    # ... etc. ...
```

❶ In the example from the docstring, index() is the function that will be called in response to the HTTP request. The response will be the string "Index page".

❷ This is the signature required for a WSGI application, as specified in PEP 333/ PEP 3333.

❸ Response subclasses BaseResponse, so response is an instance of BaseResponse.

❹ See how the 404 response just requires the status keyword to be set.

❺ And, voilà, the response instance is itself callable, with all of the accompanying headers and details set to sensible default values (or overrides in the case where the path is not "/").

So, how is an instance of a class callable? Because the `BaseRequest.__call__` method has been defined. We show just that method in the following code example.

```python
class BaseResponse(object):
    #
    # ... skip everything else ...
    #

    def __call__(self, environ, start_response):    ❶
        """Process this response as WSGI application.

        :param environ: the WSGI environment.
        :param start_response: the response callable provided by the WSGI
                               server.
        :return: an application iterator
        """
        app_iter, status, headers = self.get_wsgi_response(environ)
        start_response(status, headers)    ❷
        return app_iter    ❸
```

❶ Here's the signature to make `BaseResponse` instances callable.

❷ Here's where the `start_response` function call requirement of WSGI apps is satisfied.

❸ And here's where the iterable of bytes is returned.

The lesson here is this: if it's possible in the language, why not do it? We promise after realizing we could add a `__call__()` method to any object and make it callable, we were inspired to go back to the original documentation for a good re-read of Python's data model (*http://docs.python.org/3/reference/datamodel.html*).

Mixins (also one honking great idea)

Mixins in Python are classes that are intended to add a specific functionality—a handful of related attributes—to a class. Python, unlike Java, allows for multiple inheritance. This means that the following paradigm, where a half-dozen different classes are subclassed simultaneously, is a possible way to modularize different functionality into separate classes. "Namespaces," sort of.

Modularization like this is useful in a utility library like Werkzeug because it communicates to the user which functions are related and not related: the developer can be confident that attributes in one mixin are not going to be modified by any functions in another mixin.

In Python, there isn't anything special to identify a mixin, other than the convention of appending `Mixin` to the end of the class name. This means if you don't want to pay attention to the order of method resolution, all of the mixins' methods should have distinct names.

In Werkzeug, sometimes methods in a mixin may require certain attributes to be present. These requirements are usually documented in the mixin's docstring:

```python
# ... in werkzeug/wrappers.py


class UserAgentMixin(object):  ❶

    """Adds a `user_agent` attribute to the request object which contains
    the parsed user agent of the browser that triggered the request as a
    :class:`~werkzeug.useragents.UserAgent` object.
    """

    @cached_property
    def user_agent(self):
        """The current user agent."""
        from werkzeug.useragents import UserAgent
        return UserAgent(self.environ)  ❷


class Request(BaseRequest, AcceptMixin, ETagRequestMixin,
              UserAgentMixin, AuthorizationMixin,  ❸
              CommonRequestDescriptorsMixin):

    """Full featured request object implementing the following mixins:

    - :class:`AcceptMixin` for accept header parsing
    - :class:`ETagRequestMixin` for etag and cache control handling
    - :class:`UserAgentMixin` for user agent introspection
    - :class:`AuthorizationMixin` for http auth handling
    - :class:`CommonRequestDescriptorsMixin` for common headers
    """
    ❹
```

❶ There is nothing special about the `UserAgentMixin`; it subclasses `object`, though, which is the default in Python 3, highly recommended for compatibility in Python 2, and which should be done explicitly because, well, "explicit is better than implicit."

❷ `UserAgentMixin.user_agent` assumes there is a `self.environ` attribute.

❸ When included in the list of base classes for `Request`, the attribute it provides becomes accessible via `Request(environ).user_agent`.

❹ Nothing else—this is the entire body of the definition of `Request`. All functionality is provided by the base class or the mixins. Modular, pluggable, and as froody as Ford Prefect.

New-Style Classes and object

The base class `object` adds default attributes that other built-in options rely on. Classes that don't inherit from `object` are called "old-style classes" or "classic classes" and are removed in Python 3. It's the default to inherit from `object` in Python 3, meaning all Python 3 classes are "new-style classes." New-style classes are available in Python 2.7 (actually with their current behavior since Python 2.3), but the inheritance must be written explicitly, and (we think) should always be written.

There are more details in the Python documentation on new-style classes (*https://www.python.org/doc/newstyle/*), a tutorial here (*http://www.python-course.eu/classes_and_type.php*), and a technical history of their creation in this post (*http://tinyurl.com/history-new-style-classes*). Here are some of the differences (in Python 2.7; all classes are new-style in Python 3):

```
>>> class A(object):
...     """New-style class, subclassing object."""
...
>>> class B:
...     """Old-style class."""
...
>>> dir(A)
['__class__', '__delattr__', '__dict__', '__doc__', '__format__',
 '__getattribute__', '__hash__', '__init__', '__module__', '__new__',
 '__reduce__', '__reduce_ex__', '__repr__', '__setattr__', '__sizeof__',
 '__str__', '__subclasshook__', '__weakref__']
>>>
>>> dir(B)
['__doc__', '__module__']
>>>
>>> type(A)
<type 'type'>
>>> type(B)
<type 'classobj'>
>>>
>>> import sys
>>> sys.getsizeof(A())   # The size is in bytes.
64
>>> sys.getsizeof(B())
72
```

Flask

Flask is a web microframework that combines Werkzeug and Jinja2, both by Armin Ronacher. It was created as a joke and released on April Fool's Day, 2010, but quickly became one of Python's most popular web frameworks. He had released Werkzeug a few years earlier in 2007 as a "Swiss Army knife of Python web development," and (we presume) was probably a little frustrated at its slow adoption. The idea for Werkzeug was to decouple the WSGI from everything else so that developers could plug in their own choice of utilities. Little did he know how much we'd appreciate a few more "rails."[19]

Reading Code in a Framework

A software framework is just like a physical framework—it provides the underlying structure to build a WSGI[20] application: the library user provides components that the main Flask application will run. Our goal in reading will be to understand the framework structure and what precisely it provides.

Get Flask from GitHub:

```
$ git clone https://github.com/pallets/flask.git
$ virtualenv venv  # Python 3 is usable but discouraged for now
$ source venv/bin/activate
(venv)$ cd flask
(venv)$ pip install --editable .
(venv)$ pip install -r test-requirements.txt  # Required for unit tests
(venv)$ py.test tests  # Run the unit tests
```

Read Flask's documentation

Flask's online documentation (*http://flask.pocoo.org/*) starts out with a seven-line implementation of a web app, and then summarizes Flask: it's a Unicode-based WSGI-compliant framework that uses Jinja2 for HTML templating and Werkzeug for WSGI utilities like URL routing. It also has built-in tools for development and testing. There are also tutorials, so the next step is easy.

---

19 A reference to Ruby on Rails, which popularized web frameworks, and which is much more similar to Django's style of "everything included," rather than Flask's style of "nearly nothing included" (until you add plugins). Django is a great choice when the things you want included are the things Django provides—it was made, and is fantastic for, hosting an online newspaper.

20 WSGI is a Python standard, defined in PEP 333 (*https://www.python.org/dev/peps/pep-0333/*) and PEP 3333 (*https://www.python.org/dev/peps/pep-3333/*) for how an application can communicate with a web server.

Use Flask

We can run the flaskr example that we downloaded with the GitHub repository. The documents say it's a small blog site. From within the top *flask* directory:

```
(venv)$ cd examples/flaskr/
(venv)$ py.test test_flaskr.py  # Tests should pass
(venv)$ export FLASK_APP=flaskr
(venv)$ flask initdb
(venv)$ flask run
```

Read Flask's code

The ultimate goal of Flask is to create a web application, so really it isn't so different from the command-line applications Diamond and HowDoI. Rather than another diagram tracing the flow of function calls through the code, this time we'll step through Flask by running the flaskr example app with a debugger; we'll use pdb—the Python debugger—in the standard library.

First, add a breakpoint to *flaskr.py*, which will be activated when that point in the code is reached, causing the interactive session to enter the debugger:

```
@app.route('/')
def show_entries():
    import pdb; pdb.set_trace()  ## This line is the breakpoint.
    db = get_db()
    cur = db.execute('select title, text from entries order by id desc')
    entries = cur.fetchall()
    return render_template('show_entries.html', entries=entries)
```

Next, close the file and type python on the command line to enter an interactive session. Rather than starting a server, use Flask's internal testing utilities to simulate an HTTP GET request to the / location where we just placed the debugger:

```
>>> import flaskr
>>> client = flaskr.app.test_client()
>>> client.get('/')
> /[... truncated path ...]/flask/examples/flaskr/flaskr.py(74)show_entries()
-> db = get_db()
(Pdb)
```

The last three lines are from pdb: we see the path (to *flaskr.py*), the line number (74), and the method name (show_entries()) where we stopped. The line (-> db = get_db()) shows the statement that will be executed next if we were to step forward in the debugger. And the (Pdb) prompt reminds us that we are using the pdb debugger.

We can navigate up or down the stack[21] by typing u or d, respectively, at the command prompt. See the pdb documentation (*https://docs.python.org/library/pdb.html*) under the header "Debugger Commands" for a complete list of the commands you can type. We can also type variable names to see them, and any other Python command; we can even set the variables to different values before we continue on in the code.

If we go up the stack one step, we see what called the show_entries() function (with the breakpoint we just installed): it's a flask.app.Flask object with a lookup dictionary named view_functions that maps string names (like 'show_entries') to functions. We also see the show_entries() function was called with **req.view_args. We can check what req.view_args is from the interactive debugger command line by just typing its name (it's the empty dictionary — {}, meaning no arguments):

```
(Pdb) u
> /[ ... truncated path ...]/flask/flask/app.py(1610)dispatch_request()
-> return self.view_functions[rule.endpoint](**req.view_args)
(Pdb) type(self)
<class 'flask.app.Flask'>
(Pdb) type(self.view_functions)
<type 'dict'>
(Pdb) self.view_functions
{'add_entry': <function add_entry at 0x108198230>,
 'show_entries': <function show_entries at 0x1081981b8>, [... truncated ...]
 'login': <function login at 0x1081982a8>}
(Pdb) rule.endpoint
'show_entries'
(Pdb) req.view_args
{}
```

We can simultaneously follow along through the source code, if we want to, by opening the appropriate file and going to the stated line. If we keep going up the stack, we can see where the WSGI application is called:

```
(Pdb) u
> /[ ... truncated path ...]/flask/flask/app.py(1624)full_dispatch_request()
-> rv = self.dispatch_request()
(Pdb) u
> /[ ... truncated path ...]/flask/flask/app.py(1973)wsgi_app()
-> response = self.full_dispatch_request()
(Pdb) u
> /[ ... truncated path ...]/flask/flask/app.py(1985)__call__()
-> return self.wsgi_app(environ, start_response)
```

---

21 The Python call stack contains the instructions that are in progress, being run by the Python interpreter. So if function f() calls function g(), then function f() will go on the stack first, and g() will be pushed on top of f() when it's called. When g() returns, it is *popped* off of (removed from) the stack, and then f() will continue where it left off. It is called a stack, because conceptually it works the same way a dish washer will approach a stack of plates—new ones go on the top, and you always deal with the top ones first.

If we type u any more, we end up in the testing module, which was used to create the fake client without having to start a server—we've gone as far up the stack as we want to go. We learned that the application flaskr is dispatched from within an instance of the `flask.app.Flask` class, on line 1985 of *flask/flask/app.py*. Here is the function:

```
class Flask:
    ## ~~ ... skip lots of definitions ...

    def wsgi_app(self, environ, start_response):
        """The actual WSGI application.   ... skip other documentation ...
        """
        ctx = self.request_context(environ)
        ctx.push()
        error = None
        try:
            try:
                response = self.full_dispatch_request()      ❶
            except Exception as e:
                error = e
                response = self.make_response(self.handle_exception(e))
            return response(environ, start_response)
        finally:
            if self.should_ignore_error(error):
                error = None
            ctx.auto_pop(error)

    def __call__(self, environ, start_response):
        """Shortcut for :attr:`wsgi_app`."""
        return self.wsgi_app(environ, start_response)      ❷
```

❶ This is line number 1973, identified in the debugger.

❷ This is line number 1985, also identified in the debugger. The WSGI server would receive the Flask instance as an application, and call it once for every request—by using the debugger, we've found the entry point for the code.

We're using the debugger in the same way as we used the call graph with HowDoI—by following function calls—which is also the same thing as reading through code directly. The value of using the debugger is that we avoid looking at all of the additional code that may distract or confuse us. Use the approach that is most effective for you.

After going up the stack using u, we can go back down the stack using d and will end up back at the breakpoint, labeled with the `*** Newest frame`:

```
> /[ ... truncated path ...]/flask/examples/flaskr/flaskr.py(74)show_entries()
-> db = get_db()
(Pdb) d
*** Newest frame
```

From there, we can advance through a function call with the n (*next*) command, or advance in as short a step as possible with the s (*step*) command:

```
(Pdb) s
--Call--
> /[ ... truncated path ... ]/flask/examples/flaskr/flaskr.py(55)get_db()
-> def get_db():
(Pdb) s
> /[ ... truncated path ... ]/flask/examples/flaskr/flaskr.py(59)get_db()
-> if not hasattr(g, 'sqlite_db'):   ❶
##~~
##~~ ... do a dozen steps to create and return the database connection...
##~~
-> return g.sqlite_db
(Pdb) n
> /[ ... truncated path ... ]/flask/examples/flaskr/flaskr.py(75)show_entries()
-> cur = db.execute('select title, text from entries order by id desc')
(Pdb) n
> /[ ... truncated path ... ]/flask/examples/flaskr/flaskr.py(76)show_entries()
-> entries = cur.fetchall()
(Pdb) n
> /[ ... truncated path ... ]/flask/examples/flaskr/flaskr.py(77)show_entries()
-> return render_template('show_entries.html', entries=entries)   ❷
(Pdb) n
--Return--
```

There's a lot more, but it's tedious to show. What we get out of it is:

❶ Awareness of the Flask.g object. A little more digging reveals it is the *global* (actually local to the Flask instance) context. It exists to contain database connections and other persistent things like cookies that need to survive outside of the life of the methods in the Flask class. Using a dictionary like this keeps variables out of the Flask app's namespace, avoiding possible name collisions.

❷ The render_template() function isn't much of a surprise, but it's at the end of the function definition in the *flaskr.py* module, meaning we're essentially done— the return value goes back to the calling function from the Flask instance that we saw when traversing up the stack. So we're skipping the rest.

The debugger is useful local to the place that you're inspecting, to find out precisely what's happening before and after an instant, the user-selected breakpoint, in the code. One of the big features is the ability to change variables on the fly (any Python code works in the debugger) and then continue on stepping through the code.

Logging in Flask

Diamond has an example of logging in an application, and Flask provides one of logging in a library. If all you want to do is avoid "no handler found" warnings, search for "logging" in the Requests library (*requests/requests/__init__.py*). But if you want to provide some logging support within your library or framework, Flask's logging provides a good example to follow.

Flask-specific logging is implemented in *flask/flask/logging.py*. It defines the logging format strings for production (with logging level ERROR) and for debugging (with logging level DEBUG), and follows the advice from the Twelve-Factor App (*http:// 12factor.net*) to log to streams (which direct to one of wsgi.errors or sys.stderr, depending on the context).

The logger is added to the main Flask application in *flask/flask/app.py* (the code snippet skips over anything that's not relevant in the file):

```
# a lock used for logger initialization
_logger_lock = Lock()  ❶


class Flask(_PackageBoundObject):

    ##~~ ... skip other definitions

    #: The name of the logger to use.  By default the logger name is the
    #: package name passed to the constructor.
    #:
    #: .. versionadded:: 0.4
    logger_name = ConfigAttribute('LOGGER_NAME')  ❷


    def __init__(self, import_name, static_path=None, static_url_path=None,
                 ##~~ ... skip the other arguments ...
                 root_path=None):
        ##~~ ... skip the rest of the initialization
        # Prepare the deferred setup of the logger.
        self._logger = None  ❸
        self.logger_name = self.import_name


    @property
    def logger(self):
        """A :class:`logging.Logger` object for this application.  The
        default configuration is to log to stderr if the application is
        in debug mode.  This logger can be used to (surprise) log messages.
        Here some examples::

            app.logger.debug('A value for debugging')
            app.logger.warning('A warning occurred (%d apples)', 42)
```

```
        app.logger.error('An error occurred')

    .. versionadded:: 0.3
    """
    if self._logger and self._logger.name == self.logger_name:
        return self._logger    ❹
    with _logger_lock:    ❺
        if self._logger and self._logger.name == self.logger_name:
            return self._logger
        from flask.logging import create_logger
        self._logger = rv = create_logger(self)
        return rv
```

❶ This lock is used toward the end of the code. Locks are objects that can only be posessed by one thread at a time. When it is being used, any other threads that want it must block.

❷ Like Diamond, Flask uses the configuration file (with sane defaults, that aren't shown here, so the user can simply do nothing and get a reasonable answer) to set the logger name.

❸ The Flask application's logger is initially set to none so that it can be created later (in step ❺).

❹ If the logger exists already, return it. The property decoration, like earlier in this chapter, exists to prevent the user from inadvertently modifying the logger.

❺ If the logger doesn't exist yet (it was initialized to None), then use the lock created in step ❶ and create it.

Style Examples from Flask

Most of the style examples from Chapter 4 have already been covered, so we'll only discuss one style example for Flask—the implementation of Flask's elegant and simple routing decorators.

Flask's routing decorators (beautiful is better than ugly)

The routing decorators in Flask add URL routing to target functions, like this:

```
@app.route('/')
def index():
    pass
```

The Flask application will, when dispatching a request, use URL routing to identify the correct function to generate the response. The decorator syntax keeps the routing code logic out of the target function, keeps the function flat, and is intuitive to use.

It's also not necessary—it exists only to provide this API feature to the user. Here is the source code, a method in the main `Flask` class defined in *flask/flask/app.py*:

```python
class Flask(_PackageBoundObject):  ❶
    """The flask object implements a WSGI application ...
     ... skip everything else in the docstring ...
    """
    ##~~ ... skip all but the routing() method.

    def route(self, rule, **options):
        """A decorator that is used to register a view function for a
        given URL rule.  This does the same thing as :meth:`add_url_rule`
        but is intended for decorator usage::

            @app.route('/')
            def index():
                return 'Hello World'

        ... skip the rest of the docstring ...
        """
        def decorator(f):  ❷
            endpoint = options.pop('endpoint', None)
            self.add_url_rule(rule, endpoint, f, **options)  ❸
            return f
        return decorator
```

❶ The `_PackageBoundObject` sets up the file structure to import the HTML templates, static files, and other content based on configuration values specifying their location relative to the location of the application module (e.g., *app.py*).

❷ Why not name it decorator? That's what it does.

❸ This is the actual function that adds the URL to the map containing all of the rules. The only purpose of `Flask.route` is to provide a convenient decorator for library users.

Structure Examples from Flask

The theme for both of the structure examples from Flask is modularity. Flask is intentionally structured to make it easy to extend and modify almost everything—from the way that JSON strings are encoded and decoded (Flask supplements the standard library's JSON capability with encodings for datetime and UUID objects) to the classes used when routing URLs.

Application specific defaults (simple is better than complex)

Flask and Werkzeug both have a *wrappers.py* module. The reason is to add appropriate defaults for Flask, a framework for web applications, on top of Werkzeug's more general utility library for WSGI applications. Flask subclasses Werkzeug's `Request` and `Response` objects to add specific features related to web applications. For example, the `Response` object in *flask/flask/wrappers.py* looks like this:

```
from werkzeug.wrappers import Request as RequestBase, Response as ResponseBase
##~~ ... skip everything else ...

class Response(ResponseBase):  ❶
    """The response object that is used by default in Flask.  Works like the
    response object from Werkzeug but is set to have an HTML mimetype by
    default.  Quite often you don't have to create this object yourself because
    :meth:`~flask.Flask.make_response` will take care of that for you.

    If you want to replace the response object used you can subclass this and
    set :attr:`~flask.Flask.response_class` to your subclass.  ❷
    """
    default_mimetype = 'text/html'  ❸
```

❶ Werkzeug's `Response` class is imported as `ResponseBase`, a nice style detail that makes its role obvious and allows the new `Response` subclass to take its name.

❷ The ability to subclass `flask.wrappers.Response`, and how to do it, is documented prominently in the docstring. When features like this are implemented, it's important to remember the documentation, or users won't know the possibility exists.

❸ This is it—the only change in the `Response` class. The `Request` class has more changes, which we're not showing to keep the length of this chapter down.

This small interactive session shows what changed between Flask's and Werkzeug's Response classes:

```
>>> import werkzeug
>>> import flask
>>>
>>> werkzeug.wrappers.Response.default_mimetype
'text/plain'
>>> flask.wrappers.Response.default_mimetype
'text/html'
>>> r1 = werkzeug.wrappers.Response('hello', mimetype='text/html')
>>> r1.mimetype
u'text/html'
>>> r1.default_mimetype
'text/plain'
>>> r1 = werkzeug.wrappers.Response('hello')
>>> r1.mimetype
'text/plain'
```

The point of changing the default mimetype was just to make a little less typing for Flask users when building response objects that contain HTML (the expected use with Flask). Sane defaults make your code much, much easier for the average user.

Sane Defaults Can Be Important

Sometimes defaults matter a lot more than just for ease of use. For example, Flask sets the key for sessionization and secure communication to `Null` by default. When the key is null, an error will be raised if the app attempts to start a secure session. Forcing this error means users will make their own secret keys—the other (bad) options would be to either silently allow a null session key and insecure sessionization, or to provide a default key like *mysecretkey* that would invariably not be updated (and thus be used in deployment) by many.

Modularity (also one honking great idea)

The docstring for `flask.wrappers.Response` let users know that they could subclass the `Response` object and use their newly defined class in the main `Flask` object.

In this excerpt from *flask/flask/app.py*, we highlight some of the other modularity built into Flask:

```
class Flask(_PackageBoundObject):
    """ ... skip the docstring ...
    """
    #: The class that is used for request objects.  See :class:`~flask.Request`
    #: for more information.
    request_class = Request      ❶

    #: The class that is used for response objects.  See
    #: :class:`~flask.Response` for more information.
    response_class = Response    ❷

    #: The class that is used for the Jinja environment.
    #:
    #: .. versionadded:: 0.11
    jinja_environment = Environment     ❸

    ##~~ ... skip some other definitions ...

    url_rule_class = Rule
    test_client_class = None
    session_interface = SecureCookieSessionInterface()

    ##~~ .. etc. ..     ❹
```

❶   Here's where the custom `Request` class can be substituted.

---

❷ And here is the place to identify the custom `Response` class. These are class attributes (rather than instance attributes) of the `Flask` class, and are named in a clear way that makes it obvious what their purpose is.

❸ The `Environment` class is a subclass of Jinja2's `Environment` that has the ability to understand Flask Blueprints, which make it possible to build larger, multifile Flask applications.

❹ There are other modular options that are not shown because it was getting repetitive.

If you search through the Flask class definition, you can find where these classes are instantiated and used. The point of showing it to you is that these class definitions didn't have to be exposed to the user—this was an explicit structural choice done to give the library user more control over how Flask behaves.

When people talk about Flask's modularity, they're not just talking about how you can use any database backend you want, they're also talking about this capability to plug in and use different classes.

You've now seen some examples of well-written, very Zen Python code.

We highly recommend you take a look at the full code of each of the programs discussed here: the best way to become a good coder is to read great code. And remember, whenever coding gets tough, *use the source, Luke!*

## CHAPTER 6

Shipping Great Code

This chapter focuses on best practices for packaging and distributing Python code. You'll either want to create a Python library to be imported and used by other developers, or create a standalone application for others to use, like pytest (*http:// pytest.org/latest/*).

The ecosystem around Python packaging has become a *lot* more straightforward in the past few years, thanks to the work of the Python Packaging Authority (PyPA) (*https://www.pypa.io/*)[1]—the people who maintain pip, the Python Package Index (PyPI), and much of the infrastructure relevant to Python packaging. Their packaging documentation (*https://packaging.python.org*) is stellar, so we won't reinvent the wheel (*http://wheel.readthedocs.org/en/latest/*) in "Packaging Your Code" on page 175, but we *will* briefly show two ways to host packages from a private site, and talk about how to upload code to Anaconda.org, the commercial analogue to PyPI run by Continuum Analytics.

The downside of distributing code through PyPI or other package repositories is that the recipient must understand how to install the required version of Python and be able and willing to use tools such as pip to install your code's other dependencies. This is fine when distributing to other developers but makes the method unsuitable for distributing applications to end users who aren't coders. For that, use one of the tools in "Freezing Your Code" on page 179.

Those making Python packages for Linux may also consider a Linux distro package (e.g., a *.deb* file on Debian/Ubuntu; called "build distributions" in Python documen-

---

tation). That route is a lot of work to maintain, but we give you some options in "Packaging for Linux-Built Distributions" on page 186. This is like freezing, but with the Python interpreter removed from the bundle.

Finally, we'll share a pro tip in "Executable ZIP Files" on page 187: if your code is in a ZIP archive (*.zip*) with a specific header, you can just execute the ZIP file. When you know your target audience has Python installed already, and your project is purely Python code, this is a fine option.

Useful Vocabulary and Concepts

Until the PyPA's formation, there wasn't actually a single, obvious way to do packaging (as can be seen from this historical discussion on Stack Overflow (*http://stackoverflow.com/questions/6344076*)). Here are the most important vocabulary words discussed in this chapter (there are more definitions in the PyPA glossary (*https://packaging.python.org/en/latest/glossary/*)):

Dependencies
> Python packages list their Python library depenencies either in a *requirements.txt* file (for testing or application deployment), or in the `install_requires` argument to `setuptools.setup()` when it is called in a *setup.py* file.
>
> In some projects there can be other dependencies, such as a Postgres database, a C compiler, or a C library shared object. These may not be explicitly stated, but if absent will break the build. If you build libraries like these, Paul Kehrer's seminar on distributing compiled modules (*http://bit.ly/kehrer-seminar*) may help.

Built distribution
> A format of distribution for a Python package (and optionally other resources and metadata) that is in a form that can be installed and then run without further compilation.

Egg
> Eggs are a built distribution format—basically, they're ZIP files with a specific structure, containing metadata for installation. They were introduced by the Setuptools library, and were the de facto standard for years, but were never an official Python packaging format. They have been replaced by wheels as of PEP 427 (*https://www.python.org/dev/peps/pep-0427/*). You can read all about the differences between the formats in "Wheel vs Egg" in the Python Packaging User Guide (*https://packaging.python.org/en/latest/wheel_egg/*).

Wheel
> Wheels are a built distribution format that is now the standard for distribution of built Python libraries. They are a packaged as ZIP files with metadata that `pip` will use to install and uninstall the package. The file has a *.whl* extension, by con-

vention, and follows a specific naming convention that communicates specifically what platform, build, and interpreter it is for.

Aside from having Python installed, regular Python packages, written only in Python, don't need anything but other Python libraries that can be downloaded from PyPI (*https://pypi.python.org/pypi*) (or eventually Warehouse (*https://warehouse.pypa.io/*)— the upcoming newer location for PyPI) to run. The difficulty (which we tried to get ahead of with the extra installation steps in Chapter 2) comes when the Python library has dependencies outside of Python—on C libraries or system executables, for example. Tools like Buildout and Conda are meant to help, when the distribution gets more complicated than even the Wheel format can handle.

Packaging Your Code

To *package* code for distribution means to create the necessary file structure, add the required files, and define the appropriate variables to comform to relevant PEPs and the current best practice described in "Packaging and Distributing Projects" (*https://packaging.python.org/en/latest/distributing/*) in the Python Packaging Guide (*https://packaging.python.org/*),[2] or the packaging requirements of other repositories, like *http://anaconda.org/*.

"Package" Versus "Distribution Package" Versus "Installation Package"

It may be confusing that we're using *package* to mean so many different things. Right now, we are talking about *distribution packages*, which include the (regular Python) packages, modules, and additional files needed to define a release. We also sometimes refer to libraries as *installation packages*; these are the top-level package directories that contain an entire library. Finally, the humble *package* is, as always, any directory containing an *__init__.py* and other modules (**.py* files). The PyPA keeps a glossary of packaging-related terms (*https://packaging.python.org/en/latest/glossary*).

Conda

If you have Anaconda's redistribution of Python installed, you can still use `pip` and PyPI, but your default package manager is `conda`, and your default package repository is *http://anaconda.org/*. We recommend following this tutorial for building packages (*http://bit.ly/building-conda*), which ends with instructions on uploading to Anaconda.org.

---

2 There appear to be two URLs mirroring the same content at the moment: *https://python-packaging-user-guide.readthedocs.org/* and *https://packaging.python.org*.

If you are making a library for scientific or statistical applications—even if you don't use Anaconda yourself—you will want to make an Anaconda distribution in order to easily reach the wide academic, commercial, and Windows-using audiences that choose Anaconda to get binaries that work without effort.

PyPI

The well-established ecosystem of tools such as PyPI and pip make it easy for other developers to download and install your package either for casual experiments, or as part of large professional systems.

If you're writing an open source Python module, PyPI (*http://pypi.python.org*), more properly known as *The Cheeseshop*, is the place to host it.[3] If your code isn't packaged on PyPI, it will be harder for other developers to find it and to use it as part of their existing process. They will regard such projects with substantial suspicion of being either badly managed, not yet ready for release, or abandoned.

The definitive souce for correct, up-to-date information about Python packaging is the PyPA-maintained Python Packaging Guide (*https://packaging.python.org/en/latest/*).

Use testPyPI for Testing and PyPI for Real

If you are just testing your packaging settings, or teaching someone how to use PyPI, you can use testPyPI (*https://testpypi.python.org*) and run your unit tests before pushing a real version to PyPI. Like with PyPI, you *must* change the version number every time you push a new file.

Sample project

The PyPA's sample project (*https://github.com/pypa/sampleproject*) demonstrates the current best practice for packaging a Python project. Comments in the *setup.py* module (*https://github.com/pypa/sampleproject/blob/master/setup.py*) give advice, and identify relevant PEPs governing options. The overall file structure is organized as required, with helpful comments about each file's purpose and what it should contain.

The project's README file links back to the packaging guide (*https://packaging.python.org/*) and to a tutorial about packaging and distribution (*https://packaging.python.org/en/latest/distributing.html*).

---

3 PyPI is in the process of being switched to the Warehouse (*https://warehouse.python.org/*), which is now in an evaluation phase. From what we can tell, they are changing the UI, but not the API. Nicole Harris, one of the PyPA developers, wrote a brief introduction to Warehouse (*http://whoisnicoleharris.com/warehouse/*), for the curious.

Use pip, not easy_install

Since 2011, the PyPA has worked to clear up considerable confusion (*http://stackoverflow.com/questions/6344076*) and considerable discussion (*http://stackoverflow.com/questions/3220404*) about the canonical way to distribute, package, and install Python libraries. pip was chosen as Python's default package installer in PEP 453 (*https://www.python.org/dev/peps/pep-0453/*), and it is installed by default with Python 3.4 (first released in 2014) and later releases.[4]

The tools have a number of nonoverlapping uses, and older systems may still need `easy_install`. This chart (*http://packaging.python.org/en/latest/pip_easy_install/*) from the PyPA compares pip and `easy_install`, identifying what each tool does and does not offer.

When developing your own code, you'll want to install using `pip install --editable .` so that you can continue to edit the code without reinstalling.

Personal PyPI

If you want to install packages from a source other than PyPI, (e.g., an internal work server for proprietary company packages, or packages checked and blessed by your security and legal teams), you can do it by hosting a simple HTTP server, running from the directory containing the packages to be installed.

For example, say you want to install a package called *MyPackage.tar.gz*, with the following directory structure:

```
.
|--- archive/
    |--- MyPackage/
        |--- MyPackage.tar.gz
```

You can run an HTTP server from the *archive* directory by typing the following in a shell:

```
$ cd archive
$ python3 -m SimpleHTTPServer 9000
```

This runs a simple HTTP server running on port 9000 and will list all packages (in this case, *MyPackage*). Now you can install *MyPackage* using any Python package installer. Using pip on the command line, you would do it like this:

```
$ pip install --extra-index-url=http://127.0.0.1:9000/ MyPackage
```

---

4 If you have Python 3.4 or higher without pip, you can install it on the command line with `python -m ensurepip`.

Having a folder with the same name as the package name is *crucial* here. But if you feel that the structure *MyPackage/MyPackage.tar.gz* is redundant, you can always pull the package out of the directory and install with a direct path:

```
$ pip install http://127.0.0.1:9000/MyPackage.tar.gz
```

Pypiserver

Pypiserver (*https://pypi.python.org/pypi/pypiserver*) is a minimal PyPI-compatible server. It can be used to serve a set of packages to `easy_install` or `pip`. It includes helpful features like an administrative command (`-U`) which will update all its packages to their latest versions found on PyPI.

S3-hosted PyPI

Another option for a personal PyPI server is to host on Amazon's Simple Storage Service, Amazon S3 (*https://aws.amazon.com/s3/*). You must first have an Amazon Web Service (AWS) account with an S3 bucket. Be sure to follow the bucket naming rules (*http://bit.ly/rules-bucket-naming*)—you'll be allowed to create a bucket that breaks the naming rules, but you won't be able to access it. To use your bucket, first create a virtual environment on your own machine and install all of your requirements from PyPI or another source. Then install pip2pi:

```
$ pip install git+https://github.com/wolever/pip2pi.git
```

And follow the pip2pi *README* file for the `pip2tgz` and `dir2pi` commands. Either you'll do:

```
$ pip2tgz packages/ YourPackage+
```

or these two commands:

```
$ pip2tgz packages/ -r requirements.txt
$ dir2pi packages/
```

Now, upload your files. Use a client like Cyberduck (*https://duck.sh/*) to sync the entire *packages* folder to your S3 bucket. Make sure you upload *packages/simple/index.html* as well as all new files and directories.

By default, when you upload new files to the S3 bucket, they will have user-only permissions. If you get HTTP 403 when trying to install a package, make sure you've set the permissions correctly: use the Amazon web console to set the `READ` permission of the files to `EVERYONE`. Your team will now be able to install your package with:

```
$ pip install \
  --index-url=http://your-s3-bucket/packages/simple/ \
  YourPackage+
```

VCS support for pip

It is possible to pull code directly from a version control system using `pip`; to do so, follow these instructions (*http://bit.ly/vcs-support*). This is another alternative to hosting a personal PyPI. An example command using `pip` with a GitHub project is:

```
$ pip install git+git://git.myproject.org/MyProject#egg=MyProject
```

In which the *egg* does not have to be an egg—it is the name of the directory in your project that you want to install.

Freezing Your Code

To *freeze* your code means to create a standalone executable bundle you can distribute to end users who do not have Python installed on their computer—the distributed file or bundle contains both the application code and the Python interpreter.

Applications such as Dropbox (*https://www.dropbox.com/en/help/65*), Eve Online (*http://www.eveonline.com/*), Civilization IV (*https://www.civilization.com/en/games/civilization-iv/*), and BitTorrent client (*http://www.bittorrent.com/*)—all primarily written in Python—do this.

The advantage of distributing this way is that your application will *just work*, even if the user doesn't already have the required (or any) version of Python installed. On Windows, and even on many Linux distributions and OS X, the right version of Python will not already be installed. Besides, end user software should always be in an executable format. Files ending in *.py* are for software engineers and system administrators.

A disadvantage of freezing is that it increases the size of your distribution by about 2–12 MB. Also, you will be responsible for shipping updated versions of your application when security vulnerabilities to Python are patched.

Check the License When Using C Libraries

You should check the licensing for every package you use all the way up your tree of dependencies, for all operating systems. But we want to particularly call out Windows because all Windows solutions need MS Visual C++ dynamically linked libraries (DLLs) to be installed on the target machine. You may or may not have permission to redistribute specific libraries and must check your license permissions before distributing your app (see Microsoft's legal message about Visual C++ files (*http://bit.ly/visual-cplusplus*) for more information). You can also optionally use the MinGW compiler (*https://sourceforge.net/projects/mingw/*) (Minimalist GNU for Windows), but because it's a GNU project, the licensing may be restrictive in the opposite (must always be open and free) way.

Also, MinGW and the Visual C++ compilers aren't completely the same, so you should check whether your unit tests still run as you expected after using a different compiler. This is getting into the weeds, so ignore all of this if you don't frequently compile C code on Windows—but, for example, there are still a few problems with MinGW and NumPy (*https://github.com/numpy/numpy/issues/5479*). There is a post recommending a MinGW build with static toolchains (*https://github.com/numpy/numpy/wiki/Mingw-static-toolchain*) on the NumPy wiki.

We compare the popular freezing tools in Table 6-1. They all interface with *distuils* in Python's Standard Library. They cannot do cross-platform freezes,[5] so you must perform each build on the target platform.

The tools are listed in the order they will appear in this section. Both PyInstaller and cx_Freeze can be used on all platforms, py2app only works on OS X, py2exe only works on Windows, and bbFreeze can work on both UNIX-like and Windows systems, but not OS X, and it has not yet been ported to Python 3. It *can* generate eggs, though, in case you need this ability for your legacy system.

Table 6-1. Freezing tools

	pyInstaller	cx_Freeze	py2app	py2exe	bbFreeze
Python 3	Yes	Yes	Yes	Yes	—
License	Modified GPL	Modified PSF	MIT	MIT	Zlib
Windows	Yes	Yes	—	Yes	Yes
Linux	Yes	Yes	—	—	Yes
OS X	Yes	Yes	Yes	—	—
Eggs	Yes	Yes	Yes	—	Yes
Support for pkg_resources[a]	—	—	Yes	—	Yes
One-file mode[b]	Yes	—	—	Yes	—

[a] pkg_resources (*https://pythonhosted.org/setuptools/pkg_resources.html*) is a separate module bundled with Setuptools that can be used to dynamically find dependencies. This is a challenge when freezing code because it's hard to discover dynamically loaded dependencies from the static code. PyInstaller, for example, only says they will get it right when the introspection is on an egg file.

[b] One-file mode is the option to bundle an application and all its dependencies into a single executable file on Windows. InnoSetup (*http://www.jrsoftware.org/isinfo.php*) and the Nullsoft Scriptable Install System (*http://nsis.sourceforge.net/Main_Page*) (NSIS) are both popular tools that create installers and can bundle code into a single .exe file.

---

5 Freezing Python code on Linux into a Windows executable was attempted in PyInstaller 1.4, but dropped in 1.5 (*https://github.com/pyinstaller/pyinstaller/wiki/FAQ#features*) because it didn't work well except for pure Python programs (so, no GUI applications).

PyInstaller

PyInstaller (*http://www.pyinstaller.org/*) can be used to make applications on OS X, Windows, and Linux. Its primary goal is to be compatible with third-party packages out of the box—so the freeze just works.[6] They have a list of PyInstaller supported packages (*https://github.com/pyinstaller/pyinstaller/wiki/Supported-Packages*). Supported graphical libraries include Pillow, pygame, PyOpenGL, PyGTK, PyQT4, PyQT5, PySide (except for Qt plug-ins), and wxPython. Supported scientific tools include NumPy, Matplotlib, Pandas, and SciPy.

PyInstaller has a modified GPL license (*https://github.com/pyinstaller/pyinstaller/wiki/License*) "with a special exception which allows [anyone] to use PyInstaller to build and distribute non-free programs (including commercial ones)"—so the license(s) you must comply with will depend on the libraries you used to develop your code. Their team even provides instructions for hiding the source code (*http://bit.ly/hiding-source-code*) for those making commercial applications or wanting to prevent others from altering the code. But *do* read the license (consult a lawyer if it's important or *https://tldrlegal.com/* if it's not that important) if you need to modify their source code to build your app, because you may be required to share that change.

The PyInstaller Manual (*http://pyinstaller.readthedocs.org/*) is well organized and detailed. Check the PyInstaller requirements page (*http://bit.ly/pyinstaller-reqs*) to confirm that your system is compatible—for Windows, you need XP or later; for Linux systems, you'll need several terminal applications (the documentation lists where you can find them); and for OS X, you need version 10.7 (Lion) or later. You *can* use Wine (a Windows emulator) to cross-compile for Windows while running under Linux or OS X.

To install PyInstaller, use pip from within the same virtual environment where you are building your app:

```
$ pip install pyinstaller
```

To create a standard executable from a module named *script.py*, use:

```
$ pyinstaller script.py
```

To create a windowed OS X or Windows application, use the `--windowed` option on the command line like this:

```
$ pyinstaller --windowed script.spec
```

---

6 As we'll see when looking at other installers, the challenge is not just in finding and bundling the compatible C libraries for the specific version of a Python library, but also in discovering peripheral configuration files, sprites or special graphics, and other files that aren't discoverable to the freezing tool by inspecting your source code.

This creates two new directories and a file in the same folder where you executed the pyinstaller command:

- A *.spec* file, which can be rerun by PyInstaller to re-create the build.
- A *build* folder that holds some log files.
- A *dist* folder, that holds the main executable and some dependent Python libraries.

PyInstaller puts all the Python libraries used by your application into the *dist* folder, so when distributing the executable, distribute the whole *dist* folder.

The *script.spec* file can be edited to customize the build (*http://pythonhosted.org/PyInstaller/#spec-file-operation*), with options to:

- Bundle data files with the executable.
- Include runtime libraries (*.dll* or *.so* files) that PyInstaller can't infer automatically.
- Add Python runtime options to the executable.

This is useful, because now the file can be stored with version control, making future builds easier. The PyInstaller wiki page contains build recipes (*https://github.com/pyinstaller/pyinstaller/wiki/Recipes*) for some common applications, including Django, PyQt4, and code signing for Windows and OS X. This is the most current set of quick tutorials for PyInstaller. Now, the edited *script.spec* can be run as an argument to pyinstaller (instead of using *script.py* again):

```
$ pyinstaller script.spec
```

 When PyInstaller is given a *.spec* file, it takes all of its options from the contents of that file and ignores command-line options, except for: --upx-dir=, --distpath=, --workpath=, --noconfirm, and --ascii.

cx_Freeze

Like PyInstaller, cx_Freeze (*https://cx-freeze.readthedocs.org/en/latest/*) can freeze Python projects on Linux, OS X, and Windows systems. However, the cx_Freeze team does not recommend compiling for Windows using Wine because they've had to manually copy some files around to get the app to work. To install it, use pip:

```
$ pip install cx_Freeze
```

The easiest way to make the executable is to run cxfreeze from the command line, but you have more options (and can use version control) if you write a *setup.py* script.

This is the same *setup.py* as is used by distutils in Python's Standard Library—cx_Freeze extends distutils to provide extra commands (and modify some others). These options can be provided at the command line or in the setup script, or in a *setup.cfg* (*https://docs.python.org/3/distutils/configfile.html*) configuration file.

The script `cxfreeze-quickstart` creates a basic *setup.py* file that can be modified and version controlled for future builds. Here is an example session for a script named *hello.py*:

```
$ cxfreeze-quickstart
Project name: hello_world
Version [1.0]:
Description: "This application says hello."
Python file to make executable from: hello.py
Executable file name [hello]:
(C)onsole application, (G)UI application, or (S)ervice [C]:
Save setup script to [setup.py]:

Setup script written to setup.py; run it as:
    python setup.py build
Run this now [n]?
```

Now we have a setup script, and can modify it to match what our app needs. The options are in the cx_Freeze documentation under "distutils setup scripts." (*https://cx-freeze.readthedocs.org/en/latest/distutils.html*) There are also example *setup.py* scripts and minimal working applications that demonstrate how to freeze applications that use PyQT4, Tkinter, wxPython, Matplotlib, Zope, and other libraries in the *samples/* directory of the cx_Freeze source code (*https://bitbucket.org/anthony_tuininga/cx_freeze/src*): navigate from the top directory to *cx_Freeze/cx_Freeze/samples/*. The code is also bundled with the installed library. You can get the path by typing:

```
$ python -c 'import cx_Freeze; print(cx_Freeze.__path__[0])'
```

Once you are done editing *setup.py*, you can use it to build your executable using one of these commands:

```
$ python setup.py build_exe   ❶
$ python setup.py bdist_msi    ❷
$ python setup.py bdist_rpm    ❸
$ python setup.py bdist_mac    ❹
$ python setup.py bdist_dmg    ❺
```

❶ This is the option to build the command-line executable.

❷ This is modified by cx_Freeze from the original distutils command to also handle Windows executables and their dependencies.

❸ This is modified from the original distutils command to ensure Linux packages are created with the proper architecture for the current platform.

❹ This creates a standalone windowed OS X application bundle (.*app*) containing the dependencies and the executable.

❺ This one creates the .*app* bundle and also creates an application bundle, then packages it into a DMG disk image.

py2app

py2app (*https://pythonhosted.org/py2app*) builds executables for OS X. Like cx_Freeze, it extends distutils, adding the new command `py2app`. To install it, use `pip`:

```
$ pip install py2app
```

Next, autogenerate a *setup.py* script using the command `py2applet`, like this:

```
$ py2applet --make-setup hello.py
Wrote setup.py
```

This makes a basic *setup.py*, which you can modify for your needs. There are examples with minimal working code and the appropriate *setup.py* scripts that use libraries including PyObjC, PyOpenGL, pygame, PySide, PyQT, Tkinter, and wxPython in py2app's source code (*https://bitbucket.org/ronaldoussoren/py2app/src/*). To find them, navigate from the top directory to *py2app/examples/*.

Then, run *setup.py* with the `py2app` command to make two directores, *build* and *dist*. Be sure to clean the directories when you rebuild; the command looks like this:

```
$ rm -rf build dist
$ python setup.py py2app
```

For additional documentation, check out the py2app tutorial (*https://pythonhos ted.org/py2app/tutorial.html*). The build may exit on an `AttributeError`. If so, read this tutorial about using py2app (*http://bit.ly/py2app-tutorial*)—the variables `scan_code` and `load_module` may need to be preceded with underscores: `_scan_code` and `_load_module`.

py2exe

py2exe (*https://pypi.python.org/pypi/py2exe*) builds executables for Windows. It is very popular, and the Windows version of BitTorrent (*http://www.bittorrent.com*) was made using py2exe. Like cx_Freeze and py2exe, it extends distutils, this time adding the command `py2exe`. If you need to use it with Python 2, download the older version of py2exe from sourceforge (*https://sourceforge.net/projects/py2exe/*). Otherwise, for Python 3.3+, use `pip`:

```
$ pip install py2exe
```

The py2exe tutorial (*http://www.py2exe.org/index.cgi/Tutorial*) is excellent (apparently what happens when documentation is hosted wiki-style rather than in source control). The most basic *setup.py* looks like this:

```
from distutils.core import setup
import py2exe

setup(
        windows=[{'script': 'hello.py'}],
)
```

The documentation lists all of the configuration options for py2exe (*http://www.py2exe.org/index.cgi/ListOfOptions*) and has detailed notes about how to (optionally) include icons (*http://www.py2exe.org/index.cgi/CustomIcons*) or create a single file executable (*http://www.py2exe.org/index.cgi/SingleFileExecutable*). Depending on your own license for Microsoft Visual C++, you may or may not be able to distribute the Microsoft Visual C++ runtime DLL with your code. If you can, here are the instructions to distribute the Visual C++ DLL alongside the *.exe* file (*http://www.py2exe.org/index.cgi/Tutorial#Step52*); otherwise, you can provide your application's users with a way to download and install the Microsoft Visual C++ 2008 redistributable packge (*http://bit.ly/ms-visual-08*) or the Visual C++ 2010 redistributable packge (*http://bit.ly/ms-visual-10*) if you're using Python 3.3 or later.

Once you have modified your setup file, you can generate the *.exe* into *dist* directory by typing:

```
$ python setup.py py2exe
```

bbFreeze

The bbFreeze (*https://pypi.python.org/pypi/bbfreeze*) library currently has no maintainer and has not been ported to Python 3, but it is still frequently downloaded. Like cx_Freeze, py2app, and py2exe, it extends distutils, adding the command bbfreeze. In fact, older versions of bbFreeze were based on cx_Freeze. The appeal here may be for those who maintain legacy systems and would like to packge built distributions into eggs to be used across their infrastructure. To install it, use pip:

```
$ pip install bbfreeze  # bbFreeze can't work with Python3
```

It is light on documentation, but has build recipes (*https://github.com/schmir/bbfreeze/blob/master/bbfreeze/recipes.py*) for Flup (*https://pypi.python.org/pypi/flup*), Django, Twisted, Matplotlib, GTK, and Tkinter, among others. To make executable binaries, use the command bdist_bbfreeze like this:

```
$ bdist_bbfreeze hello.py
```

It will create a directory *dist* in the location where `bbfreeze` was run that contains a Python interpreter and an executable with the same name as the script (*hello.py* in this case).

To generate eggs, use the new distutils command:

```
$ python setup.py bdist_bbfreeze
```

There are other options, like tagging builds as snapshots or daily builds. Get more usage information using the standard `--help` option:

```
$ python setup.py bdist_bbfreeze --help
```

For fine-tuning, you can use the `bbfreeze.Freezer` class, which is the preferred way to use bbfreeze. It has flags for whether to use compression in the created ZIP file, whether to include a Python interpreter, and which scripts to include.

Packaging for Linux-Built Distributions

Creating a Linux *built distribution* is arguably the "right way" to distribute code on Linux: a built distribution is like a frozen package, but it doesn't include the Python interpreter, so the download and install are about 2 MB smaller than when using freezing.[7] Also, if a distribution releases a new security update for Python, your application will automatically start using that new version of Python.

The `bdist_rpm` command from the distutils module in Python's Standard Library makes it trivially easy to produce an RPM file (*https://docs.python.org/3/distutils/ builtdist.html#creating-rpm-packages*) for use by Linux distributions like Red Hat or SuSE.

Caveats to Linux Distribution Packages

Creating and maintaining the different configurations required for each distribution's format (e.g., **.deb* for Debian/Ubuntu, **.rpm* for Red Hat/Fedora, etc.) is a fair amount of work. If your code is an application that you plan to distribute on other platforms, then you'll also have to create and maintain the separate config required to freeze your application for Windows and OS X. It would be much less work to simply create and maintain a single config for one of the cross-platform freezing tools described in "Freezing Your Code" on page 179, which produce standalone executables for all distributions of Linux, as well as Windows and OS X.

---

7 Some people may have heard these called "binary packages" or "installers"; the official Python name for them is "built distributions"—meaning RPMs, or Debian packages, or executable installers for Windows. The wheel format is also a type of built distribution, but for various reasons touched on in a micro-rant about wheels (*http://bit.ly/python-on-wheels*) it is often better to make platform-specific Linux distributions like described in this section.

Creating a distribution package is also problematic if your code is for a version of Python that isn't currently supported by a distribution. Having to tell end users of some Ubuntu versions that they need to add the "dead-snakes" PPA (*http://bit.ly/dead-snakes-ppas*) using sudo apt-repository commands before they can install your *.deb* file makes for an unpleasant user experience. Not only that, but you'd have to maintain a custom equivalent of these instructions for every distribution, and worse, have your users read, understand, and act on them.

Having said all that, here are links to the Python packaging instructions for some popular Linux distributions:

- Fedora (*https://fedoraproject.org/wiki/Packaging:Python*)
- Debian and Ubuntu (*http://bit.ly/debian-and-ubuntu*)
- Arch (*https://wiki.archlinux.org/index.php/Python_Package_Guidelines*)

If you want a faster way to package code for all of the flavors of Linux out there, you may want to try the effing package manager (fpm) (*https://github.com/jordansissel/fpm*). It's written in Ruby and shell, but we like it because it packages code from multiple source types (including Python) into targets including Debian (*.deb*), RedHat (*.rpm*), OS X (*.pkg*), Solaris, and others. It's a great fast hack but does not provide a tree of dependencies, so package maintainers may frown upon it. Or Debian users can try Alien (*http://joeyh.name/code/alien/*), a Perl program that converts between Debian, RedHat, Stampede (*.slp*), and Slackware (*.tgz*) file formats, but the code hasn't been updated since 2014, and the maintainer has stepped down.

For those interested, Rob McQueen posted some insights about deploying server apps at work (*https://nylas.com/blog/packaging-deploying-python*), on Debian.

Executable ZIP Files

It's a little-known secret that Python has been able to execute ZIP files containing a *__main__.py* since version 2.6. This is a great way to package pure Python apps (applications that don't require platform-specific binaries). So, if you have a single file *__main__.py* like this:

```
if __name__ == '__main__':
    try:
        print 'ping!'
    except SyntaxError:  # Python 3
        print('ping!')
```

And you create a ZIP file containing it by typing this on the command line:

```
$ zip machine.zip __main__.py
```

You can then send that ZIP file to other people, and so long as they have Python, they can execute it on the command line like this:

```
$ python machine.zip
ping!
```

Or if you want to make it an executable, you can prepend a POSIX "shebang" (#!) to the ZIP file—the ZIP file format allows this—and you now have a self-contained app (provided Python is reachable via the path in the shebang). Here is an example that continues on from the previous code:

```
$ echo '#!/usr/bin/env python' > machine
$ cat machine.zip >> machine
$ chmod u+x machine
```

And now it's an executable:

```
$ ./machine
ping!
```

 Since Python 3.5, there is also a module zipapp (*https://docs.python.org/3/library/zipapp.html*) in the Standard Library that makes it more convenient to create these ZIP files. It also adds flexibility so that the main file need no longer be called *__main__.py*.

If you vendorize your dependencies by placing them inside your current directory, and change your import statements, you can make an executable ZIP file with all dependencies included. So, if your directory structure looks like this:

```
.
|--- archive/
     |--- __main__.py
```

and you are running inside a virtual environment that has only your dependencies installed, you can type the following in the shell to include your dependencies:

```
$ cd archive
$ pip freeze | xargs pip install --target=packages
$ touch packages/__init__.py
```

The xargs commands takes standard input from pip freeze and turns it into the argument list for the pip command, and the --target=packages option sends the installation to a new directory, *packages*. The touch command creates an empty file if none exists; otherwise, it updates the file's timestamp to the current time. The directory structure will now look something like this:

```
.
|--- archive/
     |--- __main__.py
     |--- packages/
```

```
|--- __init__.py
|--- dependency_one/
|--- dependency_two/
```

If you do this, make sure to also change your import statements to use the *packages* directory you just created:

```
#import dependency_one  # not this
import packages.dependency_one as dependency_one
```

And then just recursively include all of the directories in the new ZIP file using zip -r, like this:

```
$ cd archive
$ zip machine.zip -r *
$ echo '#!/usr/bin/env python' > machine
$ cat machine.zip >> machine
$ chmod ug+x machine
```

## PART III

Scenario Guide

At this point, you have Python installed, you've selected an editor, you know what it means to be *Pythonic*, you've read a few lines of great Python code, and you can share your own code with the rest of the world. This part of the guide will help you choose libraries to use in your project, whatever you decide to do, by sharing our community's most common approaches to specific coding scenarios, grouped by similar use:

Chapter 7, User Interaction
    We cover libraries for all types of user interaction, from console applications to GUIs, and web applications.

Chapter 8, Code Management and Improvement
    We describe tools for systems administration, tools to interface with C and C++ libraries, and ways to improve Python's speed.

Chapter 9, Software Interfaces
    We summarize libraries used for for networking, including asynchronous libraries and libraries for serialization and cryptography.

Chapter 10, Data Manipulation
    We survey the libraries that provide symbolic and numerical algorithms, plots, and tools for image and audio processing.

Chapter 11, Data Persistence
    Last, we highlight some of the differences between the popular ORM libraries that interact with databases.

## CHAPTER 7

User Interaction

Libraries in this chapter help developers write code that interacts with end users. We describe the Jupyter project—it's unique—then cover the more typical command-line and graphical user interfaces (GUIs), and finish with a discussion of tools for web applications.

Jupyter Notebooks

Jupyter (*http://jupyter.org/*) is a web application that allows you to display and execute Python interactively. It's listed here because it's a user-to-user interface.

Users view Jupyter's client interface—written in CSS, HTML, and JavaScript—in a web browser on the client machine. The client communicates with a a kernel written in Python (or a number of other languages) that executes blocks of code and responds with the result. Content is stored on the server machine in "notebook" (**.nb*) format—text-only JSON divided into a series of "cells" that can contain HTML, Markdown (a human-readable markup language like what's used on wiki pages), raw notes, or executable code. The server can be local (on the user's own laptop), or remote like the sample notebooks at *https://try.jupyter.org/*.

The Jupyter server requires at least Python 3.3 and has been made compatible with Python 2.7. It comes bundled with the most recent versions of commercial Python redistributions (described in "Commercial Python Redistributions" on page 19) such as Canopy and Anaconda, so no further installation is required with these tools, provided you can compile and build C code on your system, as we discussed in Chapter 2. After the proper setup, you can install Jupyter from the command line with `pip`:

```
$ pip install jupyter
```

A recent study using Jupyter in the classroom (*http://bit.ly/jupyter-classroom*) found it to be an effective and popular way to create interactive lectures for students new to coding.

Command-Line Applications

Command-line (also called console) applications are computer programs designed to be used from a text interface, such as a shell (*http://en.wikipedia.org/wiki/Shell_(computing)*). They can be simple commands—such as pep8 or virtualenv—or interactive, like the python interpreter or ipython. Some have subcommands, such as pip install, pip uninstall, or pip freeze—all of which have their own options in addition to pip's general options. All of them are likely started in a main() function; our BDFL has shared his opinion (*http://bit.ly/python-main-functions*) about what makes a good one.

We'll use an example pip call to name the components that can be present when invoking a command-line application:

```
   ❶   ❷      ❸
$ pip install --user -r requirements.txt
```

❶ The *command* is the name of the executable being invoked.

❷ *Arguments* come after the command and do not begin with a dash. They may also be referred to as parameters or subcommands.

❸ *Options* begin with either one dash (for single characters, such as -h) or else with two dashes (for words, such as --help). They may also be referred to as flags or switches.

The libraries in Table 7-1 all provide different options for parsing arguments or provide other useful tools for command-line applications.

Table 7-1. Command-line tools

Library	License	Reasons to use
argparse	PSF license	• In the Standard Library.
		• Gives you standard argument and option parsing.
docopt	MIT license	• Gives you control over the layout of your help message.
		• Parses the command line according to the utility conventions defined in the POSIX standard (*http://bit.ly/utility-conventions*).

Library	License	Reasons to use
plac	BSD 3-clause license	• Autogenerates the help message from an existing function signature. • Parses the command-line arguments behind the scenes, passing them directly to your function.
click	BSD 3-clause license	• Provides decorators to make the help message and parser (a lot like plac) • Lets you compose multiple subcommands together • Interfaces with other Flask plug-ins (Click is independent from Flask, but originally written to help users compose together command-line tools from different Flask plug-ins without breaking things, so it is already used in the Flask ecosystem)
clint	Internet Software Consortium (ISC) license	• Provides formatting features like colors, indentation, and columnar displays for your text output • Also provides type checking (e.g., check against a regex, for an integer, or a path) in your interactive input • Gives you direct access to the argument list, with some simple filtering and grouping tools
cliff	Apache 2.0 license	• Provides a structured framework for a large Python project with multiple subcommands • Builds an interactive environment to use the subcommands, with no additional coding

In general, you should try and use tools provided in Python's Standard Library first, and only add other libraries to your project when they offer something you want that the Standard Library doesn't have.

The following sections provide more details about each of the command-line tools listed in Table 7-1.

argparse

The module *argparse* (which replaces the now deprecated *optparse*) exists in Python's Standard Library to help with parsing command-line options. The command-line interface provided by the HowDoI project uses argparse—you can refer to it when building your own command-line interface.

Here is the code to generate the parser:

```
import argparse
#
# ... skip a lot of code ...
#

def get_parser():
    parser = argparse.ArgumentParser(description='...truncated for brevity...')
    parser.add_argument('query', metavar='QUERY', type=str, nargs='*',
```

```
                                    help='the question to answer')
        parser.add_argument('-p','--pos',
                                    help='select answer in specified position (default: 1)',
                                    default=1, type=int)
        parser.add_argument('-a','--all', help='display the full text of the answer',
                                    action='store_true')
        parser.add_argument('-l','--link', help='display only the answer link',
                                    action='store_true')
        parser.add_argument('-c', '--color', help='enable colorized output',
                                    action='store_true')
        parser.add_argument('-n','--num-answers', help='number of answers to return',
                                    default=1, type=int)
        parser.add_argument('-C','--clear-cache', help='clear the cache',
                                    action='store_true')
        parser.add_argument('-v','--version',
                                    help='displays the current version of howdoi',
                                    action='store_true')
        return parser
```

The parser will parse the command line and create a dictionary that maps each argument to a value. The `action='store_true'` indicates the option is intended as a flag that, if present on the command line, will be stored as `True` in the parser's dictionary.

docopt

docopt (*http://docopt.org*)'s core philosophy is that documentation should be beautiful and understandable. It provides one main command, `docopt.docopt()`, plus a few convenience functions and classes for power users. The function `docopt.docopt()` takes developer-written POSIX-style usage instructions, uses them to interpret the user's command-line arguments, and returns a dictionary with all of the arguments and options parsed from the command line. It also appropriately handles the `--help` and `--version` options.

In the following example, the value of the variable `arguments` is a dictionary with keys *name*, `--capitalize`, and `--num_repetitions`:

```
#!/usr/bin env python3
"""Says hello to you.

    Usage:
      hello <name>... [options]
      hello -h | --help | --version

      -c, --capitalize  whether to capitalize the name
      -n REPS, --num_repetitions=REPS number of repetitions [default: 1]
"""

__version__ = "1.0.0"  # Needed for --version

def hello(name, repetitions=1):
```

```
    for rep in range(repetitions):
        print('Hello {}'.format(name))

if __name__ == "__main__":
    from docopt import docopt
    arguments = docopt(__doc__, version=__version__)
    name = ' '.join(arguments['<name>'])
    repetitions = arguments['--num_repetitions']
    if arguments['--capitalize']:
        name = name.upper()
    hello(name, repetitions=repetitions)
```

Since version 0.6.0, docopt can be used to create complex programs with subcommands that behave like the git (*https://git-scm.com*) command or Subversion's (*https://subversion.apache.org*) svn command. It can even be used when a subcommand is written in different languages. There is a complete example application (*https://github.com/docopt/docopt/tree/master/examples/git*) that mocks up a reimplementation of the git command that explains how.

Plac

Plac's (*https://pypi.python.org/pypi/plac*) philosophy is that all of the information necessary to parse a command invocation is in the target function's signature. It is a lightweight (around 200 lines) wrapper around the Python Standard Library's argparse (*http://docs.python.org/2/library/argparse.html*) and provides one main command, plac.plac(), which infers the argument parser from the function signature, parses the command line, and then invokes the function.

The library was supposed to be named Command-Line Argument Parser (clap) but that ended up becoming taken a few days after its author chose the name, so it's Plac —clap in reverse. The usage statements aren't informative, but look how few lines this example takes:

```
# hello.py

def hello(name, capitalize=False, repetitions=1):
    """Says hello to you."""
    if capitalize:
        name = name.upper()
    for rep in range(repetitions):
        print('Hello {}'.format(name))


if __name__ == "__main__":
    import plac
    plac.call(hello)
```

The usage statement looks like this:

```
$ python hello.py --help
usage: hello.py [-h] name [capitalize] [repetitions]

Says hello to you.

positional arguments:
  name
  capitalize   [False]
  repetitions  [1]

optional arguments:
  -h, --help   show this help message and exit
```

If you want to typecast (convert to the correct type) any of the arguments before you pass them to the function, use the `annotations` decorator:

```
import plac

@plac.annotations(
    name = plac.Annotation("the name to greet", type=str),
    capitalize = plac.Annotation("use allcaps", kind="flag", type=bool),
    repetitions = plac.Annotation("total repetitions", kind="option", type=int)
def hello(name, capitalize=False, repetitions=1):
    """Says hello to you."""
    if capitalize:
        name = name.upper()
    for rep in range(repetitions):
        print('Hello {}'.format(name))
```

Also, `plac.Interpreter` provides a lightweight way to make a very quick interactive command-line application. Examples are with plac's interactive mode documentation (*https://github.com/kennethreitz-archive/plac/blob/master/doc/plac_adv.txt*).

Click

The main purpose of Click (*http://click.pocoo.org/*) (the "Command Line-Interface Creation Kit") is to help developers create composable command-line interfaces with as little code as possible. The Click documentation clarifies its relation to docopt:

> The aim of Click is to make composable systems, whereas the aim of docopt is to build the most beautiful and hand-crafted command-line interfaces. These two goals conflict with one another in subtle ways. Click actively prevents people from implementing certain patterns in order to achieve unified command-line interfaces. You have very little input on reformatting your help pages for instance.

Its defaults will satisfy most developers' needs, but it's highly configurable for power users. Like Plac, it uses decorators to tie the parser definitions to the functions that will use them, keeping command-line argument management out of the functions themselves.

The *hello.py* application with Click looks like this:

```
import click

@click.command()
@click.argument('name', type=str)
@click.option('--capitalize', is_flag=True)
@click.option('--repetitions', default=1,
              help="Times to repeat the greeting.")
def hello(name, capitalize, repetitions):
    """Say hello, with capitalization and a name."""
    if capitalize:
        name = name.upper()
    for rep in range(repetitions):
        print('Hello {}'.format(name))

if __name__ == '__main__':
    hello()
```

Click parses the description from the command's docstring and creates its help message using a custom parser derived from the Python Standard Library's now deprecated *optparse*, which was more compliant with the POSIX standard than *argparse*.[1] The help message looks like this:

```
$ python hello.py --help
Usage: hello.py [OPTIONS] NAME

  Say hello, with capitalization and a name.

Options:
  --capitalize
  --repetitions INTEGER  Times to repeat the greeting.
  --help                 Show this message and exit.
```

But the real value of Click is its modular composability—you can add an outer grouping function, and then any other click-decorated functions in your project will become subcommands to that top-level command:

```
import click

@click.group()  ❶
@click.option('--verbose', is_flag=True)
@click.pass_context  ❷
def cli(ctx, verbose):
    ctx.obj = dict(verbose = verbose)  ❸
    if ctx.obj['verbose']:
        click.echo("Now I am verbose.")

# The 'hello' function is the same as before...
```

---

1 docopt uses neither optparse nor argparse and relies on regular expressions to parse the docstring.

```
if __name__ == '__main__':
    cli()  ❹
```

❶ The `group()` decorator makes a top-level command that runs first, before executing the invoked subcommand.

❷ The `pass_context` decorator is how to (optionally) pass objects from the grouped command to a subcommand, by making the first argument a `click.core.Context` object.

❸ That object has a special attribute `ctx.obj` that can be passed to subcommands that use an `@click.pass_context` decorator.

❹ Now instead of calling the function `hello()`, call the function that was decorated with `@click.group()`—in our case, `cli()`.

Clint

The Clint (*https://pypi.python.org/pypi/clint/*) library is, like its name says, a collection of "Command-Line INterface Tools." It supports features such as CLI colors and indentation, a simple and powerful column printer, iterator-based progress bars, and implicit argument handling. This example shows the colorization and indentation tools:

```
"""Usage string."""
from clint.arguments import Args
from clint.textui import colored, columns, indent, puts

def hello(name, capitalize, repetitions):
    if capitalize:
        name = name.upper()
    with indent(5, quote=colored.magenta(' ~*~', bold=True)):  ❶
        for i in range(repetitions):
            greeting = 'Hello {}'.format(colored.green(name))  ❷
            puts(greeting)  ❸


if __name__ == '__main__':
    args = Args()  ❹
    # First check and display the help message
    if len(args.not_flags) == 0 or args.any_contain('-h'):
        puts(colored.red(__doc__))
        import sys
        sys.exit(0)

    name = " ".join(args.grouped['_'].all)  ❺
    capitalize = args.any_contain('-c')
    repetitions = int(args.value_after('--reps') or 1)
    hello(name, capitalize=capitalize, repetitions=repetitions)
```

❶ Clint's `indent` is a context manager—intuitive to use in the `with` statement. The `quote` option prefixes each line with a bold magenta ~*~.

❷ The `colored` module has eight color functions and an option to turn coloring off.

❸ The `puts()` function is like `print()` but also handles the indentation and quoting.

❹ `Args` provides some simple filtering tools for the argument list. It returns another `Args` object, to make it possible to chain the filters.

❺ Here's how to use the `args` made by `Args()`.

cliff

cliff (*https://pypi.python.org/pypi/cliff*) (the Command-Line Interface Formulation Framework) is a framework for building command-line programs. The framework is meant to be used to create multilevel commands that behave like `svn` (Subversion) or `git`, and interactive programs like a Cassandra shell or a SQL shell.

cliff's functionality is grouped into abstract base classes. You have to implement `cliff.command.Command` once for every subcommand, and then `cliff.commandman ager.CommandManager` will delegate to the correct command. Here is a minimal *hello.py*:

```
import sys

from argparse import ArgumentParser  ❶
from pkg_resources import get_distribution

from cliff.app import App
from cliff.command import Command
from cliff.commandmanager import CommandManager

__version__ = get_distribution('HelloCliff').version  ❷


class Hello(Command):
    """Say hello to someone."""

    def get_parser(self, prog_name):  ❸
        parser = ArgumentParser(description="Hello command", prog=prog_name)
        parser.add_argument('--num', type=int, default=1, help='repetitions')
        parser.add_argument('--capitalize', action='store_true')
        parser.add_argument('name', help='person\'s name')
        return parser

    def take_action(self, parsed_args):  ❹
```

```
        if parsed_args.capitalize:
            name = parsed_args.name.upper()
        else:
            name = parsed_args.name
        for i in range(parsed_args.num):
            self.app.stdout.write("Hello from cliff, {}.\n".format(name))


class MyApp(cliff.app.App):    ❺
    def __init__(self):
        super(MyApp, self).__init__(
            description='Minimal app in Cliff',
            version=__version__,
            command_manager=CommandManager('named_in_setup_py'),    ❻
        )


def main(argv=sys.argv[1:]):
    myapp = MyApp()
    return myapp.run(argv)
```

❶ cliff uses `argparse.ArgumentParser` directly for its command-line interface.

❷ Get the version from *setup.py* (the last time `pip install` was run).

❸ `get_parser()` is required by the abstract base class—it should return an `arg parse.ArgumentParser`.

❹ `take_action()` is required by the abstract base class—it runs when the `Hello` command is invoked.

❺ The main application subclasses `cliff.app.App`, and is responsible for setting up logging, I/O streams, and anything else that globally applies to all subcommands.

❻ The `CommandManager` manages all of the `Command` classes. It uses the `entry_points` content from *setup.py* to find the command names.

GUI Applications

In this section, we first list widget libraries—toolkits and frameworks that provide buttons, scroll bars, progress bars, and other prebuilt components. We also quickly list game libraries at the end.

Widget Libraries

In the context of GUI development, *widgets* are buttons, sliders, scroll bars, and other commonly used UI control and display elements. With them, you don't have to deal with low-level coding like identifying which button (if any) was underneath the mouse when it was clicked, or even lower-level tasks, like the different windowing APIs used by each operating system.

When you're new to GUI development, the first thing you want is something that's easy to use—so that you can learn how to make GUIs. For that we recommend Tkinter, already in Python's Standard Library. After that, you probably care about the structure and function of the toolkit underlying the library, so we group libraries by toolkits, listing the more popular ones first.

Table 7-2. GUI widget libraries

Underlying library (language)	Python library	License	Reasons to use
Tk (Tcl)	tkinter	Python Software Foundation license	• All of the dependencies are already bundled with Python. • It provides standard UI widgets like buttons, scroll bars, text boxes, and a drawing canvas.
SDL2 (C)	Kivy	MIT, or LGPL3 (before 1.7.2)	• It can be used to make an Android app. • It has multitouch features. • It is optimized to C when possible, and uses the GPU.
Qt (C++)	PyQt	GNU General Public License (GPL) or Commercial	• It provides a consistent look and feel across platforms. • Many applications and libraries already rely on Qt, (e.g., the Eric IDE, Spyder, and/or Matplotlib), so it may already be installed. • Qt5 (which can't be used alongside Qt4) provides utilities to make an Android app.
Qt (C++)	PySide	GNU Lesser General Public License (LGPL)	• It's a drop-in replacement for PyQt with a more permissive license.
GTK (C) (GIMP Toolkit)	PyGObject (PyGi)	GNU Lesser General Public License (LGPL)	• It provides Python bindings for GTK+ 3. • It should be familiar to those who already develop for the GNOME desktop system.
GTK (C)	PyGTK	GNU Lesser General Public license (LGPL)	• Only use this if your project already uses PyGTK; you should be porting old PyGTK code to PyGObject.
wxWindows (C++)	wxPython	wxWindows license (a modified LGPL)	• Provides a native look and feel by directly exposing the various windowing libraries for each platform. • This means parts of your code will be different for each platform.

Underlying library (language)	Python library	License	Reasons to use
Objective C	PyObjC	MIT license	• Provides an interface to (and from) Objective C. • Will give a native feel for your OS X project. • It cannot be used on other platforms.

The following sections provide more detail on the different GUI options for Python, grouped by each one's underlying toolkit.

Tk

The module Tkinter in Python's Standard Library is a thin object-oriented layer on top of Tk, the widget library written in the language Tcl. (Both are usually written together as Tcl/Tk.[2]) Because it's in the Standard Library, it's the most convenient and compatible GUI toolkit in this list. Both Tk and Tkinter are available on most Unix platforms, as well as on Windows and OS X.

There's a good multilanguage Tk tutorial with Python examples at TkDocs (*http://www.tkdocs.com/tutorial/index.html*), and more information available on the Python wiki (*http://wiki.python.org/moin/TkInter*).

Also, if you have a standard distribution of Python, you shoud have IDLE, a GUI interactive coding environment written entirely in Python that is part of Python's Standard Library—you can launch it from the command line by typing idle, or view all of its source code. You can find the path where it's installed by typing this in a shell:

```
$ python -c"import idlelib; print(idlelib.__path__[0])"
```

There are many files in the directory; the main IDLE application is launched from module *PyShell.py*.

Likewise, for an example use of the drawing interface, tkinter.Canvas, see the code for the turtle module (*https://docs.python.org/3/library/turtle.html*). You can find it by typing this in a shell:

```
$ python -c"import turtle; print(turtle.__file__)"
```

---

2 Tcl (*https://www.tcl.tk/about/language.html*), originally Tool Command Language, is a lightweight language created by John Ousterhout (*http://web.stanford.edu/~ouster/cgi-bin/tclHistory.php*) in the early 1990s for integrated circuit design.

Kivy

Kivy (*http://kivy.org*) is a Python library for development of multitouch enabled media rich applications. Kivy is actively being developed by a community, has a permissive BSD-like license, and operates on all major platforms (Linux, OS X, Windows, and Android). It's written in Python and does not use any underlying windowing toolkit—it interfaces directly with SDL2 (Simple DirectMedia Layer) (*https://www.libsdl.org/*), a C library that provides low-level access to user input devices,[3] and audio, plus access to 3D rendering using OpenGL (or Direct3D for Windows). It has some widgets (they're in the module kivy.uix (*https://kivy.org/docs/api-kivy.uix.html*)), but not nearly as many as the most popular alternatives, Qt and GTK. If you're developing a traditional desktop business application, Qt or GTK are probably better.

To install it, go to the Kivy downloads page (*https://kivy.org/#download*), find your operating system, download the correct ZIP file for your version of Python, and follow the instructions linked for your operating system. The code comes with a directory of over a dozen examples that demonstrate different parts of the API.

Qt

Qt (*http://qt-project.org/*) (pronounced "cute") is a cross-platform application framework that is widely used for developing software with a GUI, but can also be used for non-GUI applications. Plus, there is a Qt5 version for Android (*http://doc.qt.io/qt-5/android-support.html*). If you already have Qt installed (because you're using Spyder, Eric IDE, Matplotlib, or other tools using Qt), you can check your version of Qt from the command line by using:

```
$ qmake -v
```

Qt is released under the LGPL license, allowing you to distribute binaries that work with Qt so long as you don't change Qt. A commercial license will get you add-on tools like data visualization and in-application purchasing. Qt is a *framework*—it provides some prebuilt scaffolding for different types of applications. Both Python interfaces to Qt, PyQt and PySide, don't do well with documentation, so your best option is Qt's actual C++ documentation (*http://doc.qt.io/*). Here are brief descriptions of each:

---

3 In addition to supporting the usual mouse, it can handle touch: TUIO (*http://www.tuio.org/*) (an open source touch and gesture protocol and API), Nintendo's Wii remote, WM_TOUCH (the Windows touch API), USB touchscreens using HidTouch (*https://sourceforge.net/projects/hidtouchsuite/*) Apple's products, and others (*https://kivy.org/docs/api-kivy.input.providers.html*).

PyQt

Riverbank Computing's PyQt is more up to date than PySide (which doesn't yet have a Qt5 version). To install, follow the documentation for PyQt4 installation (*http://pyqt.sourceforge.net/Docs/PyQt4/installation.html*) or PyQt5 installation (*http://pyqt.sourceforge.net/Docs/PyQt5/installation.html*). PyQt4 only works with Qt4, and PyQt5 only works with Qt5. (We suggest Docker, a user-space isolation tool discussed in "Docker" on page 42, if you really have to develop using both—just to not have to deal with changing your library paths.)

Riverbank Computing also publishes pyqtdeploy (*https://pypi.python.org/pypi/pyqtdeploy*), a PyQt5-only GUI tool that generates platform-specific C++ code you can use to build binaries for distribution. For more information, check out these PyQt4 tutorials (*https://pythonspot.com/en/pyqt4/*) and PyQt5 examples (*https://github.com/baoboa/pyqt5/tree/master/examples*).

PySide

PySide (*https://wiki.qt.io/PySideDocumentation*) was released while Nokia owned Qt, because they couldn't get Riverside Computing, the makers of PyQt, to change PyQt's license from GPL to LGPL. It is intended to be a drop-in replacement for PyQt, but tends to lag PyQt in development. This wiki page describes the differences between PySide and PyQt (*http://bit.ly/differences-pyside-pyqt*).

To install PySide, follow the instructions in the Qt documentation (*https://wiki.qt.io/Setting_up_PySide*); there is also a page to help you write your first PySide application (*https://wiki.qt.io/Hello-World-in-PySide*).

GTK+

The GTK+ toolkit (*http://www.gtk.org/*) (which stands for the GIMP[4] Toolkit) provides an API to the backbone of the GNOME desktop environment. Programmers might choose GTK+ over Qt either because they prefer C and are more comfortable looking in GTK+'s source code when they have to, or because they have programmed GNOME applications before and are comfortable with the API. The two libraries with Python bindings to GTK+ are:

pyGTK

PyGTK provides Python bindings for GTK+ but only currently supports the GTK+ 2.x API (not GTK+ 3+). It is no longer being developed, and its team recommends PyGTK not be used for new projects and that existing applications be ported from PyGTK to PyGObject.

---

4 GIMP stands for GNU Image Manipulation Program. GTK+ was built to support drawing in GIMP, but became popular enough that people wanted to make a whole desktop windowing environment with it—hence GNOME.

PyGObject (aka PyGI)

PyGObject (*https://wiki.gnome.org/Projects/PyGObject*) provides Python bindings that give access to the entire GNOME software platform. It is also known as PyGI because it makes use of, and provides a Python API (*http://lazka.github.io/pgi-docs/*) for, GObject Introspection (*https://wiki.gnome.org/Projects/GObjectIntrospection*), which is an API bridge between other languages and GNOME's core C libraries, GLib (*https://developer.gnome.org/glib/*), provided they follow the convention used to define a GObject (*https://developer.gnome.org/gobject/stable/pt02.html*). It is fully compatible with GTK+ 3. The Python GTK+ 3 Tutorial (*http://python-gtk-3-tutorial.readthedocs.org/en/latest/*) is a good place to start.

To install, get the binaries from the PyGObject download site (*http://bit.ly/pygobject-download*), or on OS X, install it with homebrew using `brew install pygobject`.

wxWidgets

The design philosophy behind wxWidgets (*https://www.wxwidgets.org/*) is that the best way for an app to get a native look and feel is to use the API native to each operating system. Both Qt and GTK+ now also can use other windowing libraries than X11 under the hood, but Qt abstracts them, and GTK makes them look like you're programming GNOME. The benefit of using wXWidgets is that you are directly interfacing with each platform, and the license is much more permissive. The problem, though, is that you now have to handle each platform slightly differently.

The Python extension module that wraps wxWidgets for Python users is called wxPython (*http://wxpython.org/*). It at one point was the most popular windowing library in Python, possibly because of its philosophy of using native interface tools, but now the workarounds in Qt and GTK+ seem to have become good enough. Still, to install it, go to *http://www.wxpython.org/download.php#stable* and download the appropriate package for your OS, and get started with their wxPython tutorial (*http://bit.ly/wxpython-getting-started*).

Objective-C

Objective-C is the proprietary language used by Apple for the OS X and iOS operating systems, and providing access to the Cocoa framework for application development on OS X. Unlike the other options, Objective-C is not cross-platform; it is only for Apple products.

PyObjC is a bidirectional bridge between the OS X Objective-C languages and Python, meaning it not only allows Python access to the Cocoa framework for application development on OS X, but allows Objective-C programmers to access Python.[5]

 The Cocoa framework is only available on OS X, so don't choose Objective-C (via PyObjC) if you're writing a cross-platform application.

You will need to have Xcode installed, as described in "Installing Python on Mac OS X" on page 9, because PyObjC needs a compiler. Also, PyObjC works only with the standard CPython distribution—not with other distributions like PyPy or Jython —and we recommend using the Python executable provided by OS X, because *that* Python was modified by Apple and configured specifically to work with OS X.

To make your virtual environment using your system's Python interpreter, use the whole path when invoking it. If you do not want to install as the super user, install using the `--user` switch, which will save the library under *$HOME/Library/ Python/2.7/lib/python/site-packages/*:

```
$ /usr/bin/python -m pip install --upgrade --user virtualenv
```

Activate the environment, enter it, and install PyObjC:

```
$ /usr/bin/python -m virtualenv venv
$ source venv/bin/activate
(venv)$ pip install pyobjc
```

This takes a while. PyObjC comes bundled with py2app (discussed in "py2app" on page 184), which is the OS X–specific tool to create distributable standalone application binaries. There are sample applications on the PyObjC examples page (*http:// pythonhosted.org/pyobjc/examples/index.html*).

Game Development

Kivy has become really popular really quickly, but has a much larger footprint than the libraries listed in this section. It was categorized as a toolkit because it provides widgets and buttons but is frequently used to build games. The Pygame community hosts a Python game developer website (*http://www.pygame.org/hifi.html*) that welcomes all game developers, whether or not they're using Pygame. The most popular game development libraries are:

---

5 But the creation of Swift (*http://www.apple.com/swift/*) may have reduced that demand—it's almost as easy as Python, so if you're just writing for OS X, why not just use Swift and do everything native (except for calculations, which still would benefit from scientific libraries like NumPy and Pandas)?

cocos2d

cocos2d (*https://pypi.python.org/pypi/cocos2d*) is released under the BSD license. It builds on top of pyglet, providing a framework to structure your game as a set of *scenes* connected via custom workflows, all managed by a *director*. Use it if you like the scene-director-workflow style they use as described in the documentation (*http://tinyurl.com/py-cocos2d-scenes*), or want pyglet for drawing, plus SDL2 for joystick and audio. You can install cocos2D using `pip`. For SDL2, check your package manager first, then download from the SDL2 site (*https://www.libsdl.org/*). The best way to get started is with their example cocos2d applications (*https://github.com/los-cocos/cocos/tree/master/samples*).

pyglet

pyglet (*https://pypi.python.org/pypi/pyglet*) is released under the BSD license. It's a set of lightweight wrappers around OpenGL, plus tools for presenting and moving sprites around a window. Just install it—`pip` should be all you need because most every computer has OpenGL—and run some of the example applications (*https://bitbucket.org/pyglet/pyglet/src/default/examples*), including a complete Asteroids clone (*http://bit.ly/astrea-py*) in fewer than 800 lines of code.

Pygame

Pygame is released under the Zlib license, plus the GNU LGPLv2.1 for SDL2. It has a large, active community, with tons of Pygame tutorials (*http://www.pygame.org/wiki/tutorials*), but it has been using SDL1, a prior version of the library. It isn't available on PyPI, so check your package manager first, and if they don't have it, download Pygame (*http://www.pygame.org/download.shtml*).

Pygame-SDL2

Pygame-SDL2 (*http://bit.ly/pygame-sdl2*) was recently announced as an effort to reimplement Pygame with an SDL2 backend. It is released under the same licenses as Pygame.

PySDL2

PySDL2 (*https://pypi.python.org/pypi/PySDL2*) runs on CPython, IronPython, and PyPy, and is a thin Python interface to the SDL2 library. If you want the lightest-weight interface to SDL2 in Python, this is your library. For more information, see the PySDL2 tutorial (*http://pysdl2.readthedocs.io/en/latest/tutorial/index.html*).

Web Applications

As a powerful scripting language adapted to both fast prototyping and bigger projects, Python is widely used in web application development (YouTube, Pinterest, Dropbox, and The Onion all use it).

Two of the libraries we profiled in Chapter 5—"Werkzeug" on page 146, and "Flask" on page 162 were related to building web applications. With them, we briefly described the Web Server Gateway Interface (WSGI), a Python standard defined in PEP 3333 (*https://www.python.org/dev/peps/pep-3333/*) that specifies how web servers and Python web applications communicate. This section will look at Python web frameworks, their templating systems, the servers they interface with, and the platforms they run on.

Web Frameworks/Microframeworks

Broadly speaking, a web framework consists of a set of libraries and a main handler within which you can build custom code to implement a web application (i.e., an interactive website providing a client interface to code running on a server). Most web frameworks include patterns and utilities to accomplish at least the following:

URL routing
Match an incoming HTTP request to a particular Python function (or callable).

Handling Request and Response objects
Encapsulate the information received from or sent to a user's browser.

Templating
Inject Python variables into HTML templates or other output, allowing programmers to separate an application's logic (in Python) from the layout (in the template).

Development web service for debugging
Run a miniature HTTP server on development machines to enable rapid development; often automatically reloading server-side code when files are updated.

You shouldn't have to code around your framework. It should already provide the things you need—tested and used by thousands of other developers—so if you still don't find what you need, keep exploring the many other available frameworks (e.g., Bottle, Web2Py, CherryPy). A technical reviewer also noted we should mention Falcon (*http://falconframework.org/*), which is a framework specifically for building RESTful APIs (i.e., not for serving HTML).

All of the libraries in Table 7-3 can be installed using `pip`:

```
$ pip install Django
$ pip install Flask
$ pip install tornado
$ pip install pyramid
```

Table 7-3. Web frameworks

Python library	License	Reasons to use
Django	BSD license	• It provides structure—a mostly prebuilt site where you design the layout and the underlying data and logic. • It also autogenerates an administrative web interface, where nonprogrammers can add or delete data (like news articles). • It is integrated with Django's object-relational mapping (ORM) tool.
Flask	BSD license	• It allows you total control over what is in your stack. • It provides elegant decorators that add URL routing to any function you choose. • It frees you from the structure provided by either Django or Pyramid.
Tornado	Apache 2.0 license	• It provides excellent asynchronous event handling—Tornado uses its own HTTP server. • It also gives you a way to handle many WebSockets (full duplex, persistent communication over TCP[a]) or other long-duration connection out of the box.
Pyramid	Modified BSD license	• It provides *some* prebuilt structure—called a *scaffolding*—but less than Django, allowing you to use any database interface or templating library you wish (if any). • It is based on the popular the Zope framework, and on Pylons, both predecessors of Pyramid.

[a] Transmission Control Protocol (TCP) is a standard protocol that defines a way for two computers to establish a connection and communicate with each other.

The following sections provide a more detailed look at the web frameworks in Table 7-3.

Django

Django (*http://www.djangoproject.com*) is a "batteries included" web application framework and is an excellent choice for creating content-oriented websites. By providing many utilities and patterns out of the box, Django aims to make it possible to build complex, database-backed web applications quickly while encouraging best practices in code that uses it.

Django has a large and active community, and many reusable modules (*http://django packages.com/*) that can be directly incorporated into a new project or customized to fit your needs.

There are annual Django conferences in the United States (*http://djangocon.us*) and in Europe (*http://djangocon.eu*)—the majority of new Python web applications today are built with Django.

Flask

Flask (*http://flask.pocoo.org/*) is a *microframework* for Python, and is an excellent choice for building smaller applications, APIs, and web services. Rather than aiming to provide everything you could possibly need, Flask implements the most commonly used core components of a web application framework, like URL routing, HTTP request and response objects, and templates. Building an app with Flask is a lot like writing standard Python modules, except some functions have routes attached to them (via a decorator, like in the code sample shown here). It's really beautiful:

```
@app.route('/deep-thought')
def answer_the_question():
    return 'The answer is 42.'
```

If you use Flask, it is up to you to choose other components for your application, if any. For example, database access or form generation/validation are not built into Flask. This is great, because many web applications don't need those features. If yours do, there are many available extensions (*http://flask.pocoo.org/extensions/*), such as SQLAlchemy (*http://flask-sqlalchemy.pocoo.org/*) for a database, or pyMongo (*https://docs.mongodb.org/getting-started/python/*) for MongoDB and WTForms (*https://flask-wtf.readthedocs.org/*) for forms.

Flask is the default choice for any Python web application that isn't a good fit for Django's prebuilt scaffolding. Try these example Flask applications (*https://github.com/pallets/flask/tree/master/examples*) for a good introduction. If you want to run multiple applications (the default for Django), use application dispatching (*http://bit.ly/application-dispatching*). If instead you want to duplicate behaviors for sets of subpages within an app, try Flask's Blueprints (*http://flask.pocoo.org/docs/0.10/blueprints/*).

Tornado

Tornado (*http://www.tornadoweb.org/*) is an asynchronous (event-driven and non-blocking, like Node.js (*https://nodejs.org/en/*)) web framework for Python that has its own event loop.[6] This allows it to natively support the WebSockets (*http://bit.ly/websockets-api*) communication protocol, for example. Unlike the other frameworks in this section, Tornado is *not* a WSGI application. It can be made to run *either* as a WSGI application *or* as a WSGI server through their module `tornado.wsgi` (*http://www.tornadoweb.org/en/stable/wsgi.html*), but even the authors ask "what's the

---

6 It was inspired by the Twisted project's Twisted Web (*http://twistedmatrix.com/trac/wiki/TwistedWeb*) server, which is a part of the Tornado networking toolkit. If you wish things existed in Tornado that don't, look into Twisted, because it's probably implemented them. But be warned that Twisted is notoriously hard for beginners.

point?"[7] seeing as WSGI is a *synchronous* interface and the purpose of Tornado is to provide an *asynchronous* framework.

Tornado is a more difficult and less frequently used web framework than Django or Flask—use it only if you know the performance gain of using an asynchronous framework is worth the additional time you will spend programming. If you do, a good place to start is with their demo applications (*https://github.com/tornadoweb/tornado/tree/master/demos*). Well-written Tornado applications are known to have excellent performance.

Pyramid

Pyramid (*http://www.pylonsproject.org/*) is a lot like Django, except with a heavier focus on modularity. It comes with a smaller number of built-in libraries (fewer "batteries" included), and encourages users to extend its base functionality through shareable templates they call *scaffolds* (*http://bit.ly/pyramid-scaffolds*). You register the scaffold, and then invoke it when creating a new project using their command `pcreate` to build your project's scaffolding—like Django's `django-admin startpro ject project-name` command, but with options for different structures, different database backends, and URL routing options.

Pyramid does not have a large user base, unlike Django and Flask, but those who use it are passionate about it. It's a very capable framework, but not as popular a choice for new Python web applications right now.

Here are a few Pyramid tutorials (*http://docs.pylonsproject.org/projects/pyramid-tutorials*) to start with. Or, for a page you can use to sell Pyramid to your boss, try this portal to all things Pyramid (*https://trypyramid.com/*).

Web Template Engines

Most WSGI applications exist to respond to HTTP requests and serve content in HTML or other markup languages. Template engines are in charge of rendering this content: they manage a suite of templating files, with a system of hierarchy and inclusion to avoid unnecessary repetition, and fill the static content of the templates with the dynamic content generated by the application. This helps us adhere to the concept of *separation of concerns*[8]—keeping only the application logic in the code, and delegating presentation to the templates.

---

7 Actually, their WSGI documentation says "Use WSGIContainer only when there are benefits to combining Tornado and WSGI in the same process that outweigh the reduced scalability."

8 Separation of concerns (*https://en.wikipedia.org/wiki/Separation_of_concerns*) is a design principle that means good code is modular—each component should do just one thing.

Template files are sometimes written by designers or frontend developers, and complexity in the pages can make coordination difficult. Here are some good practices both for the application passing dynamic content to the template engine, and for the templates themselves:

Never is often better than right now
> Template files should be passed only the dynamic content that is needed for rendering the template. Avoid the temptation to pass additional content "just in case": it is easier to add some missing variable when needed than to remove a likely unused variable later.

Try to keep logic out of the template
> Many template engines allow for complex statements or assignments in the template itself, and many allow some Python code to be evaluated in the templates. This convenience can lead to uncontrolled growth in complexity and often makes it harder to find bugs. We're not 100% against it—practicality beats purity —just contain yourself.

Keep the JavaScript separate from the HTML
> It is often necessary to mix JavaScript templates with HTML templates. Preserve your sanity, and isolate the parts where the HTML template passes variables to the JavaScript code.

All of the template engines listed in Table 7-4 are second-generation, with good rendering speed[9] and features added thanks to experience with older template languages.

Table 7-4. Template engines

Python library	License	Reasons to use
Jinja2	BSD license	• It's Flask's default and bundled with Django. • It is based on the Django Template Language, with just a *little* more logic allowed in the templates. • Jinja2 is the default engine for Sphinx, Ansible, and Salt—if you've used them, you know Jinja2.
Chameleon	Modified BSD license	• The templates are themselves valid XML/HTML. • It is similar to the Template Attribute Language (TAL) and its derivatives.

---

9 Rendering is rarely the bottleneck in a web app, though—it's usually the data access.

Python library	License	Reasons to use
Mako	MIT license	• It's Pyramid's default.
		• It's designed for speed—for when your template rendering is actually a bottleneck.
		• It allows you to put a *lot* of code in your templates—Mako is kind of like a Python version of PHP (*http://php.net/*).

The following sections describe the libraries in Table 7-4 in more detail.

Jinja2

Jinja2 (*http://jinja.pocoo.org/*) is our recommended templating library for new Python web applications. It is Flask's default engine, the default engine for the Python documentation generator Sphinx (*http://www.sphinx-doc.org/*) and can be used in Django, Pyramid, and Tornado. It uses a text-based template language and can thus be used to generate any type of markup, not just HTML. It allows customization of filters, tags, tests, and globals. Inspired by the Django template language, it adds features like a little bit of in-template logic, which saves tons of code.

Here are some important Jinja2 tags:

```
{# This is a comment -- because of the hash + curly braces. #}

{# This is how to insert a variable: #}
{{title}}

{# This defines a named block, replaceable by a child template. #}
{% block head %}
<h1>This is the default heading.</h1>
{% endblock %}

{# This is how to do iteration: #}
{% for item in list %}
<li>{{ item }}</li>
{% endfor %}
```

Here's an example of a website in combination with the Tornado web server, described in "Tornado" on page 212:

```
# import Jinja2
from jinja2 import Environment, FileSystemLoader

# import Tornado
import tornado.ioloop
import tornado.web

# Load template file templates/site.html
TEMPLATE_FILE = "site.html"
```

```
templateLoader = FileSystemLoader( searchpath="templates/" )
templateEnv = Environment( loader=templateLoader )
template = templateEnv.get_template(TEMPLATE_FILE)

# List for famous movie rendering
movie_list = [
    [1,"The Hitchhiker's Guide to the Galaxy"],
    [2,"Back to the Future"],
    [3,"The Matrix"]
]

# template.render() returns a string containing the rendered HTML
html_output = template.render(list=movie_list, title="My favorite movies")

# Handler for main page
class MainHandler(tornado.web.RequestHandler):
    def get(self):
        # Returns rendered template string to the browser request
        self.write(html_output)

# Assign handler to the server root  (127.0.0.1:PORT/)
application = tornado.web.Application([
    (r"/", MainHandler),
])
PORT=8884
if __name__ == "__main__":
    # Set up the server
    application.listen(PORT)
    tornado.ioloop.IOLoop.instance().start()
```

A *base.html* file can be used as base for all site pages. In this example, they would be implemented in the (currently empty) content block:

```
<!DOCTYPE HTML PUBLIC "-//W3C//DTD HTML 4.01//EN">
<html lang="en">
<html xmlns="http://www.w3.org/1999/xhtml">
<head>
    <link rel="stylesheet" href="style.css" />
    <title>{{title}} - My Web Page</title>
</head>
<body>
<div id="content">
    {# In the next line, the content from the site.html template will be added #}
    {% block content %}{% endblock %}
</div>
<div id="footer">
    {% block footer %}
    &copy; Copyright 2013 by <a href="http://domain.invalid/">you</a>.
    {% endblock %}
</div>
</body>
```

The next code example is our site page (*site.html*), which extends *base.html*. The content block here will be automatically inserted into the corresponding block in *base.html*:

```
<!{% extends "base.html" %}
{% block content %}
    <p class="important">
    <div id="content">
        <h2>{{title}}</h2>
        <p>{{ list_title }}</p>
        <ul>
            {% for item in list %}
            <li>{{ item[0]}} :  {{ item[1]}}</li>
            {% endfor %}
        </ul>
    </div>
    </p>
{% endblock %}
```

Chameleon

Chameleon (*https://chameleon.readthedocs.org/*) Page Templates (with file extension **.pt*) are an HTML/XML template engine implementation of the Template Attribute Language (TAL) (*http://en.wikipedia.org/wiki/Template_Attribute_Language*), TAL Expression Syntax (TALES) (*http://bit.ly/expression-tales*), and Macro Expansion TAL (Metal) (*http://bit.ly/macros-metal*) syntaxes. Chameleon parses the Page Templates and "compiles" them into Python bytecode to increase loading speed. It is available for Python 2.5 and up (including 3.x and PyPy) and is one of the two default rendering engines used by "Pyramid" on page 213. (The other is Mako, described in the next section.)

Page Templates add special element attributes and text markup to your XML document: a set of simple language constructs let you control the document flow, element repetition, text replacement, and translation. Because of the attribute-based syntax, unrendered page templates are valid HTML and can be viewed in a browser and even edited in WYSIWYG (what you see is what you get) editors. This can make round-trip collaboration with designers and prototyping with static files in a browser easier. The basic TAL language is simple enough to grasp from an example:

```
<html>
  <body>
  <h1>Hello, <span tal:replace="context.name">World</span>!</h1>
    <table>
      <tr tal:repeat="row 'apple', 'banana', 'pineapple'">
        <td tal:repeat="col 'juice', 'muffin', 'pie'">
          <span tal:replace="row.capitalize()" /> <span tal:replace="col" />
        </td>
      </tr>
    </table>
```

```
  </body>
</html>
```

The `<span tal:replace="expression" />` pattern for text insertion is common enough that if you do not require strict validity in your unrendered templates, you can replace it with a more terse and readable syntax using the pattern `${expression}`, as follows:

```
<html>
  <body>
    <h1>Hello, ${world}!</h1>
    <table>
      <tr tal:repeat="row 'apple', 'banana', 'pineapple'">
        <td tal:repeat="col 'juice', 'muffin', 'pie'">
          ${row.capitalize()} ${col}
        </td>
      </tr>
    </table>
  </body>
</html>
```

But remember the full `<span tal:replace="expression">Default Text</span>` syntax also allows for default content in the unrendered template.

Being from the Pyramid world, Chameleon is not widely used.

Mako

Mako (*http://www.makotemplates.org/*) is a template language that compiles to Python for maximum performance. Its syntax and API are borrowed from the best parts of other templating languages like Django and Jinja2 templates. It is the default template language included with the Pyramid web framework (discussed in "Pyramid" on page 213) web framework. An example template in Mako looks like this:

```
<%inherit file="base.html"/>
<%
    rows = [[v for v in range(0,10)] for row in range(0,10)]
%>
<table>
    % for row in rows:
        ${makerow(row)}
    % endfor
</table>

<%def name="makerow(row)">
    <tr>
    % for name in row:
        <td>${name}</td>\
    % endfor
    </tr>
</%def>
```

It is a text markup language, like Jinja2, so it can be used for anything, not just XML/HTML documents. To render a very basic template, you can do the following:

```
from mako.template import Template
print(Template("hello ${data}!").render(data="world"))
```

Mako is well respected within the Python web community. It is fast and allows developers to embed a lot of Python logic into the page, which we know we cautioned against—but in times when you think it's necessary, this is the tool that allows it.

Web Deployment

The two options we'll cover for web deployment are either to use web hosting (i.e., pay a vendor like Heroku, Gondor, or PythonAnywhere to manage your server and your database for you), or to set up your own infrastructure on a machine provided by a virtual private server (VPS) host like Amazon Web Services (*http://aws.amazon.com/*) or Rackspace (*https://www.rackspace.com*). We'll quickly cover both.

Hosting

Platform as a Service (PaaS) is a type of cloud computing infrastructure which abstracts and manages infrastructure (e.g., setting up the database and web server, and keeping up with security patches), routing, and scaling of web applications. When using a PaaS, application developers can focus on writing application code rather than concerning themselves with deployment details.

There are dozens of competing PaaS providers, but the ones in this list specifically focus on the Python community. Most offer some sort of free tier or trial to start:

Heroku
> Heroku (*http://www.heroku.com/python*) is our recommended PaaS for deploying Python web applications. It supports Python 2.7–3.5 applications of all types: web applications, servers, and frameworks. A set of command-line tools (*https://toolbelt.heroku.com/*) is provided for interfacing with both your Heroku account and the actual database and web servers that support your application, so you can make changes without using a web interface. Heroku maintains detailed articles (*https://devcenter.heroku.com/categories/python*) on using Python with Heroku, as well as step-by-step instructions (*https://devcenter.heroku.com/articles/getting-started-with-python*) on how to set up your first application.

Gondor
> Gondor (*https://gondor.io/*) is run by a small company and focuses on helping businesses find success with Python and Django. Its platform is specialized for

deploying Django and Pinax[10] applications and uses. Gondor's platform is Ubuntu 12.04 with Django 1.4, 1.6, and 1.7 and a subset of Python 2 and 3 implementation listed here (*https://gondor.io/support/runtime-environment/*). It can automatically configure your Django site if you use *local_settings.py* for site-specific configuration information. For more information, see Gondor's guide to deploying Django projects (*https://gondor.io/support/django/setup/*); a command-line interface tool (*https://gondor.io/support/client/*) is also available.

PythonAnywhere

PythonAnywhere (*https://www.pythonanywhere.com/*) supports Django, Flask, Tornado, Pyramid, and many of the other web application frameworks we didn't describe, like Bottle (no framework, like Flask, but with a much smaller community) and web2py (great for teaching). Its pricing model is related to compute time—rather than charging more, computations are throttled once they go over a daily maximum—which is good for cost-conscious developers.

Web servers

With the exception of Tornado (which comes with its own HTTP server), all of the web application frameworks we discussed are WSGI applications. This means they must interact with a WSGI server as defined in PEP 3333 (*https://www.python.org/dev/peps/pep-3333/*) in order to receive an HTTP request and send back an HTTP response.

The majority of self-hosted Python applications today are hosted with a WSGI server such as Gunicorn, either by itself—WSGI servers can often be used as standalone HTTP servers—or behind a lightweight web server such as Nginx. When both are used, the WSGI servers interact with the Python applications while the web server handles tasks better suited for it—static file serving, request routing, distributed denial-of-service (DDoS) protection, and basic authentication. The two most popular web servers are Nginx and Apache, described here:

Nginx

Nginx (*http://nginx.org/*) (pronounced "engine-x") is a web server and reverse proxy[11] for HTTP, SMTP, and other protocols. It is known for its high performance, relative simplicity, and compatibility with many application servers (like WSGI servers). It also includes handy features like load balancing,[12] basic authen-

---

10 Pinax bundles popular Django templates, apps, and infrastructure to make starting a Django project faster.

11 A reverse proxy fetches information from another server on behalf of a client and returns it to the client as if it come from the reverse proxy.

12 Load balancing optimizes performance by delegating work across multiple computing resources.

tication, streaming, and others. Designed to serve high-load websites, Nginx is gradually becoming quite popular.

Apache HTTP server

Apache is the most popular HTTP server (*http://w3techs.com/technologies/over view/web_server/all*) in the world, but we prefer Nginx. Still, those new to deployment may want to start with Apache and mod_wsgi (*https://pypi.python.org/pypi/ mod_wsgi*), which is regarded as the easiest WSGI interface out there. There are tutorials in each framework's documentation for mod_wsgi with Pyramid (*http:// bit.ly/pyramidwsgi*), mod_wsgi with Django (*http://bit.ly/django-mod_wsgi*), and mod_wsgi with Flask (*http://bit.ly/flask-mod_wsgi*).

WSGI servers

Standalone WSGI servers typically use less resources than traditional web servers and provide top performance benchmarks for Python WSGI Servers (*http://nichol.as/ benchmark-of-python-web-servers*). They can also be used in conjunction with Nginx or Apache, which would serve as reverse proxies. The most popular WSGI servers are:

Gunicorn (Green Unicorn)

Gunicorn (*http://gunicorn.org/*) is the recommended choice for new Python web applications—a pure-Python WSGI server used to serve Python applications. Unlike other Python web servers, it has a thoughtful user interface and is extremely easy to use and configure. Gunicorn has sane and reasonable defaults for configurations. However, some other servers, like uWSGI, are tremendously more customizable (but therefore are much more difficult to effectively use).

Waitress

Waitress (*http://waitress.readthedocs.org*) is a pure-Python WSGI server that claims "very acceptable performance." Its documentation is not very detailed, but it does offer some nice functionality that Gunicorn doesn't have (e.g., HTTP request buffering); it doesn't block when a slow client takes time to respond— hence the name "Wait"-ress. Waitress is gaining popularity within the Python web development community.

uWSGI

uWSGI (*https://uwsgi-docs.readthedocs.org*) is a full stack for building hosting services. We don't recommend using it as a standalone web router unless you know why you need it.

But uWSGI can also run behind a full web server (such as Nginx or Apache)—a web server can configure uWSGI and an application's operation over the uwsgi protocol (*http://bit.ly/uwsgi-protocol*). uWSGI's web server support allows for dynamically configuring Python, passing environment variables and further tuning. For full details, see uWSGI magic variables (*http://bit.ly/uwsgimagicvar*).

## CHAPTER 8

Code Management and Improvement

This chapter covers libraries used to manage or simplify the development and build process, system integration, server management, and performance optimization.

Continuous Integration

Nobody describes *continuous integration* better than Martin Fowler:[1]

> Continuous Integration is a software development practice where members of a team integrate their work frequently, usually each person integrates at least daily—leading to multiple integrations per day. Each integration is verified by an automated build (including test) to detect integration errors as quickly as possible. Many teams find that this approach leads to significantly reduced integration problems and allows a team to develop cohesive software more rapidly.

The three most popular tools for CI right now are Travis-CI, Jenkins, and Buildbot—which are all listed in the following sections. They are frequently used with Tox, a Python tool to manage virtualenv and tests from the command line. Travis is for multiple Python interpreters on a single platform, and Jenkins (most popular) and Buildbot (written in Python) can manage builds on multiple machines. Many also use Buildout (discussed in "Buildout" on page 40) and Docker (discussed in "Docker" on page 42) to rapidly and repeatably build complex environments for their test battery.

---

1 Fowler is an advocate for best practices in software design and development, and one of continuous integration's most vocal proponents. The quote is excerpted from his blog post on continuous integration (*http://martinfowler.com/articles/continuousIntegration.html*). He hosted a series of discussions about *test-driven development* (TDD) (*http://martinfowler.com/articles/is-tdd-dead/*) and its relationship to extreme development with David Heinemeier Hansson (creator of Ruby on Rails) and Kent Beck (instigator of the *extreme programming* (XP) movement (*https://en.wikipedia.org/wiki/Extreme_programming*), with CI as one of its cornerstones).

Tox

Tox (*http://tox.readthedocs.org/en/latest/*) is an automation tool providing packaging, testing, and deployment of Python software right from the console or CI server. It is a generic virtualenv management and test command-line tool that provides the following features:

- Checks that packages install correctly with different Python versions and interpreters
- Runs tests in each of the environments, configuring your test tool of choice
- Acts as a frontend to continuous integration servers, reducing boilerplate and merging CI and shell-based testing

Install it using `pip`:

```
$ pip install tox
```

System Administration

The tools in this section are for managing and monitoring systems—server automation, system monitoring, and workflow management.

Travis-CI

Travis-CI (*https://travis-ci.org/*) is a distributed CI server which builds tests for open source projects for free. It provides multiple workers that run Python tests and seamlessly integrates with GitHub. You can even have it comment on your pull requests[2] whether this particular set of changes breaks the build or not. So if you are hosting your code on GitHub, Travis-CI is a great and easy way to get started with continuous integration. Travis-CI can build your code on a virtual machine that is running Linux, OS X, or iOS.

To get started, add a *.travis.yml* file to your repository with this example content:

```
language: python
python:
  - "2.6"
  - "2.7"
  - "3.3"
  - "3.4"
script: python tests/test_all_of_the_units.py
branches:
```

---

2 On GitHub, other users submit *pull requests* to notify owners of another repository that they have changes they'd like to merge.

```
only:
  - master
```

This will get your project tested on all the listed Python versions by running the given script and will only build the master branch. There are a lot more options you can enable, like notifications, before and after steps, and much more. The Travis-CI docs (*http://about.travis-ci.org/docs/*) explain all of these options and are very thorough. To use Tox with Travis-CI, add a Tox script to your repository, and change the line with `script:` in it to become:

```
install:
  - pip install tox
script:
  - tox
```

In order to activate testing for your project, go to the Travis-CI site (*https://travis-ci.org/*) and log in with your GitHub account. Then activate your project in your profile settings and you're ready to go. From now on, your project's tests will be run on every push to GitHub.

Jenkins

Jenkins CI (*http://jenkins.io*) is an extensible continuous integration engine and currently the most popular CI engine. It works on Windows, Linux, and OS X and plugs in to "every Source Code Management (SCM) tool that exists." Jenkins is a Java servlet (the Java equivalent of a Python WSGI application) that ships with its own servlet container, so you can run it directly using `java --jar jenkins.war`. For more information, refer to the Jenkins installation instructions (*https://wiki.jenkins-ci.org/display/JENKINS/Installing+Jenkins*); the Ubuntu page has instructions for how to place Jenkins behind an Apache or Nginx reverse proxy.

You interact with Jenkins via a web-based dashboard, or its HTTP-based *RESTful API*[3] (e.g., at *http://myServer:8080/api*), meaning we can use HTTP to communicate with the Jenkins server from remote machines. For examples, look at Apache's Jenkins Dashboard (*https://builds.apache.org/*) or the Pylons project's Jenkins Dashboard (*http://jenkins.pylonsproject.org/*).

The most frequently used Python tool to interact with the Jenkins API is python-jenkins (*https://pypi.python.org/pypi/python-jenkins*), created by the OpenStack

---

[3] REST stands for "representational state transfer." It's not a standard or a protocol, just a set of design principles developed during the creation of the HTTP 1.1 standard. A list of relevant architectural constraints for REST (*https://en.wikipedia.org/wiki/Representational_state_transfer#Architectural_constraints*) is available on Wikipedia.

(*https://www.openstack.org/*)[4] infrastructure team. Most Python users configure Jenkins to run a Tox script as part of the build process. For more information, see the documentation for using Tox with Jenkins (*http://tox.readthedocs.io/en/latest/example/jenkins.html*) and this guide to set up Jenkins with multiple build machines (*http://tinyurl.com/jenkins-setup-master-slave*).

Buildbot

Buildbot (*http://docs.buildbot.net/current/*) is a Python system to automate the compile/test cycle to validate code changes. It works like Jenkins in that it polls your source control manager for changes, builds and test your code on multiple computers according to your instructions (with built-in support for Tox), and then tells you what happened. It runs behind a Twisted web server. For an example of what the web interface looks like, here is Chromium's public buildbot dashboard (*https://build.chromium.org/p/chromium/waterfall*) (Chromium powers the Chrome browser).

Because Buildbot is pure Python, it's installed via `pip`:

```
$ pip install buildbot
```

The 0.9 version has a REST API (*http://docs.buildbot.net/latest/developer/apis.html*), but it is still in beta, so you won't be able to use it unless you expressly specify the version number (e.g., `pip install buildbot==0.9.00.9.0rc1`). Buildbot has a reputation for being the most powerful, but also the most complex of the continuous integration tools. To get started, follow their excellent tutorial (*http://docs.buildbot.net/current/tutorial*).

Server Automation

Salt, Ansible, Puppet, Chef, and CFEngine are server automation tools that provide an elegant way for system administrators to manage their fleet of physical and virtual machines. They all can manage Linux, Unix-like systems, and Windows machines. We're of course partial to Salt and Ansible, as they're written in Python. But they're still new, and the other options are more widely used. The following sections provide a quick summary of these options.

 For the record, folks at Docker say that they expect system automation tools like Salt, Ansible, and the rest to be *complemented by*, and not *replaced by* Docker—see this post about how Docker fits into the rest of DevOps (*http://stackshare.io/posts/how-docker-fits-into-the-current-devops-landscape*).

---

4 OpenStack provides free software for cloud networking, storage, and computation so that organizations can host private clouds for themselves or public clouds that third parties can pay to use.

Salt

Salt (*http://saltstack.org/*) calls its master node the *master* and its agent nodes *minions*, or *minion hosts*. Its main design goal is speed—networking by default is done using ZeroMQ, with TCP connections between the master and its "minions," and members of the Salt team have even written their own (optional) transmission protocol, RAET (*https://github.com/saltstack/raet*), which is faster than TCP and not as lossy as UDP.

Salt supports Python versions 2.6 and 2.7 and can be installed via `pip`:

```
$ pip install salt  # No Python 3 yet ...
```

After configuring a master server and any number of minion hosts, we can run arbitrary shell commands or use prebuilt modules of complex commands on our minions. The following command lists all available minion hosts, using `ping` in salt's `test` module:

```
$ salt '*' test.ping
```

You can filter minion hosts by either matching the minion ID, or by using the *grains* system (*http://docs.saltstack.org/en/latest/topics/targeting/grains.html*), which uses static host information like the operating system version or the CPU architecture to provide a host taxonomy for the Salt modules. For example, the following command uses the grains system to list only the available minions running CentOS:

```
$ salt -G 'os:CentOS' test.ping
```

Salt also provides a state system. States can be used to configure the minion hosts. For example, when a minion host is ordered to read the following state file, it will install and start the Apache server:

```
apache:
  pkg:
    - installed
  service:
    - running
    - enable: True
    - require:
      - pkg: apache
```

State files can be written using YAML, augmented by the Jinja2 template system, or can be pure Python modules. For more information, see the Salt documentation (*http://docs.saltstack.com*).

Ansible

The biggest advantage of Ansible (*http://ansible.com/*) over the other system automation tools is that it does not require anything (except Python) to be permanently installed on client machines. All of the other options[5] keep daemons running on the clients to poll the master. Their configuration files are in the YAML format. *Playbooks* are Ansible's configuration, deployment, and orchestration documents, and are written in YAML with Jinja2 for templating. Ansible supports Python versions 2.6 and 2.7 and can be installed via `pip`:

```
$ pip install ansible  # No Python 3 yet...
```

Ansible requires an inventory file that describes the hosts to which it has access. The following code is an example of a host and playbook that will ping all the hosts in the inventory file. Here is an example inventory file (*hosts.yml*):

```
[server_name]
127.0.0.1
```

Here is an example playbook (*ping.yml*):

```
---
- hosts: all

  tasks:
    - name: ping
      action: ping
```

To run the playbook:

```
$ ansible-playbook ping.yml -i hosts.yml --ask-pass
```

The Ansible playbook will ping all of the servers in the *hosts.yml* file. You can also select groups of servers using Ansible. For more information about Ansible, read the Ansible documentation (*http://docs.ansible.com/*). The Servers for Hackers Ansible tutorial (*https://serversforhackers.com/an-ansible-tutorial/*) is also a great and detailed introduction.

Puppet

Puppet (*http://puppetlabs.com*) is written in Ruby and provides its own language—PuppetScript—for configuration. It has a designated server, the *Puppet Master*, that's responsible for orchestrating its *Agent* nodes. *Modules* are small, shareable units of code written to automate or define the state of a system. Puppet Forge (*https:// forge.puppetlabs.com/*) is a repository for modules written by the community for Open Source Puppet and Puppet Enterprise.

Agent nodes send basic facts about the system (e.g., the operating system, kernel, architecture, IP address, and hostname) to the Puppet Master. The Puppet Master then compiles a catalog with information provided by the agents on how each node

---

5 Except for Salt-SSH, which is an alternative Salt architecture, probably created in response to users wanting an Ansible-like option from Salt.

should be configured and sends it to the agent. The agent enforces the change as prescribed in the catalog and sends a report back to the Puppet Master.

Facter (yes, spelled with an "-er") is an interesting tool that ships with Puppet and pulls basic facts about the system. These facts can be referenced as a variable while writing your Puppet modules:

```
$ facter kernel
Linux
$
$ facter operatingsystem
Ubuntu
```

Writing Modules in Puppet is pretty straightforward: Puppet Manifests (files with the extension *.pp) together form Puppet Modules. Here is an example of *Hello World* in Puppet:

```
notify { 'Hello World, this message is getting logged into the agent node':

    #As nothing is specified in the body, the resource title
    #is the notification message by default.
}
```

Here is another example, with system-based logic. To reference other facts, prepend a $ sign to the variable name—for instance, $hostname, or in this case, $operatingsystem:

```
notify{ 'Mac Warning':
    message => $operatingsystem ? {
        'Darwin' => 'This seems to be a Mac.',
        default  => 'I am a PC.',
    },
}
```

There are several resource types for Puppet, but the package-file-service paradigm is all you need for for the majority of the configuration management. The following Puppet code makes sure that the OpenSSH-Server package is installed in a system and the sshd service (the SSH server daemon) is notified to restart every time the sshd configuration file is changed:

```
package { 'openssh-server':
    ensure => installed,
}

file { '/etc/ssh/sshd_config':
    source   => 'puppet:///modules/sshd/sshd_config',
    owner    => 'root',
    group    => 'root',
    mode     => '640',
    notify   => Service['sshd'], # sshd will restart
                                 # whenever you edit this
                                 # file
```

```
    require => Package['openssh-server'],

}

service { 'sshd':
    ensure    => running,
    enable    => true,
    hasstatus => true,
    hasrestart=> true,
}
```

For more information, refer to the Puppet Labs documentation (*http://docs.puppet labs.com*).

Chef

If Chef (*https://www.chef.io/chef/*) is your choice for configuration management, you will primarily use Ruby to write your infrastructure code. Chef is similar to Puppet, but designed with the opposite philosophy: Puppet provides a framework that simplifies things at the expense of flexibility, while Chef provides nearly no framework—its goal is to be very extensible, and so it is more difficult to use.

Chef *clients* run on every node in your infrastructure and regularly check with your Chef *server* to ensure your system is always aligned and represents the desired state. Each individual Chef client configures itself. This distributed approach makes Chef a scalable automation platform.

Chef works by using custom *recipes* (configuration elements), implemented in *cookbooks*. Cookbooks, which are basically packages for infrastructure choices, are usually stored in your Chef server. Read DigitalOcean's tutorial series on Chef (*http://tinyurl.com/digitalocean-chef-tutorial*) to learn how to create a simple Chef server.

Use the knife (*https://docs.chef.io/knife.html*) command to create a simple cookbook:

```
$ knife cookbook create cookbook_name
```

Andy Gale's "Getting started with Chef" (*http://gettingstartedwithchef.com/first-steps-with-chef.html*) is a good starting point for Chef beginners. Many community cookbooks can be found on the Chef Supermarket (*https://supermarket.chef.io/cookbooks*) —they're a good starting point for your own cookbooks. For more information, check out the full Chef documentation (*https://docs.chef.io/*).

CFEngine

CFEngine has a tiny footprint because it's written in C. Its main design goal is robustness to failure, accomplished via autonomous agents operating in a distributed network (as opposed to a master/client architecture) that communicate using Promise Theory (*https://en.wikipedia.org/wiki/Promise_theory*). If you want a headless architecture, try this system.

System and Task Monitoring

The following libraries all help system administrators monitor running jobs but have very different applications: Psutil provides information in Python that can be obtained by Unix utility functions, Fabric makes it easy to define and execute commands on a list of remote hosts via SSH, and Luigi makes it possible to schedule and monitor long-running batch processes like chained Hadoop commands.

Psutil

Psutil (*https://pythonhosted.org/psutil/*) is a cross-platform (including Windows) interface to different system information (e.g., CPU, memory, disks, network, users, and processes)—it makes accessible within Python information that many of us are accustomed to obtaining via Unix commands (*https://en.wikipedia.org/wiki/List_of_Unix_commands*) such as top, ps, df, and netstat. Get it using pip:

```
$ pip install psutil
```

Here is an example that monitors for server overload (if any of the tests—net, CPU—fail, it will send an email):

```python
# Functions to get system values:
from psutil import cpu_percent, net_io_counters
# Functions to take a break:
from time import sleep
# Package for email services:
import smtplib
import string

MAX_NET_USAGE = 400000
MAX_ATTACKS = 4
attack = 0
counter = 0
while attack <= MAX_ATTACKS:
    sleep(4)
    counter = counter + 1
    # Check the CPU usage
    if cpu_percent(interval = 1) > 70:
        attack = attack + 1
    # Check the net usage
    neti1 = net_io_counters()[1]
    neto1 = net_io_counters()[0]
    sleep(1)
    neti2 = net_io_counters()[1]
    neto2 = net_io_counters()[0]
    # Calculate the bytes per second
    net = ((neti2+neto2) - (neti1+neto1))/2
    if net > MAX_NET_USAGE:
        attack = attack + 1
    if counter > 25:
        attack = 0
```

```
        counter = 0

    # Write a very important email if attack is higher than 4
    TO = "you@your_email.com"
    FROM = "webmaster@your_domain.com"
    SUBJECT = "Your domain is out of system resources!"
    text = "Go and fix your server!"
    BODY = string.join(
            ("From: %s" %FROM,"To: %s" %TO,"Subject: %s" %SUBJECT, "",text), "\r\n")
    server = smtplib.SMTP('127.0.0.1')
    server.sendmail(FROM, [TO], BODY)
    server.quit()
```

For a good example use of Psutil, see glances (*https://github.com/nicolargo/glances/*), a full terminal application that behaves like a widely extended top (which lists running process by CPU use or a user-specified sort order), with the ability of a client-server monitoring tool.

Fabric

Fabric (*http://docs.fabfile.org*) is a library for simplifying system administration tasks. It allows you to SSH to multiple hosts and execute tasks on each one. This is convenient for system administration or application deployment. Use pip to install Fabric:

```
$ pip install fabric
```

Here is a complete Python module defining two Fabric tasks—memory_usage and deploy:

```
# fabfile.py
from fabric.api import cd, env, prefix, run, task

env.hosts = ['my_server1', 'my_server2']    # Where to SSH

@task
def memory_usage():
    run('free -m')

@task
def deploy():
    with cd('/var/www/project-env/project'):
        with prefix('. ../bin/activate'):
            run('git pull')
            run('touch app.wsgi')
```

The with statement just nests the commands in so that in the end deploy() becomes this for each host:

```
$ ssh hostname cd /var/ww/project-env/project && ../bin/activate && git pull
$ ssh hostname cd /var/ww/project-env/project && ../bin/activate && \
> touch app.wsgi
```

With the previous code saved in a file named *fabfile.py* (the default module name `fab` looks for), we can check memory usage with our new `memory_usage` task:

```
$ fab memory_usage
[my_server1] Executing task 'memory'
[my_server1] run: free -m
[my_server1] out:                total    used    free  shared  buffers   cached
[my_server1] out: Mem:            6964    1897    5067       0      166      222
[my_server1] out: -/+ buffers/cache:     1509    5455
[my_server1] out: Swap:              0       0       0

[my_server2] Executing task 'memory'
[my_server2] run: free -m
[my_server2] out:                total    used    free  shared  buffers   cached
[my_server2] out: Mem:            1666     902     764       0      180      572
[my_server2] out: -/+ buffers/cache:      148    1517
[my_server2] out: Swap:            895       1     894
```

and we can deploy with:

```
$ fab deploy
```

Additional features include parallel execution, interaction with remote programs, and host grouping. The examples in the Fabric documentation (*http://docs.fabfile.org*) are easy to follow.

Luigi

Luigi (*https://pypi.python.org/pypi/luigi*) is a pipeline management tool developed and released by Spotify. It helps developers manage the entire pipeline of large, long-running batch jobs, stitching together things such as Hive queries, database queries, Hadoop Java jobs, pySpark jobs, and any tasks you want to write yourself. They don't all have to be big data applications—the API allows you to schedule anything. But Spotify made it to run their jobs over Hadoop, so they provide all of these utilities already in `luigi.contrib` (*http://luigi.readthedocs.io/en/stable/api/luigi.contrib.html*). Install it with `pip`:

```
$ pip install luigi
```

It includes a web interface, so users can filter for their tasks and view dependency graphs of the pipeline workflow and its progress. There are example Luigi tasks (*https://github.com/spotify/luigi/tree/master/examples*) in their GitHub repository, or see the Luigi documentation (*http://luigi.readthedocs.io/*).

Speed

This chapter lists the Python community's most common approaches to speed optimization. Table 8-1 shows your optimization options, after you've done the simple things like profiling your code (*https://docs.python.org/3.5/library/profile.html*) and comparing options for code snippets (*https://docs.python.org/3.5/library/timeit.html*) to first get all of the performance you can directly from Python.

You may have already heard of the global interpreter lock (*http://wiki.python.org/moin/GlobalInterpreterLock*) (GIL)—it is how the C implementation of Python allows multiple threads to operate at the same time. Python's memory management isn't entirely thread-safe, so the GIL is required to prevent multiple threads from running the same Python code at once.

The GIL is often cited as a limitation of Python, but it's not really as big of a deal as it's made out to be—it's only a hindrance when processes are CPU bound (in which case, like with NumPy or the cryptography libraries discussed soon, the code is rewritten in C and exposed with Python bindings). For anything else (like network I/O or file I/O), the bottleneck is the code blocking in a single thread while waiting for the I/O. You can solve blocking problems using threads or event-driven programming.

We should also note that in Python 2, there were slower and faster versions of libraries—StringIO and cStringIO, ElementTree and cElementTree. The C implementations are faster, but had to be imported explicitly. Since Python 3.3, the regular versions import from the faster implementation whenever possible, and the C-prefixed libraries are deprecated.

Table 8-1. Speed options

Option	License	Reasons to use
Threading	PSFL	• Allows you to create multiple execution threads.
		• Threading (when using CPython, because of the GIL) does not use multiple processes; the different threads switch when one is blocking, which is useful when your bottleneck is some blocking task, like wating on I/O.
		• There is no GIL in some other implementations of Python, like Jython and IronPython.
Multiprocessing/ subprocess	PSFL	• Tools in the multiprocessing library allow you to actually spawn other Python processes, bypassing the GIL.
		• And subprocess allows you to launch multiple command-line processes.
PyPy	MIT license	• It's a Python interpreter (Python 2.7.10 or 3.2.5 right now) that provides just-in-time compilation to C when possible.
		• Effortless: no coding necessary, and it usually gives a good boost.
		• It's a drop-in replacement for CPython that usually works—any C libraries should use the CFFI, or be on the PyPy compatibility list (*http://pypy.org/compat.html*).

Option	License	Reasons to use
Cython	Apache license	• It provides two ways to statically compile Python code: the first choice is to use an annotation language, Cython (*.pxd). • The second choice is to statically compile pure Python and use Cython's provided decorators to specify object type.
Numba	BSD license	• It provides both a static (via its `pycc` tool) or a just-in-time runtime compiler to *machine code* that uses NumPy arrays. • It requires Python 2.7 or 3.4+, the llvmlite (*http://llvmlite.pydata.org/en/latest/install/index.html*) library, and its dependency, the LLVM (Low-Level Virtual Machine) compiler infrastructure.
Weave	BSD license	• It provides a way to "weave" a few lines of C into Python, but only use it if you're already using Weave. • Otherwise, use Cython—Weave is now deprecated.
PyCUDA/gnumpy/ TensorFlow/ Theano/PyOpenCL	MIT/ modified BSD/BSD/ BSD/MIT	• These libraries provide different ways to use a NVIDIA GPU, provided you have one installed, and can install NVIDIA's CUDA toolchain (*http://docs.nvidia.com/cuda/*). • PyOpenCL can use processors other than NVIDIA's use other processors • They each have a different application—for example, gnumpy is intended to be a drop-in replacement for NumPy.
Direct use of C/C++ libraries	—	• The speed improvement is worth the extra time you'll need to spend coding in C/C++.

Jeff Knupp, author of *Writing Idiomatic Python* (*http://bit.ly/writing-idiomatic-python*), wrote a blog post about getting around the GIL (*http://bit.ly/pythons-hardest-problems*), citing David Beazley's deep look[6] into the subject.

Threading and the other optimization options in Table 8-1 are discussed in more detail in the following sections.

Threading

Python's threading library allows you to create multiple threads. Because of the GIL (at least in CPython), there will only be one Python process running per Python interpreter, meaning there will only be a performance gain when at least one thread is

---

6 David Beazley has a great guide (PDF) (*http://www.dabeaz.com/python/UnderstandingGIL.pdf*) that describes how the GIL operates. He also covers the new GIL (PDF) (*http://www.dabeaz.com/python/NewGIL.pdf*) in Python 3.2. His results show that maximizing performance in a Python application requires a strong understanding of the GIL, how it affects your specific application, how many cores you have, and where your application bottlenecks are.

blocking (e.g., on I/O). The other option for I/O is to use event handling. For that, see the paragraphs on asyncio in "Performance networking tools in Python's Standard Library" on page 259.

What happens in Python when you have multiple threads is the kernel notices that one thread is blocking on I/O, and it switches to allow the next thread to use the processor until it blocks or is finished. All of this happens automatically when you start your threads. There's a good example use of threading on Stack Overflow (*http://bit.ly/threading-in-python*), and the Python Module of the Week series has a great threading introduction (*https://pymotw.com/2/threading/*). Or see the threading documentation in the Standard Library (*https://docs.python.org/3/library/threading.html*).

Multiprocessing

The multiprocessing module (*https://docs.python.org/3/library/multiprocessing.html*) in Python's Standard Library provides a way to bypass the GIL—by launching additional Python interpreters. The separate processes can communicate using a `multiprocessing.Pipe`, or by a `multiprocessing.Queue`, or share memory via a `multiprocessing.Array` and `multiprocessing.Value`, which implement locking automatically. Share data sparingly; these objects implement locking to prevent simultaneous access by different processes.

Here's an example to show that the speed gain from using a pool of worker processes isn't always proportional to the number of workers used. There's a trade-off between the computational time saved and the time it takes to launch another interpeter. The example uses the Monte Carlo method (of drawing random numbers) to estimate the value of Pi:[7]

```
>>> import multiprocessing
>>> import random
>>> import timeit
>>>
>>> def calculate_pi(iterations):
...     x = (random.random() for i in range(iterations))
...     y = (random.random() for i in range(iterations))
...     r_squared = [xi**2 + yi**2 for xi, yi in zip(x, y)]
...     percent_coverage = sum([r <= 1 for r in r_squared]) / len(r_squared)
...     return 4 * percent_coverage
...
>>>
>>> def run_pool(processes, total_iterations):
...     with multiprocessing.Pool(processes) as pool:    ❶
...         # Divide the total iterations among the processes.
```

---

[7] Here is a full derivation of the method (*http://bit.ly/monte-carlo-pi*). Basically you're throwing darts at a 2 x 2 square, with a circle that has radius = 1 inside. If the darts land with equal likelihood anywhere on the board, the percent that are in the circle is equal to Pi / 4. Which means 4 times the percent in the circle is equal to Pi.

```
...        iterations = [total_iterations // processes] * processes  ❷
...        result = pool.map(calculate_pi, iterations)  ❸
...     print( "%0.4f" % (sum(result) / processes), end=',  ')
...
>>>
>>> ten_million = 10000000        ❹
>>> timeit.timeit(lambda: run_pool(1, ten_million), number=10)
3.141,  3.142,  3.142,  3.141,  3.141,  3.142,  3.141,  3.141,  3.142,  3.142,
134.48382110201055  ❺
>>>                              ❻
>>> timeit.timeit(lambda: run_pool(10, ten_million), number=10)
3.142,  3.142,  3.142,  3.142,  3.142,  3.142,  3.141,  3.142,  3.142,  3.141,
74.38514468498761  ❼
```

❶ Using the `multiprocessing.Pool` within a context manager reinforces that the pool should only be used by the process that creates it.

❷ The total iterations will always be the same; they'll just be divided between a different number of processes.

❸ `pool.map()` creates the multiple processes—one per item in the `iterations` list, up to the maximum number stated when the pool was initialized (in `multiproc essing.Pool(processes)`).

❹ There is only one process for the first `timeit` trial.

❺ 10 repetitions of one single process running with 10 million iterations took 134 seconds.

❻ There are 10 processes for the second `timeit` trial.

❼ 10 repetitions of 10 processes each running with one million iterations took 74 seconds.

The point of all this was that there is overhead in making the multiple processes, but the tools for runing multiple processes in Python are robust and mature. See the multiprocessing documentation in the Standard Library (*https://docs.python.org/3.5/ library/multiprocessing.html*) for more information, and check out Jeff Knupp's blog post about getting around the GIL (*http://bit.ly/pythons-hardest-problems*), because it has a few paragraphs about multiprocessing.

Subprocess

The subprocess library (*https://docs.python.org/3/library/subprocess.html*) was introduced into the Standard Library in Python 2.4 and defined in PEP 324 (*https:// www.python.org/dev/peps/pep-0324*). It launches a system call (like `unzip` or `curl`) as if called from the command line (by default, without calling the system shell (*http://bit.ly/subprocess-security*)), with the developer selecting what to do with the subprocess's input and output pipes. We recommend Python 2 users get an updated version with some bugfixes from the subprocess32 (*https://pypi.python.org/pypi/subprocess32/*) package. Install it using `pip`:

```
$ pip install subprocess32
```

There is a great subprocess tutorial (*https://pymotw.com/2/subprocess/*) on the Python Module of the Week blog.

PyPy

PyPy (*http://pypy.org*) is a pure-Python implementation of Python. It's fast, and when it works, you don't have to do anything to your code, and it just runs faster for free. You should try this option before anything else.

You can't get it using `pip`, because it's actually another implementation of Python. Scroll through the PyPy downloads page (*http://pypy.org/download.html*) for your correct version of Python and your operating system.

Here is a slightly modified version of David Beazley's (*http://www.dabeaz.com/GIL/gilvis/measure2.py*) CPU bound test code, with an added loop for multiple tests. You can see the difference between PyPy and CPython. First it's run using the CPython:

```
$ # CPython
$ ./python -V
Python 2.7.1
$
$ ./python measure2.py
1.06774401665
1.45412397385
1.51485204697
1.54693889618
1.60109114647
```

And here is the same script, and the only thing different is the Python interpreter—it's running with PyPy:

```
$ # PyPy
$ ./pypy -V
Python 2.7.1 (7773f8fc4223, Nov 18 2011, 18:47:10)
[PyPy 1.7.0 with GCC 4.4.3]
$
$ ./pypy measure2.py
0.0683999061584
0.0483210086823
0.0388588905334
0.0440690517426
0.0695300102234
```

So, just by downloading PyPy, it went from an average of about 1.4 seconds to around 0.05 seconds—more than 20 times faster. Sometimes your code won't even double in speed, but other times you really do get a big boost. And with no effort outside of downloading the PyPy interpreter. If you want your C library to be compatible with PyPy, follow PyPy's advice (*http://pypy.org/compat.html*) and use the CFFI instead of ctypes in the Standard Library.

Cython

Unfortunately, PyPy doesn't work with all libraries that use C extensions. For those cases, Cython (*http://cython.org/*) (pronounced "PSI-thon"—*not* the same as CPython, the standard C implementation of Python) implements a superset of the Python language that lets you write C and C++ modules for Python. Cython also allows you to call functions from compiled C libraries, and provides a context, `nogil`, that allows you to release the GIL (*http://tinyurl.com/cython-nogil*) around a section of code, provided it does not manipulate Python objects in any way. Using Cython allows you to take advantage of Python's strong typing[8] of variables and operations.

Here's an example of strong typing with Cython:

```
def primes(int kmax):
"""Calculation of prime numbers with additional Cython keywords"""

    cdef int n, k, i
    cdef int p[1000]
    result = []
    if kmax > 1000:
        kmax = 1000
    k = 0
    n = 2
    while k < kmax:
        i = 0
        while i < k and n % p[i] != 0:
            i = i + 1
        if i == k:
            p[k] = n
            k = k + 1
            result.append(n)
        n = n + 1
    return result
```

This implementation of an algorithm to find prime numbers has some additional keywords compared to the next one, which is implemented in pure Python:

---

8 It *is* possible for a language to both be strongly and dynamically typed, as described in this Stack Overflow discussion (*http://stackoverflow.com/questions/11328920/*).

```
def primes(kmax):
"""Calculation of prime numbers in standard Python syntax"""

    p= range(1000)
    result = []
    if kmax > 1000:
        kmax = 1000
    k = 0
    n = 2
    while k < kmax:
        i = 0
        while i < k and n % p[i] != 0:
            i = i + 1
        if i == k:
            p[k] = n
            k = k + 1
            result.append(n)
        n = n + 1
    return result
```

Notice that in the Cython version you declare integers and integer arrays to be compiled into C types while also creating a Python list:

```
# Cython version

def primes(int kmax):    ❶
    """Calculation of prime numbers with additional Cython keywords"""
    cdef int n, k, i    ❷
    cdef int p[1000]    ❸
    result = []
```

❶ The type is declared to be an integer.

❷ The upcoming variables n, k, and i are declared as integers.

❸ And we then have preallocated a 1000-long array of integers for p.

What is the difference? In the Cython version, you can see the declaration of the variable types and the integer array in a similar way as in standard C. For example, the addtional type declaration (of integer) in the cdef int n,k,i allows the Cython compiler to generate more efficient C code than it could without type hints. Because the syntax is incompatible with standard Python, it is not saved in *.py files—instead, Cython code is saved in *.pyx files.

What's the difference in speed? Let's try it!

```
import time
# activate pyx compiler
import pyximport    ❶
pyximport.install()    ❷
# primes implemented with Cython
```

```
import primesCy
# primes implemented with Python
import primes

print("Cython:")
t1 = time.time()
print primesCy.primes(500)
t2 = time.time()
print("Cython time: %s" %(t2-t1))
print("")
print("Python")
t1 = time.time()    ❸
print(primes.primes(500))
t2 = time.time()
print("Python time: {}".format(t2-t1))
```

❶ The *pyximport* module allows you to import **.pyx* files (e.g., *primesCy.pyx*) with the Cython-compiled version of the primes function.

❷ The pyximport.install() command allows the Python interpreter to start the Cython compiler directly to generate C-code, which is automatically compiled to a **.so* C-library. Cython is then able to import this library for you in your Python code, easily and efficiently.

❸ With the time.time() function, you are able to compare the time between these two different calls to find 500 prime numbers. On a standard notebook (dual-core AMD E-450 1.6 GHz), the measured values are:

```
Cython time: 0.0054 seconds
```

```
Python time: 0.0566 seconds
```

And here the output of an embedded ARM BeagleBone (*http://beagleboard.org/Prod ucts/BeagleBone*) machine:

```
Cython time: 0.0196 seconds
```

```
Python time: 0.3302 seconds
```

Numba

Numba (*http://numba.pydata.org*) is a NumPy-aware Python compiler (just-in-time [JIT] specializing compiler) that compiles annotated Python (and NumPy) code to LLVM (Low-Level Virtual Machine) (*http://llvm.org/*) through special decorators. Briefly, Numba uses LLVM to compile Python down to machine code that can be natively executed at runtime.

If you use Anaconda, install Numba with conda install numba; if not, install it by hand. You must already have NumPy and LLVM installed before installing Numba.

Check the LLVM version you need (it's on the PyPI page for llvmlite (*https://pypi.python.org/pypi/llvmlite*)), and download that version from whichever place matches your OS:

- LLVM builds for Windows (*http://llvm.org/builds/*).
- LLVM builds for Debian/Ubuntu (*http://llvm.org/apt/*).
- LLVM builds for Fedora (*https://apps.fedoraproject.org/packages/llvm*).
- For a discussion of how to build from source for other Unix systems, see "Building the Clang + LLVM compilers" (*http://ftp.math.utah.edu/pub/llvm/*).
- On OS X, use `brew install homebrew/versions/llvm37` (or whatever version number is now current).

Once you have LLVM and NumPy, install Numba using `pip`. You may need to help the installer find the *llvm-config* file by providing an environment variable `LLVM_CON FIG` with the appropriate path, like this:

```
$ LLVM_CONFIG=/path/to/llvm-config-3.7 pip install numba
```

Then, to use it in your code, just decorate your functions:

```
from numba import jit, int32

@jit  ❶
def f(x):
    return x + 3

@jit(int32(int32, int32))  ❷
def g(x, y):
    return x + y
```

❶ With no arguments, the `@jit` decorator does *lazy compilation*—deciding itself whether to optimize the function, and how.

❷ For *eager compilation*, specify types. The function will be compiled with the given specialization, and no other will be allowed—the return value and the two arguments will all have type `numba.int32`.

There is a `nogil` flag that can allow code to ignore the Global Interpreter Lock, and a module `numba.pycc` that can be used to compile the code ahead of time. For more information, see Numba's user manual (*http://numba.pydata.org/numba-doc/latest/user*).

GPU libraries

Numba can optionally be built with capacity to run on the computer's *graphics processing unit* (GPU), a chip optimized for the fast, parallel computation used in modern video games. You'll need to have a NVIDIA GPU, with NVIDIA's CUDA Toolkit (*https://developer.nvidia.com/cuda-downloads*) installed. Then follow the documentation for using Numba's CUDA JIT (*http://numba.pydata.org/numba-doc/0.13/CUDAJit.html*) with the GPU.

Outside of Numba, the other popular library with GPU capability is TensorFlow (*https://www.tensorflow.org*), released by Google under the Apache v2.0 license. It provides tensors (mutidimensional matrices) and a way to chain tensor operations together, for fast matrix math. Currently it can only use the GPU on Linux operating systems. For installation instructions, see the following pages:

- Installing TensorFlow with GPU support (*http://bit.ly/tensorflow-gpu-support*)
- TensorFlow installation without GPU support (*http://bit.ly/tensorflow-no-gpu*)

For those not on Linux, Theano (*http://deeplearning.net/software/theano/*), from the University of Montréal, was the de facto matrix-math-over-GPU libary in Python until Google posted TensorFlow. Theano is still under active development. It has a page dedicated to using the GPU (*http://deeplearning.net/software/theano/tutorial/using_gpu.html*). Theano supports Windows, OS X, and Linux operating systems, and is available via pip:

```
$ pip install Theano
```

For lower-level interaction with the GPU, you can try PyCUDA (*https://developer.nvidia.com/pycuda*).

Finally, people without a NVIDIA GPU can use PyOpenCL (*https://pypi.python.org/pypi/pyopencl*), a wrapper for Intel's OpenCL library (*https://software.intel.com/en-us/intel-opencl*), which is compatible with a number of different hardware sets (*https://software.intel.com/en-us/articles/opencl-drivers*).

Interfacing with C/C++/FORTRAN Libraries

Each of the libraries described in the following sections are very different: both CFFI and ctypes are Python libraries, F2PY is for FORTRAN, SWIG can make C objects available in multiple languages (not just Python), and Boost.Python is a C++ library that can expose C++ objects to Python and vice versa. Table 8-2 goes into a little more detail.

Table 8-2. C and C++ interfaces

Library	License	Reasons to use
CFFI	MIT license	• It provides the best compatibility with PyPy. • It allows you to write C code from within Python that can be compiled to build a shared C library with Python bindings.
ctypes	Python Software Foundation license	• It's in the Python Standard Library. • It allows you to wrap existing DLLs or shared objects that you didn't write or don't have control over. • It provides the second-best compatibility with PyPy.
F2PY	BSD license	• This lets you use a FORTRAN library. • F2PY is a part of NumPy, so you should be using NumPy.
SWIG	GPL (output is not restricted)	• It provides a way to autogenerate libraries in multiple languages, using a special file format that is neither C nor Python.
Boost.Python	Boost Software license	• It's not a command-line tool; it's a C++ library that can be included in the C++ code and used to identify which objects to expose to Python.

C Foreign Function Interface

The CFFI (*https://cffi.readthedocs.org/en/latest/*) package provides a simple mechanism to interface with C from both CPython and PyPy. CFFI is recommended by PyPy (*http://doc.pypy.org/en/latest/extending.html*) for the best compatibility between CPython and PyPy. It supports two modes: the inline *application binary interface* (ABI) compatibility mode (see the following code example) allows you to dynamically load and run functions from executable modules (essentially exposing the same functionality as LoadLibrary or dlopen), and an API mode, which allows you to build C extension modules.[9]

Install it using `pip`:

```
$ pip install cffi
```

Here is an example with ABI interaction:

```
from cffi import FFI
ffi = FFI()
ffi.cdef("size_t strlen(const char*);")   ❶
```

---

9 Special care (*http://docs.python.org/c-api/init.html#threads*) must be taken when writing C extensions to make sure you register your threads with the interpreter.

```
clib = ffi.dlopen(None)  ❷
length = clib.strlen("String to be evaluated.")  ❸
# prints: 23
print("{}".format(length))
```

❶ The string here could be lifted from a function declaration from a C header file.

❷ Open the shared library (*.DLL or *.so).

❸ Now we can treat `clib` as if it were a Python module and just call functions we defined with dot notation.

ctypes

ctypes (*https://docs.python.org/3/library/ctypes.html*) is the de facto library for interfacing with C/C++ from CPython, and it's in the Standard Library. It provides full access to the native C interface of most major operating systems (e.g., kernel32 on Windows, or libc on *nix), plus support for loading and interfacing with dynamic libraries—shared objects (*.so*) or DLLs—at runtime. It brings along with it a whole host of types for interacting with system APIs and allows you to easily define your own complex types, such as structs and unions, and allows you to modify things like padding and alignment if needed. It can be a bit crufty to use (because you have to type so many extra characters), but in conjunction with the Standard Library's struct module (*https://docs.python.org/3.5/library/struct.html*), you are essentially provided full control over how your data types get translated into something usable by a pure C/C++ method.

For example, a C struct defined like this in a file named *my_struct.h*:

```
struct my_struct {
    int a;
    int b;
};
```

could be implemented as shown in a file named *my_struct.py*:

```
import ctypes
class my_struct(ctypes.Structure):
    _fields_ = [("a", c_int),
                ("b", c_int)]
```

F2PY

The Fortran-to-Python interface generator (F2PY) (*http://docs.scipy.org/doc/numpy/f2py/*) is a part of NumPy, so to get it, install NumPy using `pip`:

```
$ pip install numpy
```

It provides a versatile command-line function, f2py, that can be used three different ways, all documented in the F2PY quickstart guide (*http://docs.scipy.org/doc/numpy/ f2py/getting-started.html*). If you have control over the source code, you can add special comments with instructions for F2PY that clarify the intent of each argument (which items are return values and which are inputs), and then just run F2PY like this:

```
$ f2py -c fortran_code.f -m python_module_name
```

When you can't do that, F2PY can generate an intermediate file with extension **.pyf* that you *can* modify, to then produce the same results. This would be three steps:

```
$ f2py fortran_code.f -m python_module_name -h interface_file.pyf  ❶
$ vim interface_file.pyf  ❷
$ f2py -c interface_file.pyf fortran_code.f  ❸
```

❶ Autogenerate an intermediate file that defines the interface between the FOR-TRAN function signatures and the Python signatures.

❷ Edit the file so that it correctly labels input and output variables.

❸ *Now* compile the code and build the extension modules.

SWIG

The Simplified Wrapper Interface Generator (SWIG) (*http://www.swig.org*) supports a large number of scripting languages, including Python. It's a popular, widely used command-line tool that generates bindings for interpreted languages from annotated C/C++ header files. To use it, first use SWIG to autogenerate an intermediate file from the header—with **.i* suffix. Next, modify that file to reflect the actual interface you want, and then run the build tool to compile the code into a shared library. All of this is done step by step in the SWIG tutorial (*http://www.swig.org/tutorial.html*).

While it does have some limits (it currently seems to have issues with a small subset of newer C++ features, and getting template-heavy code to work can be a bit verbose), SWIG provides a great deal of power and exposes lots of features to Python with little effort. Additionally, you can easily extend the bindings SWIG creates (in the interface file) to overload operators and built-in methods, and effectively re-cast C++ exceptions to be catchable by Python.

Here is an example that shows how to overload __repr__. This excerpt would be from a file named *MyClass.h*:

```
#include <string>
class MyClass {
private:
    std::string name;
public:
```

```
    std::string getName();
};
```

And here is *myclass.i* :

```
%include "string.i"

%module myclass
%{
#include <string>
#include "MyClass.h"
%}

%extend MyClass {
    std::string __repr__()
    {
        return $self->getName();
    }
}

%include "MyClass.h"
```

There are more Python examples (*https://github.com/swig/swig/tree/master/Examples/
python*) in the SWIG GitHub repository. Install SWIG using your package manager, if
it's there (`apt-get install swig`, `yum install swig.i386`, or `brew install swig`),
or else use this link to download SWIG (*http://www.swig.org/survey.html*), then follow
the installation instructions (*http://www.swig.org/Doc3.0/Preface.html#Preface_instal
lation*) for your operating system. If you're missing the Perl Compatible Regular
Expressions (PCRE) library in OS X, use Homebrew to install it:

```
$ brew install pcre
```

Boost.Python

Boost.Python (*http://www.boost.org/doc/libs/1_60_0/libs/python/doc/*) requires a bit
more manual work to expose C++ object functionality, but it is capable of providing
all the same features SWIG does and then some—for example, wrappers to access
Python objects as PyObjects in C++, as well as the tools to expose C++ objects to
Python. Unlike SWIG, Boost.Python is a library, not a command-line tool, and there
is no need to create an intermediate file with different formatting—it's all written
directly in C++. Boost.Python has an extensive, detailed tutorial (*http://bit.ly/boost-
python-tutorial*) if you wish to go this route.

## CHAPTER 9

Software Interfaces

This chapter will first show you how to use Python to get information from APIs that are used now to share data between organizations, and then highlight the tools that most Python-powered organizations would use to support communication within their own infrastructure.

We already discussed Python's support for pipes and queues across processes in "Multiprocessing" on page 236. Communicating *between computers* requires the computers at both ends of the conversation use a defined set of protocols—the Internet adheres to the TCP/IP suite (*https://en.wikipedia.org/wiki/Internet_protocol_suite*).[1] You can implement UDP yourself (*https://pymotw.com/2/socket/udp.html*) over sockets, Python provides a library called ssl for TLS/SSL wrappers over sockets, and asyncio to implement asynchronous transports (*https://docs.python.org/3/library/asyncio-protocol.html*) for TCP, UDP, TLS/SSL, and subprocess pipes.

But most of us will be using the higher-level libraries that provide clients implementing various application-level protocols: ftplib, poplib, imaplib, nntplib, smtplib, telnetlib, and xmlrpc. All of them provide classes for both regular and TLS/SSL wrapped clients (and urllib exists for HTTP requests, but recommends the Requests library for most uses).

---

1 The TCP/IP (or Internet Protocol) suite has four conceptual parts: *Link layer* protocols specify how to get information between a computer and the Internet. Within the computer, they're the responsibility of network cards and the operating system, not of the Python program. *Internet layer* protocols (IPv4, IPv6, etc.) govern the delivery of packages of bits from a source to a destination—the standard options are in Python's socket library (*https://docs.python.org/3/library/socket.html*). *Transport layer* protocols (TCP, UDP, etc.) specify how the two endpoints will communicate. The options are also in the socket library (*https://docs.python.org/3/library/socket.html*). Finally, *application layer* protocols (FTP, HTTP, etc.) specify what the data should look like to be used by an intended application (e.g., FTP is used for file transfer, and HTTP is used for hypertext transfer)—Python's Standard Library provides separate modules implementing the most common protocols.

The first section in this chapter covers HTTP requests—how to get data from public APIs on the Web. Next is a brief aside about serialization in Python, and the third section describes popular tools used in enterprise-level networking. We'll try to explicitly say when something is only available in Python 3. If you're using Python 2 and can't find a module or class we're talking about, we recommend checking this list of changes between the Python 2 and Python 3 Standard Libraries (*http://python3port ing.com/stdlib.html*).

Web Clients

The Hypertext Transfer Protocol (HTTP) is an application protocol for distributed, collaborative, hypermedia information systems and is the foundation of data communication for the World Wide Web. We're focusing this entire section on how to get data from the Web using the Requests library.

Python's standard urllib module provides most of the HTTP capabilities you need, but at a low level, that requires quite a bit of work to perform seemingly simple tasks (like getting data from an HTTPS server that requires authentication). The documentation for the `urllib.request` module actually says to use the Requests library instead.

Requests (*http://pypi.python.org/pypi/requests*) takes all of the work out of Python HTTP requests—making your integration with web services seamless. There's no need to manually add query strings to your URLs, or to form-encode your POST data. Keep-alive (persistent HTTP connections) and HTTP connection pooling are available through the `request.sessions.Session` class, powered by urllib3 (*https:// pypi.python.org/pypi/urllib3*), which is embedded within Requests (meaning you don't need to install it separately). Get it using `pip`:

```
$ pip install requests
```

The Requests documentation (*http://docs.python-requests.org/en/latest/index.html*) goes into more detail than what we'll cover next.

Web APIs

Nearly everybody, from the US Census (*https://www.census.gov/developers/*) to the Dutch National Library (*http://bit.ly/early-dutch-books*), has an API that you can use to get the data they want to share; and some, like Twitter and Facebook, allow you (or the apps you use) to also modify that data. You may hear the term *RESTful* API. REST stands for representational state transfer—it is a paradigm that informed how HTTP 1.1 was designed, but is not a standard, protocol, or requirement. Still, most web service API providers follow the RESTful design principles. We'll use some code to illustrate common terms:

```
import requests
         ❶                  ❷          ❸        ❹
result = requests.get('http://pypi.python.org/pypi/requests/json')
```

❶   The *method* is part of the HTTP protocol. In a RESTful API, the API designer chooses what action the server will take, and tells you in their API documentation. Here is a list of all of the methods (*http://bit.ly/http-method-defs*), but the ones commonly available in RESTful APIs are GET, POST, PUT, and DELETE. Usually, these "HTTP verbs" do what their meaning implies, getting data, changing data, or deleting it.

❷   The *base URI* is the root of the API.

❸   Clients would specify a specific *element* they want data on.

❹   And there may be an option for different *media types*.

That code actually performed an HTTP request to *http://pypi.python.org/pypi/ requests/json*, which is the JSON backend for PyPI. If you look at it in your browser, you will see a large JSON string. In Requests, the return value of an HTTP request is a Response object:

```
>>> import requests
>>> response = requests.get('http://pypi.python.org/pypi/requests/json')
>>> type(response)
<class 'requests.models.Response'>
>>> response.ok
True
>>> response.text    # This gives all of the text of the response
>>> response.json()  # This converts the text response into a dictionary
```

PyPI gave us the text in JSON format. There isn't a rule about the format to send data in, but many APIs use JSON or XML.

JSON parsing

Javascript Object Notation (JSON) is exactly what it says—the notation used to define objects in JavaScript. The Requests library has built a JSON parser into its Response object.

The json (*https://docs.python.org/3/library/json.html*) library can parse JSON from strings or files into a Python dictionary (or list, as appropriate). It can also convert Python dictionaries or lists into JSON strings. For example, the following string contains JSON data:

```
json_string = '{"first_name": "Guido", "last_name":"van Rossum"}'
```

It can be parsed like this:

```
import json
parsed_json = json.loads(json_string)
```

and can now be used as a normal dictionary:

```
print(parsed_json['first_name'])
"Guido"
```

You can also convert the following to JSON:

```
d = {
    'first_name': 'Guido',
    'last_name': 'van Rossum',
    'titles': ['BDFL', 'Developer'],
}

print(json.dumps(d))
'{"first_name": "Guido", "last_name": "van Rossum",
  "titles": ["BDFL", "Developer"]}'
```

---

simplejson for Earlier Versions of Python

The json library was added to Python 2.6. If you're using an earlier version of Python, the simplejson (*https://simplejson.readthedocs.org/en/latest/*) library is available via PyPI.

simplejson provides the same API as the json module in Python's Standard Library but is updated more frequently than Python is. Also, developers who use older versions of Python can still use the features available in the json library by importing simplejson. You can use simplejson as a drop-in replacement for json like this:

```
import simplejson as json
```

After importing simplejson as json, the preceding examples will all work as if you were using the standard json library.

XML parsing

There is an XML parser in the Standard Library (xml.etree.ElementTree's parse() and fromstring() methods), but this uses the Expat library (*http://bit.ly/xml-expat*) and creates an ElementTree object that preserves the structure of the XML, meaning we have to iterate down it and look into its children to get content. When all you want is to get the data, try either untangle or xmltodict. You can get both using pip:

```
$ pip install untangle
$ pip install xmltodict
```

untangle

untangle (*https://github.com/stchris/untangle*) takes an XML document and returns a Python object whose structure mirrors the nodes and attributes. For example, an XML file like this:

```
<?xml version="1.0" encoding="UTF-8"?>
<root>
    <child name="child1" />
</root>
```

can be loaded like this:

```
import untangle
obj = untangle.parse('path/to/file.xml')
```

and then you can get the child element's name like this:

```
obj.root.child['name']  # is 'child1'
```

xmltodict

xmltodict (*http://github.com/martinblech/xmltodict*) converts the XML to a dictionary. For example, an XML file like this:

```
<mydocument has="an attribute">
  <and>
    <many>elements</many>
    <many>more elements</many>
  </and>
  <plus a="complex">
    element as well
  </plus>
</mydocument>
```

can be loaded into an `OrderedDict` instance (from the collections module in Python's Standard Library) like this:

```
import xmltodict

with open('path/to/file.xml') as fd:
    doc = xmltodict.parse(fd.read())
```

and then you can access elements, attributes, and values like this:

```
doc['mydocument']['@has']  # is u'an attribute'
doc['mydocument']['and']['many']  # is [u'elements', u'more elements']
doc['mydocument']['plus']['@a']  # is u'complex'
doc['mydocument']['plus']['#text']  # is u'element as well'
```

With xmltodict, you can also roundtrip the dictionary back to XML with the `unparse()` function. It has a streaming mode suitable for handling files that don't fit in memory, and it supports namespaces.

Web scraping

Websites don't always provide their data in comfortable formats such as CSV or JSON, but HTML is also structured data—this is where web scraping comes in.

Web scraping is the practice of using a computer program to sift through a web page and gather the data that you need in a format most useful to you while at the same time preserving the structure of the data.

 More and more now, as sites offer APIs, they explicitly request you to not scrape their data—the API presents the data they are willing to share, and that's it. Before getting started, check around the website you're looking at for a Terms of Use statement, and be a good citizen of the Web.

lxml

lxml (*http://lxml.de/*) is a pretty extensive library written for parsing XML and HTML documents very quickly, even handling some amount of incorrectly formatted markup in the process. Get it using `pip`:

```
$ pip install lxml
```

Use `requests.get` to retrieve the web page with our data, parse it using the `html` module, and save the results in `tree`:

```
from lxml import html
import requests

page = requests.get('http://econpy.pythonanywhere.com/ex/001.html')  ❶
tree = html.fromstring(page.content)  ❷
```

❶ This is a real web page, and the data we show are real—you can visit the page in your browser.

❷ We use `page.content` rather than `page.text` because `html.fromstring()` implicitly expects `bytes` as input.

Now, `tree` contains the whole HTML file in a nice tree structure that we can go over in two different ways: XPath (*http://lxml.de/xpathxslt.html*) or CSSSelect (*http://lxml.de/cssselect.html*). They are both standard ways to specify a path through an HTML tree, defined and maintained by the World Wide Web Consortium (W3C), and implemented as modules in lxml. In this example, we will use XPath. A good introduction is W3Schools XPath tutorial (*http://www.w3schools.com/xsl/xpath_intro.asp*).

There are also various tools for obtaining the XPath of elements from inside your web browser, such as Firebug for Firefox or the Chrome Inspector. If you're using

Chrome, you can right-click an element, choose "Inspect element", highlight the code, right-click again and choose "Copy XPath".

After a quick analysis, we see that in our page the data is contained in two elements—one is a div with title *buyer-name*, and the other is a span with the class *item-price*:

```
<div title="buyer-name">Carson Busses</div>
<span class="item-price">$29.95</span>
```

Knowing this, we can create the correct XPath query and use lxml's xpath function like this:

```
# This will create a list of buyers:
buyers = tree.xpath('//div[@title="buyer-name"]/text()')
# This will create a list of prices
prices = tree.xpath('//span[@class="item-price"]/text()')
```

Let's see what we got exactly:

```
>>> print('Buyers: ', buyers)
Buyers:  ['Carson Busses', 'Earl E. Byrd', 'Patty Cakes',
'Derri Anne Connecticut', 'Moe Dess', 'Leda Doggslife', 'Dan Druff',
'Al Fresco', 'Ido Hoe', 'Howie Kisses', 'Len Lease', 'Phil Meup',
'Ira Pent', 'Ben D. Rules', 'Ave Sectomy', 'Gary Shattire',
'Bobbi Soks', 'Sheila Takya', 'Rose Tattoo', 'Moe Tell']
>>>
>>> print('Prices: ', prices)
Prices:  ['$29.95', '$8.37', '$15.26', '$19.25', '$19.25',
'$13.99', '$31.57', '$8.49', '$14.47', '$15.86', '$11.11',
'$15.98', '$16.27', '$7.50', '$50.85', '$14.26', '$5.68',
'$15.00', '$114.07', '$10.09']
```

Data Serialization

Data serialization is the concept of converting structured data into a format that allows it to be shared or stored—retaining the information necessary to reconstruct the object in memory at the receiving end of the transmission (or upon read from storage). In some cases, the secondary intent of data serialization is to minimize the size of the serialized data, which then minimizes disk space or bandwidth requirements.

The sections that follow cover the Pickle format, which is specific to Python, some cross-language serialization tools, compression options in Python's Standard Library, and Python's buffer protocol, which can reduce the number of times an object is copied before transmission.

Pickle

The native data serialization module for Python is called Pickle (*https://docs.python.org/2/library/pickle.html*). Here's an example:

```
import pickle

# Here's an example dict
grades = { 'Alice': 89, 'Bob': 72, 'Charles': 87 }

# Use dumps to convert the object to a serialized string
serial_grades = pickle.dumps( grades )

# Use loads to de-serialize an object
received_grades = pickle.loads( serial_grades )
```

Some things cannot be pickled—functions, methods, classes, and ephemeral things like pipes.

 According to Python's Pickle documentation, "The pickle module is not secure against erroneous or maliciously constructed data. Never unpickle data received from an untrusted or unauthenticated source."

Cross-language serialization

If you're looking for a serialization module that has support in multiple languages, two popular options are Google's Protobuf (*https://developers.google.com/protocol-buffers/docs/pythontutorial*) and Apache's Avro (*https://avro.apache.org/docs/1.7.6/gettingstartedpython.html*).

Also, Python's Standard Library includes xdrlib (*https://docs.python.org/3/library/xdrlib.html*) to pack and unpack Sun's External Data Representation (*https://en.wikipedia.org/wiki/External_Data_Representation*) (XDR) format, which is independent of operating system and transport protocol. It's much lower level than the preceding options and just concatenates packed bytes together, so both the client and server must know the type and order of packing. Here's an example of what a server receiving data in XDR format could look like:

```
import socketserver
import xdrlib

class XdrHandler(socketserver.BaseRequestHandler):
    def handle(self):
        data = self.request.recv(4)   ❶
        unpacker = xdrlib.Unpacker(data)
        message_size = self.unpacker.unpack_uint()   ❷
        data = self.request.recv(message_size)   ❸
        unpacker.reset(data)   ❹
        print(unpacker.unpack_string())   ❺
        print(unpacker.unpack_float())
        self.request.sendall(b'ok')
```

```
server = socketserver.TCPServer(('localhost', 12345), XdrHandler)
server.serve_forever()
```

❶ The data could be of variable length, so we added a packed unsigned integer (4 bytes) with the message size first.

❷ We had to already know we were receiving an unsigned int.

❸ Read the rest of the message on this line first,…

❹ …and on the next line, reset the unpacker with the new data.

❺ We must know a priori that we'll receive one string and then one float.

Of course, if both sides were actually Python programs, you'd be using Pickles. But if the server was from something totally different, this would be the corresponding code for a client sending the data:

```
import socket
import xdrlib

p = xdrlib.Packer()
p.pack_string('Thanks for all the fish!')   ❶
p.pack_float(42.00)
xdr_data = p.get_buffer()
message_length = len(xdr_data)

p.reset()   ❷
p.pack_uint(message_length)
len_plus_data = p.get_buffer() + xdr_data   ❸

with socket.socket() as s:
    s.connect(('localhost', 12345))
    s.sendall(len_plus_data)
    if s.recv(1024):
      print('success')
```

❶ Pack all of the data to be sent first.

❷ Next, pack the message length separately…

❸ …and prepend it to the whole message.

Compression

Python's Standard Library also contain support for data compression and decompression using the zlib, gzip, bzip2, and lzma algorithms, and the creation of ZIP- and tar-format archives. To zip a Pickle, for example:

```
import pickle
import gzip

data = "my very big object"

# To zip and pickle:
with gzip.open('spam.zip', 'wb') as my_zip:
    pickle.dump(data, my_zip)

# And to unzip and unpickle:
with gzip.open('spam.zip', 'rb') as my_zip:
    unpickled_data = pickle.load(my_zip)
```

The buffer protocol

Eli Bendersky, one of Python's core developers, wrote a blog post about reducing the number of in-memory copies Python makes of the same data by using memory buffers (*http://tinyurl.com/bendersky-buffer-protocol*). With his technique, you can even read from a file or socket into an existing buffer. For more information, see Python's buffer protocol documentation (*https://docs.python.org/3/c-api/buffer.html*) and PEP 3118 (*http://legacy.python.org/dev/peps/pep-3118/*), which suggested enhancements that were implemented in Python 3 and backported to Python 2.6 and above.

Distributed Systems

Distributed computer systems collectively accomplish a task (like game play, or an Internet chat room, or a Hadoop calculation) by passing information to each other. This section first lists our most popular libraries for common networking tasks, and then discusses cryptography, which comes hand in hand with this kind of communication.

Networking

In Python, communication for connected networks is usually handled with asynchronous tools or threads, to get around the single-thread limitation of the Global Interpreter Lock. All of the libraries in Table 9-1 solve the same problem—getting around the GIL—with different numbers and with varying amounts of additional features.

Table 9-1. Networking

Library	License	Reasons to use
asyncio	PSF license	• Provides an asynchronous event loop to manage communication with nonblocking sockets and queues, as well as any user-defined coroutines. • Also includes asynchronous sockets and queues.

Library	License	Reasons to use
gevent	MIT license	• Is tightly coupled with libev, the C library for asynchronous I/O. • Provides a fast WSGI server built on libev's HTTP server. • It also has this great gevent.monkey (*http://www.gevent.org/gevent.monkey.html*) module that has patching functions for the standard library, so third-party modules written with blocking sockets can still be used with gevent.
Twisted	MIT license	• Provides asynchronous implementations of newer protocols—for example, GPS, Internet of Connected Products (IoCP), and a Memcached (*https://memcached.org/*) protocol. • It has integrated its event loop with various other event-driven frameworks, like wxPython or GTK. • It also has a built in SSH server and client tools.
PyZMQ	LGPL (ZMQ) and BSD (Python part) license	• Lets you set up and interface with nonblocking message queues using a socket-style API. • It provides socket behaviors (request/response, publish/subscribe, and push/pull) that support distributed computing. • Use this when you want to build your own communication infrastructure; it has "Q" in its name, but is not like RabbitMQ—it could be used to build something like RabbitMQ, or something with a totally different behavior (depending on the socket patterns chosen).
pika	BSD license	• Provides a lightweight AMQP (communication protocol) client to connect with RabbitMQ or other message brokers. • Also includes adapters for use in Tornado or Twisted event loops. • Use this with a message broker like RabbitMQ when you want a lighter weight library (no web dashboard or other bells and whistles) that lets you push content to an external message broker like RabbitMQ.
Celery	BSD license	• Provides an AMQP client to connect with RabbitMQ or other message brokers. • Also has an option to store task states in a backend that can use different popular options like a database connection via SQLAlchemy, Memcached, or others. • Also has an optional web administration and monitoring tool called Flower. • Can be used with a message broker like RabbitMQ for an out-of-the-box message broker system.

Performance networking tools in Python's Standard Library

asyncio (*https://docs.python.org/3/library/asyncio.html*) was introduced in Python 3.4 and includes ideas learned from the developer communities, like those maintaining Twisted and gevent. It's a concurrency tool, and a frequent application of concurrency is for network servers. Python's own documentation for asyncore (a predecessor to asyncio), states:

> There are only two ways to have a program on a single processor do "more than one thing at a time." Multi-threaded programming is the simplest and most popular way to

do it, but there is another very different technique, that lets you have nearly all the advantages of multi-threading, without actually using multiple threads. It's really only practical if your program is largely I/O bound. If your program is processor bound, then pre-emptive scheduled threads are probably what you really need. Network servers are rarely processor bound, however.

asyncio is still only in the Python Standard Library on a provisional basis—the API may change in backward-incompatible ways—so don't get too attached.

Not all of it is new—asyncore (deprecated in Python 3.4) has an event loop, asynchronous sockets[2] and asynchronous file I/O, and asynchat (also deprecated in Python 3.4) had asynchronous queues.[3] The big thing asyncio adds is a formalized implementation of *coroutines*. In Python, this is formally defined as both a *coroutine function*—a function definition beginning with `async def` rather than just `def` (or uses the older syntax, and is decorated with `@asyncio.coroutine`)—and also the object obtained by calling a coroutine function (which is usually some sort of computation or I/O operation). The coroutine can yield the processor and thus be able to participate in an asynchronous event loop, taking turns with other coroutines.

The documentation has pages and pages of detailed examples to help the community, as it's a new concept for the language. It's clear, thorough, and very much worth checking out. In this interactive session, we just want to show the functions for the event loop and some of the classes available:

```
>>> import asyncio
>>>
>>> [l for l in asyncio.__all__ if 'loop' in l]
['get_event_loop_policy', 'set_event_loop_policy',
 'get_event_loop', 'set_event_loop', 'new_event_loop']
>>>
>>> [t for t in asyncio.__all__ if t.endswith('Transport')]
['BaseTransport', 'ReadTransport', 'WriteTransport', 'Transport',
 'DatagramTransport', 'SubprocessTransport']
>>>
>>> [p for p in asyncio.__all__ if p.endswith('Protocol')]
['BaseProtocol', 'Protocol', 'DatagramProtocol',
 'SubprocessProtocol', 'StreamReaderProtocol']
>>>
>>> [q for q in asyncio.__all__ if 'Queue' in q]
['Queue', 'PriorityQueue', 'LifoQueue', 'JoinableQueue',
 'QueueFull', 'QueueEmpty']
```

---

2 A socket is three things: an IP address including port, a transport protocol (like TCP / UDP), and an I/O channel (some sort of file-like object). The Python documentation includes a great intro to sockets (*https:// docs.python.org/3/howto/sockets.html*).

3 The queue doesn't require an IP address or protocol, as it's on the same computer—you just write some data to it and another process can read it. It's like the `multiprocessing.Queue`, but here the I/O is done asynchronously.

gevent

gevent (*http://www.gevent.org/*) is a coroutine-based Python networking library that uses greenlets to provide a high-level synchronous API on top of the C library libev (*http://software.schmorp.de/pkg/libev.html*) event loop. Greenlets are based on the greenlet (*http://greenlet.readthedocs.io/en/latest/*) library—miniature green threads (*https://en.wikipedia.org/wiki/Green_threads*) (or user-level threads, as opposed to threads controlled by the kernel) that the developer has the freedom to explicitly suspend, jumping between greenlets. For a great deep dive into gevent, check out Kavya Joshi's seminar "A Tale of Concurrency Through Creativity in Python." (*http://bit.ly/kavya-joshi-seminar*)

People use gevent because it is lightweight and tightly coupled to its underlying C library, libev, for high performance. If you like the idea of integrating asynchronous I/O and greenlets, this is the library to use. Get it using `pip`:

```
$ pip install gevent
```

Here's an example from the greenlet documentation:

```
>>> import gevent
>>>
>>> from gevent import socket
>>> urls = ['www.google.com', 'www.example.com', 'www.python.org']
>>> jobs = [gevent.spawn(socket.gethostbyname, url) for url in urls]
>>> gevent.joinall(jobs, timeout=2)
>>> [job.value for job in jobs]
['74.125.79.106', '208.77.188.166', '82.94.164.162']
```

The documentation offers many more examples (*https://github.com/gevent/gevent/tree/master/examples*).

Twisted

Twisted (*http://twistedmatrix.com/trac/*) is an event-driven networking engine. It can be used to build applications around many different networking protocols, including HTTP servers and clients, applications using SMTP, POP3, IMAP or SSH protocols, instant messaging and much more (*http://twistedmatrix.com/trac/wiki/Documentation*). Install it using `pip`:

```
$ pip install twisted
```

Twisted has been around since 2002 and has a loyal community. It's like the Emacs of coroutine libraries—with everything built in—because all of these things have to be asynchronous to work together. Probably the most useful tools are an asynchronous wrapper for database connections (in `twisted.enterprise.adbapi`), a DNS server (in `twisted.names`), direct access to packets (in `twisted.pair`), and additional protocols like AMP, GPS, and SOCKSv4 (in `twisted.protocols`). Most of Twisted now works with Python 3—when you `pip install` in a Python 3 environment, you'll get

get everything that's currently been ported. If you find something you wanted in the API (*http://twistedmatrix.com/documents/current/api/moduleIndex.html*) that's not in your Twisted, you should still use Python 2.7.

For more information, consult Jessica McKellar and Abe Fettig's *Twisted* (O'Reilly). In addition, this webpage shows over 42 Twisted examples (*http://twistedmatrix.com/documents/current/core/examples/*), and this one shows their latest speed performance (*http://speed.twistedmatrix.com/*).

PyZMQ

PyZMQ (*http://zeromq.github.com/pyzmq/*) is the Python binding for ZeroMQ (*http://www.zeromq.org/*). You can get it using `pip`:

```
$ pip install pyzmq
```

ØMQ (also spelled ZeroMQ, 0MQ, or ZMQ) describes itself as a messaging library designed to have a familiar socket-style API, and aimed at use in scalable distributed or concurrent applications. Basically, it implements asynchronous sockets with queues attached and provides a custom list of socket "types" that determine how the I/O on each socket behaves. Here's an example:

```
import zmq
context = zmq.Context()
server = context.socket(zmq.REP)   ❶
server.bind('tcp://127.0.0.1:5000')   ❷

while True:
    message = server.recv().decode('utf-8')
    print('Client said: {}'.format(message))
    server.send(bytes('I don't know.', 'utf-8'))

# ~~~~~ and in another file ~~~~~

import zmq
context = zmq.Context()
client = context.socket(zmq.REQ)   ❸
client.connect('tcp://127.0.0.1:5000')   ❹

client.send(bytes("What's for lunch?", 'utf-8'))
response = client.recv().decode('utf-8')
print('Server replied: {}'.format(response))
```

❶ The socket type `zmq.REP` corresponds to their "request-response" paradigm.

❷ Like with normal sockets, you bind the server to an IP and port.

❸ The client type is `zmq.REQ`—that's all, ZMQ defines a number of these as constants: `zmq.REQ`, `zmq.REP`, `zmq.PUB`, `zmq.SUB`, `zmq.PUSH`, `zmq.PULL`, `zmq.PAIR`. They determine how the socket's sending and receiving behaves.

❹ As usual, the client connects to the server's bound IP and port.

So, these look and quack like sockets, enhanced with queues and various I/O patterns. The point of the patterns is to provide the building blocks for a distributed network. The basic patterns for the socket types are:

request-reply
> `zmq.REQ` and `zmq.REP` connect a set of clients to a set of services. This can be for a remote procedure call pattern or a task distribution pattern.

publish-subscribe
> `zmq.PUB` and `zmq.SUB` connect a set of publishers to a set of subscribers. This is a data distribution pattern—one node is distributing data to other nodes, or this can be chained to fan out into a distribution tree.

push-pull (or pipeline)
> `zmq.PUSH` and `zmq.PULL` connect nodes in a fan-out/fan-in pattern that can have multiple steps, and loops. This is a parallel task distribution and collection pattern.

One great advantage of ZeroMQ over message-oriented middleware is that it can be used for message queuing without a dedicated message broker. PyZMQ's documentation (*http://pyzmq.readthedocs.io/*) notes some enhancements they added, like tunneling via SSH. The rest of the documentation for the ZeroMQ API is better on the main ZeroMQ guide. (*http://zguide.zeromq.org/page:all*)

RabbitMQ

RabbitMQ (*http://www.rabbitmq.com/*) is an open source message broker software that implements the Advanced Message Queuing Protocol (AMQP). A message broker is an intermediary program that receives messages from senders and sends them to receivers according to a protocol. Any client that also implements AMQP can communicate with RabbitMQ. To get RabbitMQ, go to the RabbitMQ download page (*https://www.rabbitmq.com/download.html*), and follow the instructions for your operating system.

Client libraries that interface with the broker are available for all major programming languages. The top two for Python are pika and Celery—either can be installed with pip:

```
$ pip install pika
$ pip install celery
```

pika

pika (*https://pypi.python.org/pypi/pika*) is a lightweight, pure-Python AMQP 0-9-1 client, preferred by RabbitMQ. RabbitMQ's introductory tutorials (*https://www.rabbitmq.com/getstarted.html*) for Python use pika. There's also an entire page of examples (*https://pika.readthedocs.io/en/0.10.0/examples.html*) to learn from. We recommend playing with pika when you first set up RabbitMQ, regardless of your final library choice, because it is straightforward without the extra features and so crystallizes the concepts.

Celery

Celery (*https://pypi.python.org/pypi/celery*) is a much more featureful AMQP client—it can use either RabbitMQ or Redis (a distributed in-memory data store) as a message broker, can track the tasks and results (and optionally store them in a user-selected backend), and has a web administration tool/task monitor, Flower (*https://pypi.python.org/pypi/flower*). It is popular in the web development community, and there are integration packages for Django, Pyramid, Pylons, web2py, and Tornado (Flask doesn't need one). Start with the Celery tutorial (*http://tinyurl.com/celery-first-steps*).

Cryptography

In 2013, the Python Cryptographic Authority (*https://github.com/pyca*) (PyCA) was formed. They are a group of developers all interested in providing high-quality cryptography libraries to the Python community.[4] They provide tools to encrypt and decrypt messages given the appropriate keys, and cryptographic hash functions to irreversibly but repeatably obfuscate passwords or other secret data.

Except for pyCrypto, all of the libraries in Table 9-2 are maintained by the PyCA. Almost all are built on the C library OpenSSL (*https://www.openssl.org/*), except when noted.

---

4 The birth of the cryptography library, and some of the backstory for the motivation behind this new effort, is described in Jake Edge's blog post "The state of crypto in Python." (*http://bit.ly/raim-kehrer-talk*) The cryptography library it describes is a lower-level library, intended to be imported by higher-level libraries like pyOpenSSL that most of us would use. Edge quotes Jarret Raim and Paul Kehrer's talk about the State of Crypto in Python (*https://www.youtube.com/watch?v=r_Pj__qjBvA*), saying their test suite has over 66,000 tests, run 77 times per build.

Table 9-2. Cryptography options

Option	License	Reason to use
ssl and hashlib (and in Python 3.6, secrets)	Python Software Foundation license	• Hashlib provides a decent password hashing algorithm, updated at the schedule of Python versions, and ssl provides an SSL/TLS client (and server, but it may not have the *latest* updates). • Secrets is a random number generator suitable for cryptographic uses.
pyOpenSSL	Apache v2.0 license	• It uses the most up-to-date version of OpenSSL in Python and provides functions in OpenSSL that aren't exposed by the Standard Library's ssl module.
PyNaCl	Apache v2.0 license	• It contains Python bindings for libsodium.[a]
libnacl	Apache license	• It's the Python interface to libsodium for people who are using the Salt Stack (*http://saltstack.com/*).
cryptography	Apache v2.0 license or BSD license	• It provides direct access to cryptographic primitives built on OpenSSL. The higher-level pyOpenSSL is what most of us would use.
pyCrypto	Public Domain	• This library is older, and built using its own C library, but was in the past the most popular cryptography library in Python.
bcrypt	Apache v2.0 license	• It provides the bcrypt hash function,[b] and is useful for people who want that or have previously used py-bcrypt.

[a] libsodium (*https://download.libsodium.org/doc/*) is a fork of the Networking and Cryptography library (NaCl, pronounced "salt"); its philosophy is to curate specific algorithms that are performant and easy to use.
[b] The library actually contains the C source code and builds it on installation using the C Fast Function Interface we described earlier. Bcrypt (*https://en.wikipedia.org/wiki/Bcrypt*) is based on the Blowfish encryption algorithm.

The following sections provide additional details about the libraries listed in Table 9-2.

ssl, hashlib, and secrets

The ssl module (*https://docs.python.org/3/library/ssl.html*) in Python's Standard Library provides a socket API (`ssl.socket`) that behaves like a standard socket, but is wrapped by the SSL protocol, plus `ssl.SSLContext`, which contains an SSL connection's configurations. And http (or httplib in Python 2) also uses it for HTTPS support. If you're using Python 3.5, you also have memory BIO support (*https://docs.python.org/3/whatsnew/3.5.html#ssl*)—so the socket writes I/O to a buffer instead of its destination, enabling things like hooks for hex encoding/decoding before write/ upon read.

Major security enhancements happened in Python 3.4—detailed in the release notes (*https://docs.python.org/3.4/whatsnew/3.4.html*)—to support newer transport protocols and hash algorithms. These issues were so important that they were backported to Python 2.7 as described in PEP 466 (*https://www.python.org/dev/peps/pep-0466/*) and PEP 476 (*https://www.python.org/dev/peps/pep-0476/*). You can learn all about them in Benjamin Peterson's talk about the state of ssl in Python (*http://bit.ly/ peterson-talk*).

 If you're using Python 2.7, be sure you have at least 2.7.9, or that your version at least has incorporated PEP 476 (*https:// www.python.org/dev/peps/pep-0476/*)—so that by default HTTP clients will perform certificate verification when connecting using the https protocol. Or, just always use Requests (*http://docs.python-requests.org/en/master/*) because that has always been its default.

The Python team recommends using the SSL defaults if you have no special requirements for your security policy for client use. This example showing a secure mail client is from the section within the documentation for the ssl library, "Security considerations," (*http://bit.ly/ssl-security-consider*) which you should read if you're going to use the library:

```
>>> import ssl, smtplib
>>> smtp = smtplib.SMTP("mail.python.org", port=587)
>>> context = ssl.create_default_context()
>>> smtp.starttls(context=context)
(220, b'2.0.0 Ready to start TLS')
```

To confirm that a message didn't get corrupted during transmission, use the hmac module, which implements the Keyed-Hashing for Message Authentication (HMAC) algorithm described in RFC 2104 (*https://tools.ietf.org/html/rfc2104.html*). It works with a message hashed with any of the algorithms in the set hashlib.algorithms_available. For more, see the Python Module of the Week's hmac example (*https://pymotw.com/2/hmac/*). And if it's installed, hmac.compare_digest() provides a constant-time comparison between digests to help protect against timing attacks— where the attacker attempts to infer your algorithm from the time it takes to run the digest comparison.

Python's hashlib module can be used to generate hashed passwords for secure storage or checksums to confirm data integrity during transmission. The Password-Based Key Derivation Function 2 (PBKDF2) (*https://en.wikipedia.org/wiki/PBKDF2*), recommended in NIST Special Publication 800-132 (*http://bit.ly/nist-recommendation*), is currently considered one of the best options for password hashing. Here's an example use of the function using a salt[5] and 10,000 iterations of the Secure Hash Algorithm 256-bit hash (SHA-256) to generate a hashed password (the choices for different hash algorithms or iterations let the programmer balance robustness with a desired response speed):

```python
import os
import hashlib

def hash_password(password, salt_len=16, iterations=10000, encoding='utf-8'):
    salt = os.urandom(salt_len)
    hashed_password = hashlib.pbkdf2_hmac(
        hash_name='sha256',
        password=bytes(password, encoding),
        salt=salt,
        iterations=iterations
    )
    return salt, iterations, hashed_password
```

The secrets library (*https://docs.python.org/3.6/library/secrets.html*) was proposed in PEP 506 (*https://www.python.org/dev/peps/pep-0506/*) and will be available starting with Python 3.6. It provides functions for generating secure tokens, suitable for applications such as password resets and hard-to-guess URLs. Its documentation contains examples and best-practice recommendations to manage a basic level of security.

pyOpenSSL

When Cryptography came out, pyOpenSSL (*https://pyopenssl.readthedocs.io/en/stable/*) updated its bindings to use Cryptography's CFFI-based bindings for the OpenSSL library and joined the PyCA umbrella. pyOpenSSL is separate from the Python Standard Library on purpose so that it can release updates at the speed of the security community[6]—it's built on the newest OpenSSL, and not, like Python is, built on the OpenSSL that comes with your operating system (unless you build it yourself against a newer version). Generally if you're building a server, you'd want to use pyOpenSSL—see Twisted's SSL documentation (*http://twistedmatrix.com/documents/12.0.0/core/howto/ssl.html*) for an example of how they use pyOpenSSL.

Install it using `pip`:

```
$ pip install pyOpenSSL
```

---

5 A *salt* is a random string that further obfuscates the hash; if everyone used the same algorithm, a nefarious actor could generate a lookup table of common passwords and their hashes, and use them to "decode" stolen password files. So, to thwart this, people append a random string (a "salt") to the password—they just also have to store that random string for future use.

6 Anybody can join the PyCA's cryptography-dev listserv (*https://mail.python.org/mailman/listinfo/cryptography-dev*) to keep up with development and other news...and the OpenSSL listserv (*https://mta.openssl.org/mailman/listinfo/openssl-announce*) for OpenSSL news.

and import it with the name OpenSSL. This example shows a couple of the functions available:

```
>>> import OpenSSL
>>>
>>> OpenSSL.crypto.get_elliptic_curve('Oakley-EC2N-3')
<Curve 'Oakley-EC2N-3'>
>>>
>>> OpenSSL.SSL.Context(OpenSSL.SSL.TLSv1_2_METHOD)
<OpenSSL.SSL.Context object at 0x10d778ef0>
```

The pyOpenSSL team maintains example code (*https://github.com/pyca/pyopenssl/ tree/master/examples*) that includes certificate generation, a way to start using SSL over an already-connected socket, and a secure XMLRPC server.

PyNaCl and libnacl

The idea behind libsodium (*http://bit.ly/introducing-sodium*), the C library backend for both PyNaCl and libnacl, is to intentionally *not* provide users with many choices —just the best one for their situation. It does not support all of the TLS protocol; if you want that, use pyOpenSSL. If all you want is an encrypted connection with some other computer you're in control of, with your own protocols of your choosing, and you don't want to deal with OpenSSL, then use this.[7]

 Pronounce *PyNaCl* as "py-salt" and *libnacl* as "lib-salt"—they're both derived from the NaCl (salt) library (*https://nacl.cr.yp.to/*).

We recommend PyNaCl (*https://pypi.python.org/pypi/PyNaCl*) over libnacl (*https:// libnacl.readthedocs.io/*) because it's under the PyCA umbrella, and you don't have to install libsodium separately. The libraries are virtually the same—PyNaCl uses CFFI bindings for the C libraries, and libnacl uses ctypes—so it really doesn't matter that much. Install PyNaCl using pip:

```
$ pip install PyNaCl
```

And follow the PyNaCl examples (*https://pynacl.readthedocs.io/en/latest/*) in its documentation.

---

7 If you're paranoid, want to be able to audit 100% of your crypto code, don't care that it's a tad slow, and aren't so interested in having the most current algorithms and defaults, try TweetNaCl (*https://tweetnacl.cr.yp.to/*), which is a single file crypto library that fits in 100 tweets. Because PyNaCl bundles libsodium in its release, you can probably just drop in TweetNaCl and still run most everything (however, we didn't try this option).

Cryptography

Cryptography (*https://cryptography.io/en/latest/*) provides cryptographic recipes and primitives. It supports Python 2.6–2.7, Python 3.3+, and PyPy. The PyCA recommends the higher-level interface in pyOpenSSL for most uses.

Cryptography is divided into two layers: recipes and hazardous materials (hazmat). The recipes layer provides a simple API for proper symmetric encryption, and the hazmat layer provides low-level cryptographic primitives. Install it using `pip`:

```
$ pip install cryptography
```

This example uses a high-level symmetric encryption recipe—the only high-level function in this library:

```
from cryptography.fernet import Fernet
key = Fernet.generate_key()
cipher_suite = Fernet(key)
cipher_text = cipher_suite.encrypt(b"A really secret message.")
plain_text = cipher_suite.decrypt(cipher_text)
```

PyCrypto

PyCrypto (*https://www.dlitz.net/software/pycrypto/*) provides secure hash functions and various encryption algorithms. It supports Python version 2.1+ and Python 3+. Because the C code is custom, the PyCA was wary of adopting it, but it was also the de facto cryptography library for Python for years, so you'll see it in older code. Install it using `pip`:

```
$ pip install pycrypto
```

And use it like this:

```
from Crypto.Cipher import AES
# Encryption
encryption_suite = AES.new('This is a key123', AES.MODE_CBC, 'This is an IV456')
cipher_text = encryption_suite.encrypt("A really secret message.")

# Decryption
decryption_suite = AES.new('This is a key123', AES.MODE_CBC, 'This is an IV456')
plain_text = decryption_suite.decrypt(cipher_text)
```

bcrypt

If you want to use the bcrypt (*https://en.wikipedia.org/wiki/Bcrypt*) algorithm for your passwords, use this library. Previous users of py-bcrypt should find it easy to transition, because it is compatible. Install it using `pip`:

```
pip install bcrypt
```

It only has two functions: bcrypt.hashpw() and bcrypt.gensalt(). The latter lets you choose how many iterations to use—more iterations will make the algorithm slower (it defaults to a reasonable number). Here's an example:

```
>>> import bcrypt
>>>>
>>> password = bytes('password', 'utf-8')
>>> hashed_pw = bcrypt.hashpw(password, bcrypt.gensalt(14))
>>> hashed_pw
b'$2b$14$qAmVOCfEmHeC8Wd5BoF1W.7ny9M7CSZpOR5WPvdKFXDbkkX8rGJ.e'
```

We store the hashed password somewhere:

```
>>> import binascii
>>> hexed_hashed_pw = binascii.hexlify(hashed_pw)
>>> store_password(user_id=42, password=hexed_hashed_pw)
```

and when it's time to check the password, use the hashed password as the second argument to bcrypt.hashpw() like this:

```
>>> hexed_hashed_pw = retrieve_password(user_id=42)
>>> hashed_pw = binascii.unhexlify(hexed_hashed_pw)
>>>
>>> bcrypt.hashpw(password, hashed_pw)
b'$2b$14$qAmVOCfEmHeC8Wd5BoF1W.7ny9M7CSZpOR5WPvdKFXDbkkX8rGJ.e'
>>>
>>> bcrypt.hashpw(password, hashed_pw) == hashed_pw
True
```

## CHAPTER 10

Data Manipulation

This chapter summarizes the popular Python libraries related to data manipulation: numeric, text, images, and audio. Almost all of the libraries described here serve a unique purpose, so this chapter's goal is to describe these libraries, not compare them. Unless noted, all of them can be installed directly from PyPI using `pip`:

```
$ pip install library
```

Table 10-1 briefly describes these libraries.

Table 10-1. Data tools

Python library	License	Reason to use
IPython	Apache 2.0 license	• Provides enhanced Python interpreter, with input history, integrated debugger, and graphics and plots in-terminal (with the Qt-enabled version).
Numpy	BSD 3-clause license	• Provides multidimensional arrays and linear algebra tools, optimized for speed.
SciPy	BSD license	• Provides functions and utilities related to engineering and science, from linear algebra to signal processing, integration, root finding, statistical distributions, and other topics.
Matplotlib	BSD license	• Provides scientific plotting.
Pandas	BSD license	• Provides series and DataFrame objects that can be sorted, merged, grouped, aggregated, indexed, windowed, and subset—a lot like an R Data Frame or the contents of a SQL query.

Python library	License	Reason to use
Scikit-Learn	BSD 3-clause license	• Provides machine learning algorithms, including dimensionality reduction classification, regression, clustering, model selection, imputing missing data, and preprocessing.
Rpy2	GPLv2 license	• Provides an interface to R that allows execution of R functions from within Python, and passing data between the two environments.
SymPy	BSD license	• Provides symbolic mathematics, including series expansions, limits, and calculus, aiming to be a full computer algebra system.
nltk	Apache license	• Provides comprehensive natural language toolkit, with models and training data in multiple languages.
pillow / PIL	Standard PIL license (like MIT)	• Provides huge number of file formats, plus some simple image filtering and other processing.
cv2	Apache 2.0 license	• Provides computer vision routines suitable for real-time analysis in videos, including already-trained face and person detection algorithms.
Scikit-Image	BSD license	• Provides image processing routines—filtering, adjustment, color separation, edge, blob, and corner detection, segmentaton, and more.

Nearly all of the libraries described in Table 10-1 and detailed in the rest of this chapter depend on C libraries, and specifically on SciPy (*https://www.scipy.org/*), or one of its dependencies, NumPy (*http://www.numpy.org/*). This means you may have trouble installing these if you're on a Windows system. If you primarily use Python for analyzing scientific data, and you're not familiar with compiling C and FORTRAN code on Windows already, we recommend using Anaconda or one of the other options discussed in "Commercial Python Redistributions" on page 19. Otherwise, always try `pip install` first and if that fails, look at the SciPy installation guide (*https://www.scipy.org/install.html*).

Scientific Applications

Python is frequently used for high-performance scientific applications. It is widely used in academia and scientific projects because it is easy to write and performs well.

Due to its high performance nature, scientific computing in Python often utilizes external libraries, typically written in faster languages (like C, or FORTRAN for matrix operations). The main libraries used are all part of the "SciPy Stack:" NumPy (*http://www.numpy.org/*), SciPy (*https://www.scipy.org/scipylib/index.html*), SymPy (*http://sympy.org/*), Pandas (*http://pandas.pydata.org/*), Matplotlib (*http://matplotlib.org/*), and IPython (*http://ipython.org/*). Going into detail about these libraries is beyond the scope of this book. However, a comprehensive introduction to the scientific Python ecosystem can be found in the Python Scientific Lecture Notes (*http://scipy-lectures.github.com/*).

IPython

IPython (*http://ipython.org/*) is an enhanced version of Python interpreter, with color interface, more detailed error messages, and an *inline mode* that allows graphics and plots to be displayed in the terminal (Qt-based version). It is the default kernel for Jupyter notebooks (discussed in "Jupyter Notebooks" on page 193), and the default interpreter in the Spyder IDE (discussed in "Spyder" on page 33). IPython comes installed with Anaconda, which we described in "Commercial Python Redistributions" on page 19.

NumPy

NumPy (*http://numpy.scipy.org/*) is part of the SciPy project but is released as a separate library so people who only need the basic requirements can use it without installing the rest of SciPy. NumPy cleverly overcomes the problem of running slower algorithms on Python by using multidimensional arrays and functions that operate on arrays. Any algorithm can then be expressed as a function on arrays, allowing the algorithms to be run quickly. The backend is the Automatically Tuned Linear Algebra Software (ATLAS) (*http://math-atlas.sourceforge.net/*) library,[1] and other low-level libraries written in C and FORTRAN. NumPy is compatible with Python versions 2.6+ and 3.2+.

Here is an example of a matrix multiplication, using `array.dot()`, and "broadcasting," which is element-wise multiplication where the row or column is repeated across the missing dimension:

```
>>> import numpy as np
>>>
>>> x = np.array([[1,2,3],[4,5,6]])
>>> x
array([[1, 2, 3],
       [4, 5, 6]])
>>>
>>> x.dot([2,2,1])
array([ 9, 24])
```

---

[1] ATLAS is an ongoing software project that provides tested, performant linear algebra libraries. It provides C and FORTRAN 77 interfaces to routines from the well-known Basic Linear Algebra Subset (BLAS) and Linear Algebra PACKage (LAPACK).

```
>>>
>>> x  *  [[1],[0]]
array([[1, 2, 3],
       [0, 0, 0]])
```

SciPy

SciPy (*http://scipy.org/*) uses NumPy for more mathematical functions. SciPy uses NumPy arrays as the basic data structure, and comes with modules for various commonly used tasks in scientific programming, including linear algebra, calculus, special functions and constants, and signal processing.

Here's an example from SciPy's set of physical constants:

```
>>> import scipy.constants
>>> fahrenheit = 212
>>> scipy.constants.F2C(fahrenheit)
100.0
>>> scipy.constants.physical_constants['electron mass']
(9.10938356e-31, 'kg', 1.1e-38)
```

Matplotlib

Matplotlib (*http://matplotlib.sourceforge.net/*) is a flexible plotting library for creating interactive 2D and 3D plots that can also be saved as manuscript-quality figures. The API in many ways reflects that of MATLAB (*http://www.mathworks.com/products/matlab/*), easing transition of MATLAB users to Python. Many examples, along with the source code to re-create them, are available in the Matplotlib gallery (*http://matplotlib.sourceforge.net/gallery.html*).

Those who work with statistics should also look at Seaborn (*https://stanford.edu/~mwaskom/software/seaborn*), a newer graphics library specifically for statistics visualization that is growing in popularity. It is featured in this blog post about getting started in data science (*http://bit.ly/data-science-python-guide*).

For web-capable plots, try Bokeh (*http://bokeh.pydata.org*), which uses its own visualization libraries, or Plotly (*https://plot.ly/*), which is based on the JavaScript library D3.js (*https://d3js.org/*), although the free version of Plotly may require storing your plots on their server.

Pandas

Pandas (*http://pandas.pydata.org/*) (the name is derived from Panel Data) is a data manipulation library based on NumPy which provides many useful functions for accessing, indexing, merging and grouping data easily. The main data structure (Data Frame) is close to what could be found in the R statistical software environment (i.e., heterogeneous data tables—with strings in some columns and numbers in others—with name indexing, time series operations and auto-alignment of data). But it also can be operated on like a SQL table or Excel Pivot Table—using methods like groupby() or functions like pandas.rolling_mean().

Scikit-Learn

Scikit-Learn (*https://pypi.python.org/pypi/scikit-learn*) is a machine learning library that provides dimension reduction, missing data imputation, regression and classification models, tree models, clustering, automatic model parameter tuning, plotting (via matplotlib), and more. It is well documented and comes with tons of examples (*http://scikit-learn.org/stable/auto_examples/index.html*). Scikit-Learn operates on NumPy arrays but can usually interface with Pandas data frames without much trouble.

Rpy2

Rpy2 (*https://pypi.python.org/pypi/rpy2*) is a Python binding for the R statistical package allowing the execution of R functions from Python and passing data back and forth between the two environments. Rpy2 is the object-oriented implementation of the Rpy (*http://rpy2.bitbucket.org/*) bindings.

decimal, fractions, and numbers

Python has defined a framework of abstract base classes to develop numeric types from Number, the root of all numeric types, to Integral, Rational, Real, and Complex. Developers can subclass these to develop other numeric types according to the instructions in the numbers library (*https://docs.python.org/3.5/library/numbers.html*).[2] There is also a decimal.Decimal class that is aware of numerical precision, for accounting and other precision-critical tasks. The type hierarchy works as expected:

```
>>> import decimal
>>> import fractions
>>> from numbers import Complex, Real, Rational, Integral
>>>
>>> d = decimal.Decimal(1.11, decimal.Context(prec=5))  # precision
>>>
>>> for x in (3, fractions.Fraction(2,3), 2.7, complex(1,2), d):
...     print('{:>10}'.format(str(x)[:8]),
...           [isinstance(x, y) for y in (Complex, Real, Rational, Integral)])
...
         3 [True, True, True, True]
```

2 One popular tool that makes use of Python numbers is SageMath (*http://www.sagemath.org/*)—a large, comprehensive tool that defines classes to represents fields, rings, algebras and domains, plus provides symbolic tools derived from SymPy and numerical tools derived from NumPy, SciPy, and many other Python and non-Python libraries.

```
       2/3 [True, True, True, False]
       2.7 [True, True, False, False]
    (1+2j) [True, False, False, False]
  1.110000 [False, False, False, False]
```

The exponential, trigonometric, and other common functions are in the *math* library, and corresponding functions for complex numbers are in *cmath*. The *random* library provides pseudorandom numbers using the Mersenne Twister (*https://en.wikipe dia.org/wiki/Mersenne_Twister*) as its core generator. As of Python 3.4, the statistics module in the Standard Library provides the mean and median, as well as the sample and population standard deviation and variance.

SymPy

SymPy (*https://pypi.python.org/pypi/sympy*) is *the* library to use when doing symbolic mathematics in Python. It is written entirely in Python, with optional extensions for speed, plotting, and interactive sessions.

SymPy's symbolic functions operate on SymPy objects such as symbols, functions, and expressions to make other symbolic expressions, like this:

```
>>> import sympy as sym
>>>
>>> x = sym.Symbol('x')
>>> f = sym.exp(-x**2/2) / sym.sqrt(2 * sym.pi)
>>> f
sqrt(2)*exp(-x**2/2)/(2*sqrt(pi))
```

These can be symbolically or numerically integrated:

```
>>> sym.integrate(f, x)
erf(sqrt(2)*x/2)/2
>>>
>>> sym.N(sym.integrate(f, (x, -1, 1)))
0.682689492137086
```

The library can also differentiate, expand expressions into series, restrict symbols to be real, commutative, or a dozen or so other categories, locate the nearest rational number (given an accuracy) to a float, and much more.

Text Manipulation and Text Mining

Python's string manipulation tools are often why people start using the language to begin with. We'll cover some highlights from Python's Standard Library quickly, and then move to the library nearly everyone in the community uses for text mining: the Natural Language ToolKit (nltk) (*https://pypi.python.org/pypi/nltk*).

String Tools in Python's Standard Library

For languages with special behavior of lowercase characters, `str.casefold()` helps with lowercase letters:

```
>>> 'Grünwalder Straße'.upper()
'GRÜNWALDER STRASSE'
>>> 'Grünwalder Straße'.lower()
'grünwalder straße'
>>> 'Grünwalder Straße'.casefold()
'grünwalder strasse'
```

Python's regular expression library *re* is comprehensive and powerful—we saw it in action in "Regular expressions (readability counts)" on page 155, so we won't add more here, except that the `help(re)` documentation is so complete that you won't need to open a browser while coding.

Finally, the *difflib* module in the Standard Library identifies differences between strings, and has a function `get_close_matches()` that can help with misspellings when there are a known set of correct answers (e.g., for error prompts on a travel website):

```
>>> import difflib
>>> capitals = ('Montgomery', 'Juneau', 'Phoenix', 'Little Rock')
>>> difflib.get_close_matches('Fenix', capitals)
['Phoenix']
```

nltk

The Natural Language ToolKit (nltk) (*https://pypi.python.org/pypi/nltk*) is *the* Python tool for text analysis: originally released by Steven Bird and Edward Loper to aid students in Bird's course on Natural Language Processing (NLP) at the University of Pennsylvania in 2001, it has grown to an expansive library covering multiple languages and containing algorithms for recent research in the field. It is available under the Apache 2.0 license and is downloaded from PyPI over 100,000 times per month. Its creators have an accompanying book, *Natural Language Processing with Python* (O'Reilly), that is accessible as a course text introducing both Python and NLP.

You can install nltk from the command line using `pip`.[3] It also relies on NumPy, so install that first:

```
$ pip install numpy
$ pip install nltk
```

---

3 On Windows, it currently appears that nltk is only available for Python 2.7. Try it on Python 3, though; the labels that say Python 2.7 may just be out of date.

If you're using Windows, and can't get the NumPy installed using `pip` to work, you can try following the instructions in this Stack Overflow post (*http://bit.ly/numpy-install-win*). The size and scope of the library may unnecessarily scare some people away, so here's a tiny example to demonstrate how easy simple uses can be. First, we need to get a dataset from the separately downloadable (*http://www.nltk.org/data.html*) collection of corpora (*http://www.nltk.org/nltk_data/*), including tagging tools for multiple languages and datasets to test algorithms against. These are licensed separate from nltk, so be sure to check your selection's individual license. If you know the name of the corpus you want to download (in our case, the Punkt tokenizer,[4] which we can use to split up text files into sentences or words), you can do it on the command line:

```
$ python3 -m nltk.downloader punkt --dir=/usr/local/share/nltk_data
```

Or you can download it in an interactive session—"stopwords" contains a list of common words that tend to overpower word counts, such as "the", "in", or "and" in many languages:

```
>>> import nltk
>>> nltk.download('stopwords', download_dir='/usr/local/share/nltk_data')
[nltk_data] Downloading package stopwords to /usr/local/share/nltk_data...
[nltk_data]    Unzipping corpora/stopwords.zip.
True
```

And if you don't know the name of the corpus you want, you can launch an interactive downloader from the Python interpreter by invoking `nltk.download()` without its first argument:

```
>>> import nltk
>>> nltk.download(download_dir='/usr/local/share/nltk_data')
```

Then we can load the dataset we care about, and process and analyze it. In this code sample, we are loading a saved copy of the Zen of Python:

```
>>> import nltk
>>> from nltk.corpus import stopwords
>>> import string
>>>
>>> stopwords.ensure_loaded()   ❶
>>> text = open('zen.txt').read()
>>> tokens = [
...     t.casefold() for t in nltk.tokenize.word_tokenize(text)   ❷
...     if t not in string.punctuation
... ]
```

---

4 The Punkt tokenizer algorithm was introduced by Tibor Kiss and Jan Strunk (*http://bit.ly/kiss-strunk-paper*) in 2006, and is a language-independent way to identify sentence boundaries—for example, "Mrs. Smith and Johann S. Bach listened to Vivaldi" would correctly be identified as a single sentence. It has to be trained on a large dataset, but the default tokenizer, in English, has already been trained for us.

```
>>>
>>> counter = {}
>>> for bigram in nltk.bigrams(tokens):    ❸
...     counter[bigram] = 1 if bigram not in counter else counter[bigram] + 1
...
>>> def print_counts(counter):  # We'll reuse this
...     for ngram, count in sorted(
...             counter.items(), key=lambda kv: kv[1], reverse=True):    ❹
...         if count > 1:
...             print ('{:>25}: {}'.format(str(ngram), '*' * count))    ❺
...
>>> print_counts(counter)
        ('better', 'than'): ********    ❻
         ('is', 'better'): *******
         ('explain', 'it'): **
             ('one', '--'): **
        ('to', 'explain'): **
             ('if', 'the'): **
   ('the', 'implementation'): **
  ('implementation', 'is'): **
>>>
>>> kept_tokens = [t for t in tokens if t not in stopwords.words()]    ❼
>>>
>>> from collections import Counter    ❽
>>> c = Counter(kept_tokens)
>>> c.most_common(5)
[('better', 8), ('one', 3), ('--', 3), ('although', 3), ('never', 3)]
```

❶ The corpora are loaded lazily, so we need to do this to actually load the stop-words corpus.

❷ The tokenizer requires a trained model—the Punkt tokenizer (default) comes with a model trained on English (also default).

❸ A bigram is a pair of adjacent words. We are iterating over the bigrams and counting how many times they occur.

❹ The sorted() function here is being keyed on the count, and sorted in reverse order.

❺ The '{:>25}' right-justifies the string with a total width of 25 characters.

❻ The most frequently occurring bigram in the Zen of Python is "better than."

❼ This time, to avoid high counts of "the" and "is", we remove the stopwords.

❽ In Python 3.1 and later, you can use collections.Counter for the counting.

There's a lot more in this library—take a weekend and go for it!

SyntaxNet

Google's SyntaxNet, built on top of TensorFlow, provides a trained English parser (named Parsey McParseface) and the framework to build other models, even in other languages, provided you have labeled data. It is currently only available for Python 2.7; detailed instructions for downloading and using it are on SyntaxNet's main GitHub page (*https://github.com/tensorflow/models/tree/master/syntaxnet*).

Image Manipulation

The three most popular image processing and manipulation libraries in Python are Pillow (a friendly fork of the Python Imaging Library [PIL]—which is good for format conversions and simple image processing), cv2 (the Python bindings for Open-Source Computer Vision [OpenCV] that can be used for real-time face detection and other advanced algorithms), and the newer Scikit-Image, which provides simple image processing, plus primitives like blob, shape, and edge detection. The following sections provide some more information about each of these libraries.

Pillow

The Python Imaging Library (*http://www.pythonware.com/products/pil/*), or PIL for short, is one of the core libraries for image manipulation in Python. Its was last released in 2009 and was never ported to Python 3. Luckily, there's an actively developed fork of PIL called Pillow (*http://python-pillow.github.io/*)—it's easier to install, runs on all operating systems, and supports Python 3.

Before installing Pillow, you'll have to install Pillow's prerequisites. Find the instructions for your platform in the Pillow installation instructions (*https://pillow.readthe docs.org/en/3.0.0/installation.html*). After that, it's straightforward:

```
$ pip install Pillow
```

Here is a brief example use of Pillow (yes, the module name to import from is `PIL` not `Pillow`):

```
from PIL import Image, ImageFilter
# Read image
im = Image.open( 'image.jpg' )
# Display image
im.show()

# Applying a filter to the image
im_sharp = im.filter( ImageFilter.SHARPEN )
#Saving the filtered image to a new file
im_sharp.save( 'image_sharpened.jpg', 'JPEG' )

# Splitting the image into its respective bands (i.e., Red, Green,
# and Blue for RGB)
r,g,b = im_sharp.split()
```

```
# Viewing EXIF data embedded in image
exif_data = im._getexif()
exif_data
```

There are more examples of the Pillow library in the Pillow tutorial (*http://bit.ly/opencv-python-tutorial*).

cv2

OpenSource Computer Vision (*http://docs.opencv.org/3.1.0/index.html*), more commonly known as OpenCV, is a more advanced image manipulation and processing software than PIL. It is written in C and C++, and focuses on real-time computer vision. For example, it has the first model used in real-time face detection (already trained on thousands of faces; this example (*https://github.com/Itseez/opencv/blob/master/samples/python/facedetect.py*) shows it being used in Python code), a face recognition model, and a person detection model, among others. It has been implemented in several languages and is widely used.

In Python, image processing using OpenCV is implemented using the cv2 and NumPy libraries. OpenCV version 3 has bindings for Python 3.4 and above, but the cv2 library is still linked to OpenCV2, which does not. The installation instructions in the OpenCV tutorial page (*http://tinyurl.com/opencv3-py-tutorial*) have explicit details for Windows and Fedora, using Python 2.7. On OS X, you're on your own.[5] Finally, here's an option using Python 3 on Ubuntu (*http://tinyurl.com/opencv3-py3-ubuntu*). If the installation becomes difficult, you can downlad Anaconda and use that instead; they have cv2 binaries for all platforms, and you consult the blog post "Up & Running: OpenCV3, Python 3, & Anaconda" (*http://tinyurl.com/opencv3-py3-anaconda*) to use cv2 and Python 3 on Anaconda.

Here's an example use of cv2:

```
from cv2 import *
import numpy as np
#Read Image
img = cv2.imread('testimg.jpg')
#Display Image
cv2.imshow('image',img)
cv2.waitKey(0)
cv2.destroyAllWindows()
```

---

5 These steps worked for us: first, use `brew install opencv` or `brew install opencv3 --with-python3`. Next, follow any additional instructions (like linking NumPy). Last, add the directory containing the OpenCV shared object file (e.g., */usr/local/Cellar/opencv3/3.1.0_3/lib/python3.4/site-packages/*) to your path; or to only use it in a virtual environment, use the `add2virtualenvironment` (*http://virtualenvwrapper.readthedocs.io/en/latest/command_ref.html#add2virtualenv*) command installed with the virtualenvwrapper library.

```
#Applying Grayscale filter to image
gray = cv2.cvtColor(img, cv2.COLOR_BGR2GRAY)

#Saving filtered image to new file
cv2.imwrite('graytest.jpg',gray)
```

There are more Python-implemented examples of OpenCV in this collection of tutorials (*http://opencv-python-tutroals.readthedocs.org/en/latest/py_tutorials/py_tutorials.html*).

Scikit-Image

A newer library, Scikit-Image (*http://scikit-image.org/*), is growing in popularity, thanks partly to having more of its source in Python and also its great documentation. It doesn't have the full-fledged algorithms like cv2, which you'd still use for algorithms that work on real-time video, but it's got enough to be useful for scientists—like blob detection and feature detection, plus it has the standard image processing tools like filtering and contrast adjustment. For example, Scikit-image was used to make the image composites of Pluto's smaller moons (*https://blogs.nasa.gov/pluto/2015/10/05/plutos-small-moons-nix-and-hydra/*). There are many more examples on the main Scikit-Image page (*http://scikit-image.org/docs/dev/auto_examples/*).

## CHAPTER 11

Data Persistence

We mentioned ZIP compression and pickling already in "Data Serialization" on page 255, so there isn't much left to cover besides databases in this chapter.

This chapter is mostly about Python libraries that interface with *relational databases*. These are the kinds of database we normally think about—they contain structured data stored in tables and are accessed using SQL.[1]

Structured Files

We already mentioned tools for JSON, XML, and ZIP files in Chapter 9, and pickling and XDR when talking about serialization. We recommend PyYAML (*http://pyyaml.org/wiki/PyYAML*) (get it via `pip install pyyaml`) to parse YAML. Python also has tools in its Standard Library for CSV, *.netrc* used by some FTP clients, *.plist* files used in OS X, and a dialect of the Windows INI format via *configparser*.[2]

---

1 Relational databases were introduced by in 1970 by Edgar F. Codd, who, while working at IBM, wrote "A Relational Model of Data for Large Share Data Banks." (*http://bit.ly/relational-model-data*) It was ignored until 1977, when Larry Ellison started a company—which would eventually become Oracle—based on its technology. Other competing ideas, like key-value stores and hierarchical database models, were largely ignored after the success of relational databases, until the recent not only SQL (NoSQL) movement revived nonrelational storage options in a cluster computing setting.

2 It's *ConfigParser* in Python 2—see the configparser documentation (*https://docs.python.org/3/library/configparser.html#supported-ini-file-structure*) for the precise dialect understood by the parser.

Also, there's a persistent key-value store available via the `shelve` module in Python's Standard Library. Its backend is the best available variant of the database manager (dbm—a key-value database) on your computer:[3]

```
>>> import shelve
>>>
>>> with shelve.open('my_shelf') as s:
...     s['d'] = {'key': 'value'}
...
>>> s = shelve.open('my_shelf', 'r')
>>> s['d']
{'key': 'value'}
```

You can check which database backend you're using like this:

```
>>> import dbm
>>> dbm.whichdb('my_shelf')
'dbm.gnu'
```

And you can get the GNU implementation of dbm here for Windows (*http://gnuwin32.sourceforge.net/packages/gdbm.htm*), or check your package manager (`brew`, `apt`, `yum`) first, then try the dbm source code (*http://www.gnu.org.ua/software/gdbm/download.html*).

Database Libraries

The Python Database API (DB-API2) defines a standard interface for database access in Python. It's documented in PEP 249 (*https://www.python.org/dev/peps/pep-0249/*) and in a more detailed introduction to Python's DB-API (*http://halfcooked.com/presentations/osdc2006/python_databases.html*). Nearly all Python database drivers conform to this interface, so when you just want to query a database in Python, choose any one that connects to the database that you are using: *sqlite3* for the SQLite database, *psycopg2* for Postgres, and *MySQL-python* for MySQL, for example.[4]

Code with lots of SQL strings and hardcoded columns and tables can quickly become messy, error-prone, and hard to debug. The libraries in Table 11-1 (except for *sqlite3*,

---

3 The dbm library stores key-value pairs in an on-disk hash table. The precise way that this happens depends on whether it's using the gdbm, ndbm, or "dumb" backend. The "dumb" one is implemented in Python and described in the documentation. The other two are in the gdbm (*http://www.gnu.org.ua/software/gdbm/manual//gdbm.html*) manual. With ndbm there's an upper bound on the value sizes stored. The file is locked when opened for writing unless (with gdbm only) you open the database file with an ru or wu, and even then, updates in write mode may not be visible on the other connections.

4 Although the Structured Query Language (SQL) is an ISO standard (*http://bit.ly/sql-iso-standard*), database vendors choose how much of the standard to implement, and can add their own features. This means a Python library that serves as a database driver must understand the dialect of SQL that is spoken by the database it interfaces with.

---

the SQLite driver) provide a *database abstraction layer* (DAL) that abstracts away the structure, grammar, and data types of SQL to present an API.

Because Python is an object-oriented language, the database abstraction can also implement object-relational mapping (ORM) to provide a mapping between the Python objects and the underlying database, plus operators on attributes in those classes that represent an abstracted version of SQL in Python.

All of the libraries in Table 11-1 (with the exception of sqlite3 and Records) provide an ORM, and their implementations use one of two patterns:[5] the *Active Record* pattern, where records simultaneously represent the abstracted data *and* interact with the database; and the *Data Mapper* pattern, where one layer interfaces with the database, another layer presents the data, and in between is a mapper function that performs the necessary logic to convert between the two (essentially performing the logic of a SQL view outside of the database).

When performing queries, both the Active Record and Data Mapper patterns behave about the same, but in the Data Mapper pattern, the user must explicitly state table names, add primary keys, and create helper tables to support many-to-many relationships (like on a receipt, where one transaction ID would be associated with multiple purchases) — all of that is done behind the scenes when using the Active Record pattern.

The most popular libraries are sqlite3, SqlAlchemy, and the Django ORM. Records is in a category of its own—as more of a SQL client that provides many options for output formatting—and the remaining libraries can be thought of as standalone, lighter weight versions of the Django ORM underneath (because they all use the ActiveRecord pattern), but with different implementations, and very different and unique APIs.

---

5 Defined in Martin Fowler's *Patterns of Enterprise Application Architecture* (*http://www.martinfowler.com/ books/eaa.html*). For more information on what goes into Python's ORM designs, we recommend the SQLAlchemy entry in the "Architecture of Open Source Applications," (*http://www.aosabook.org/en/ sqlalchemy.html*) and this comprehensive list of links related to Python ORMs from FullStack Python (*https:// www.fullstackpython.com/object-relational-mappers-orms.html*).

Table 11-1. Database libraries

Library	License	Reasons to use
sqlite3 (driver, not ORM)	PSFL	• It's in the Standard Library. • It's good for sites with low or moderate traffic that only need the simpler data types and a few queries—it's got low latency because there's no network communication. • It's good for learning SQL or Python's DB-API, or prototyping a database application.
SQLAlchemy	MIT license	• It provides a Data Mapper pattern with a two-layer API that has an ORM top layer resembling the API in other libraries, plus a low-level layer of tables directly attached to the database. • It gives you explicit control (via the lower level *Classical Mappings* API) over the structure and schemas in your database; this is useful, for example, if your database administrators are not the same people as your web developers. • Dialects: SQLite, PostgreSQL, MySQL, Oracle, MS-SQL Server, Firebird, or Sybase (or register your own).
Django ORM	BSD license	• It provides the Active Record pattern that can generate the database infrastructure implicitly from the user-defined models in the application. • It's tightly coupled with Django. • Dialects: SQLite, PostgreSQL, MySQL, or Oracle; alternatively, use a third-party library: SAP SQL Anywhere, IBM DB2, MS-SQL Server, Firebird, or ODBC.
peewee	MIT license	• It provides an Active Record pattern, but that's because the tables you define in the ORM *are* the tables you see in the database (plus an index column). • Dialects: SQLite, MySQL, and Postgres (or add your own).
PonyORM	AGPLv3	• It provides an Active Record pattern with an intuitive generator-based syntax. • There is also an online GUI Entity-Relationship diagram editor (to draw the data model that defines the tables in a database and their relationship to each other) that can be translated to SQL code that will create the tables. • Dialects: SQLite, MySQL, Postgres, and Oracle (or add your own).
SQLObject	LGPL	• It was one of the first to use the ActiveRecord pattern in Python. • Dialects: SQLite, MySQL, Postgres, Firebird, Sybase, MAX DB, MS-SQL Server (or add your own).
Records (query interface, not ORM)	ISC license	• It provides a simple way to query a database and generate a report document: SQL in, XLS (or JSON or YAML or CSV or LaTex) out. • Plus a command-line interface that can be used for interactive querying or one-line report generation. • It uses the powerful SQLAlchemy as its backend.

The following sections provide additional details about the libraries listed in Table 11-1.

sqlite3

SQLite is a C library that provides the database behind sqlite3 (*https://docs.python.org/3/library/sqlite3.html*). The database is stored as a single file, by convention with the extension *.db*. The "when to use SQLite" page (*https://www.sqlite.org/whentouse.html*) says it's been demonstrated to work as a database backend for websites with hundreds of thousands of hits per day. Their page also has a list of SQL commands that SQLite understands (*https://www.sqlite.org/lang.html*), and you can consult the W3Schools' quick SQL reference (*http://www.w3schools.com/sql/sql_quickref.asp*) for instructions on how to use them. Here's an example:

```
import sqlite3
db = sqlite3.connect('cheese_emporium.db')

db.execute('CREATE TABLE cheese(id INTEGER, name TEXT)')
db.executemany(
    'INSERT INTO cheese VALUES (?, ?)',
    [(1, 'red leicester'),
     (2, 'wensleydale'),
     (3, 'cheddar'),
    ]
)
db.commit()
db.close()
```

The allowable SQLite types are NULL, INTEGER, REAL, TEXT, and BLOB (bytes), or you can do other stuff that's in the sqlite3 documentation to register new data types (e.g., they implement a datetime.datetime type that is stored as TEXT).

SQLAlchemy

SQLAlchemy (*http://www.sqlalchemy.org/*) is a very popular database toolkit—Django comes with an option to switch from its own ORM to SQLAchemy, it's the backend for the Flask mega-tutorial (*http://blog.miguelgrinberg.com/post/the-flask-mega-tutorial-part-i-hello-world*) to build your own blog, and Pandas uses it as its SQL backend (*http://bit.ly/pandas-sql-query*).

SQLAlchemy is the only library listed here to follow Martin Fowler's Data Mapper pattern (*http://martinfowler.com/eaaCatalog/dataMapper.html*) instead of the more frequently implemented Active Record pattern (*http://martinfowler.com/eaaCatalog/activeRecord.html*). Unlike the other libraries, SQLAlchemy not only provides an ORM layer but also a generalized API (called the *Core* layer) for writing database-agnostic code without SQL. The ORM layer is stacked on top of the Core layer, which uses Table objects that directly map to the underlying database. The mapping between these objects and the ORM must be done explicitly by the user, so it takes more code to get started, and can be frustrating for those who are new to relational databases. The benefit is a far greater control over the database—nothing is created unless you explicitly put it there.

SQLAlchemy can run on Jython and PyPy, and supports Python 2.5 through the latest 3.x versions. The next few code snippets will show the work required to create a many-to-many object mapping. We'll create three objects in the ORM layer: Customer, Cheese, and Purchase. There can be many purchases for one customer (a many-to-one relation), and the purchase can be for many types of cheese (a many-to-many relation). The reason we're doing this in such detail is to show the unmapped table purchases_cheeses—it does not need to be present in the ORM because its only purpose is to provide a linkage between the types of cheese and the purchases. Other ORMs would create this table silently in the background—so this shows one of the big differences between SQLAlchemy and the other libraries:

```python
from sqlalchemy.ext.declarative import declarative_base
from sqlalchemy import Column, Date, Integer, String, Table, ForeignKey
from sqlalchemy.orm import relationship

Base = declarative_base()  ❶

class Customer(Base):  ❷
    __tablename__ = 'customers'
    id = Column(Integer, primary_key=True)
    name = Column(String, nullable=False)
    def __repr__(self):
        return "<Customer(name='%s')>" % (self.name)

purchases_cheeses = Table(  ❸
    'purchases_cheeses', Base.metadata,
    Column('purch_id', Integer, ForeignKey('purchases.id', primary_key=True)),
    Column('cheese_id', Integer, ForeignKey('cheeses.id', primary_key=True))
)

class Cheese(Base):  ❹
    __tablename__ = 'cheeses'
    id = Column(Integer, primary_key=True)
    kind = Column(String, nullable=False)
    purchases = relationship(  ❺
        'Purchase', secondary='purchases_cheeses', back_populates='cheeses'  ❻
    )
    def __repr__(self):
        return "<Cheese(kind='%s')>" % (self.kind)

class Purchase(Base):
    __tablename__ = 'purchases'
    id = Column(Integer, primary_key=True)
    customer_id = Column(Integer, ForeignKey('customers.id', primary_key=True))
    purchase_date = Column(Date, nullable=False)
```

```
        customer = relationship('Customer')
        cheeses = relationship(  ❼
            'Cheese', secondary='purchases_cheeses', back_populates='purchases'
        )
        def __repr__(self):
            return ("<Purchase(customer='%s', dt='%s')>" %
                    (self.customer.name, self.purchase_date))
```

❶   The *declarative base* object is a metaclass[6] that intercepts the creation of each mapped table in the ORM and defines a corresponding table in the Core layer.

❷   Objects in the ORM layer inherit from the declarative base.

❸   This is an *unmapped table* in the core layer—it's not a class and not derived from the declarative base. It will correspond the table `purchases_cheeses` in the database and exists to provide the many-to-many mapping between cheeses and purchase IDs.

❹   Compare that with `Cheese`—a mapped table in the ORM layer. Under the hood, `Cheese.__table__` is created in the core layer. It will correspond to a table named `cheeses` in the database.

❺   This `relationship` explicitly defines the relationship between the mapped classes `Cheese` and `Purchase`: they are related indirectly through the secondary table `pur chases_cheeses` (as opposed to directly via a `ForeignKey`).

❻   `back_populates` adds an event listener so that when a new `Purchase` object is added to `Cheese.purchases`, the `Cheese` object will also appear in `Pur chase.cheeses`.

❼   This is the other half of the plumbing for the many-to-many relationship.

Tables are explicitly created by the declarative base:

```
from sqlalchemy import create_engine
engine = create_engine('sqlite://')
Base.metadata.create_all(engine)
```

And *now* the interaction, using objects in the ORM layer, looks the same as in the other libraries with ORMs:

```
from sqlalchemy.orm import sessionmaker
Session = sessionmaker(bind=engine)
sess = Session()
```

---

6 There's a great explanation of Python metaclasses (*http://stackoverflow.com/a/6581949*) on Stack Overflow.

```
leicester = Cheese(kind='Red Leicester')
camembert = Cheese(kind='Camembert')
sess.add_all((camembert, leicester))
cat = Customer(name='Cat')
sess.add(cat)
sess.commit()   ❶

import datetime
d = datetime.date(1971, 12, 18)
p = Purchase(purchase_date=d, customer=cat)
p.cheeses.append(camembert)   ❷
sess.add(p)
sess.commit()
```

❶ You must explicitly commit() to push changes to the database.

❷ Objects in the many-to-many relationship aren't added during instantiation—
    they have to be appended after the fact.

Here are a few sample queries:

```
>>> for row in sess.query(Purchase,Cheese).filter(Purchase.cheeses):   ❶
...     print(row)
...
(<Purchase(customer='Douglas', dt='1971-12-17')>, <Cheese(kind='Camembert')>)
(<Purchase(customer='Douglas', dt='1971-12-17')>, <Cheese(kind='Red Leicester')>)
(<Purchase(customer='Cat', dt='1971-12-18')>, <Cheese(kind='Camembert')>)
>>>
>>> from sqlalchemy import func
>>> (sess.query(Purchase,Cheese)   ❷
...     .filter(Purchase.cheeses)
...     .from_self(Cheese.kind, func.count(Purchase.id))
...     .group_by(Cheese.kind)
... ).all()
[('Camembert', 2), ('Red Leicester', 1)]
```

❶ This is how to do the many-to-many join across the purchases_cheeses table,
    which is not mapped to a top-level ORM object.

❷ This query counts the number of purchases of each kind of cheese.

To learn more, see the SQLAlchemy documentation (*http://docs.sqlalchemy.org/en/
rel_1_0/*).

Django ORM

The Django ORM (*https://docs.djangoproject.com/en/1.9/topics/db/*) is the interface
used by Django (*http://www.djangoproject.com*) to provide database access. Their

implementation of the Active Record pattern is probably the closest one in our list to the Ruby on Rails ActiveRecord library.

It is tightly integrated with Django, so usually you only use it because you're making a Django web application. Try the Django ORM tutorial (*http://bit.ly/django-orm-tutorial*) from Django Girls if you want to follow along while building a web application.[7]

If you want to try out Django's ORM without making a whole web app, copy this skeleton GitHub project to use *only* Django's ORM (*https://github.com/mick/django_orm_only*), and follow its instructions. There may be some differences across versions of Django. Ours *settings.py* looks like this:

```python
# settings.py
DATABASES = {
    'default': {
        'ENGINE': 'django.db.backends.sqlite3',
        'NAME': 'tmp.db',
    }
}
INSTALLED_APPS = ("orm_only",)
SECRET_KEY = "A secret key may also be required."
```

Every abstracted table in the Django ORM subclasses the Django Model object, like this:

```python
from django.db import models

class Cheese(models.Model):
    type = models.CharField(max_length=30)

class Customer(models.Model):
    name = models.CharField(max_length=50)

class Purchase(models.Model):
    purchase_date = models.DateField()
    customer = models.ForeignKey(Customer)     ❶
    cheeses = models.ManyToManyField(Cheese)    ❷
```

❶ The ForeignKey relationship denotes a many-to-one relationship—the customer can make many purchases, but a purchase is associated with a single customer. Use OneToOneField for a one-to-one relation.

❷ And use ManyToManyField to denote a many-to-many relationship.

---

7 Django Girls (*https://djangogirls.org/*) is a phenomenal charity organization of brilliant programmers dedicated to providing free Django training in a celebratory environment to women around the world.

Next, we have to execute a command to build the tables. On the command line, with the virtual environment activated, and in the same directory as *manage.py*, type:

```
(venv)$ python manage.py migrate
```

With the tables created, here's how to add data to the database. Without the *instance*.save() method, the data in the new row will not make it to the database:

```
leicester = Cheese.objects.create(type='Red Leicester')
camembert = Cheese.objects.create(type='Camembert')
leicester.save()    ❶
camembert.save()

doug = Customer.objects.create(name='Douglas')
doug.save()

# Add a time of purchase
import datetime
now = datetime.datetime(1971, 12, 18, 20)
day = datetime.timedelta(1)

p = Purchase(purchase_date=now - 1 * day, customer=doug)
p.save()
p.cheeses.add(camembert, leicester)    ❷
```

❶   Objects must be saved to be added to the database and must be saved to be added in inserts that cross-reference other objects.

❷   You must add objects in a many-to-many mapping separately.

Querying via the ORM looks like this in Django:

```
# Filter for all purchases that happened in the past 7 days:
queryset = Purchase.objects.filter(purchase_date__gt=now - 7 * day)    ❶

# Show who bought what cheeses in the query set:
for v in queryset.values('customer__name', 'cheeses__type'):    ❷
    print(v)

# Aggregate purchases by cheese type:
from django.db.models import Count
sales_counts = (    ❸
    queryset.values('cheeses__type')
    .annotate(total=Count('cheeses'))    ❹
    .order_by('cheeses__type')
)
for sc in sales_counts:
    print(sc)
```

❶ In Django, the filtering operator (gt, greater than) is appended after a double underscore to the table's attribute purchase_date—Django parses this under the hood.

❷ Double underscores after a foreign key identifier will access the attribute in the corresponding table.

❸ In case you haven't seen the notation, you can put parentheses around a long statement and break it across lines for legibility.

❹ The query set's annotate clause adds extra fields to each result.

peewee

The primary goal of peewee (*http://docs.peewee-orm.com/en/latest/*) is to be a light-weight way for people who know SQL to interact with a database. What you see is what you get (you neither manually build a top layer that abstracts the table structure behind the scenes, like SQLAlchemy, nor does the library magically build a bottom layer underneath your tables, like Django ORM). Its goal is to fill a different niche than SQLAlchemy—doing a few things, but doing them quickly, simply, and Pythonically.

There is very little "magic," except to create primary keys for the tables if the user didn't. You'd create a table like this:

```
import peewee
database = peewee.SqliteDatabase('peewee.db')

class BaseModel(peewee.Model):
    class Meta:  ❶
        database = database  ❷

class Customer(BaseModel):
    name = peewee.TextField()  ❸

class Purchase(BaseModel):
    purchase_date = peewee.DateField()
    customer = peewee.ForeignKeyField(Customer, related_name='purchases')  ❹

class Cheese(BaseModel):
    kind = peewee.TextField()

class PurchaseCheese(BaseModel):
    """For the many-to-many relationship."""
    purchase = peewee.ForeignKeyField(Purchase)
    cheese = peewee.ForeignKeyField(Cheese)

database.create_tables((Customer, Purchase, Cheese, PurchaseCheese))
```

❶ peewee keeps model configuration details in a namespace called `Meta`, an idea borrowed from Django.

❷ Associate every `Model` with a database.

❸ A primary key is added implicitly if you don't explicitly add it.

❹ This adds the attribute `purchases` to `Customer` records for easy access but doesn't do anything to the tables.

Initialize data and add it to the database in one step with the `create()` method, or initialize it first, and add it later—there are configuration options to control autocommitting and utilities to do transactions. Here it's done in one step:

```
leicester = Cheese.create(kind='Red Leicester')
camembert = Cheese.create(kind='Camembert')
cat = Customer.create(name='Cat')

import datetime
d = datetime.date(1971, 12, 18)

p = Purchase.create(purchase_date=d, customer=cat)   ❶
PurchaseCheese.create(purchase=p, cheese=camembert)   ❷
PurchaseCheese.create(purchase=p, cheese=leicester)
```

❶ Directly add an object (like `cat`), and peewee will use its primary key.

❷ There's no magic for the many-to-many mapping—just add new entries manually.

And query like this:

```
>>> for p in Purchase.select().where(Purchase.purchase_date > d - 1 * day):
...     print(p.customer.name, p.purchase_date)
...
Douglas 1971-12-18
Cat 1971-12-19
>>>
>>> from peewee import fn
>>> q = (Cheese
...     .select(Cheese.kind, fn.COUNT(Purchase.id).alias('num_purchased'))
...     .join(PurchaseCheese)
...     .join(Purchase)
...     .group_by(Cheese.kind)
...     )
>>> for chz in q:
...     print(chz.kind, chz.num_purchased)
...
Camembert 2
Red Leicester 1
```

There is a collection of add-ons (*https://peewee.readthedocs.org/en/latest/peewee/play house.html#playhouse*) available, that include advanced transaction support[8] and support for custom functions that can hook data and execute prior to storage—for example, compression or hashing.

PonyORM

PonyORM (*http://ponyorm.com/*) takes a different approach to the query grammar: instead of writing an SQL-like language or boolean expressions, it uses Python's generator syntax. There's also a graphical schema editor that can generate PonyORM entities for you. It supports Python 2.6+ and Python 3.3+.

To accomplish its intuitive syntax, Pony requires that all relationships between tables be bidirectional—all related tables must explicitly refer to each other, like this:

```
import datetime
from pony import orm

db = orm.Database()
db.bind('sqlite', ':memory:')

class Cheese(db.Entity):     ❶
    type = orm.Required(str)     ❷
    purchases = orm.Set(lambda: Purchase)     ❸

class Customer(db.Entity):
    name = orm.Required(str)
    purchases = orm.Set(lambda: Purchase)     ❹

class Purchase(db.Entity):
    date = orm.Required(datetime.date)
    customer = orm.Required(Customer)     ❺
    cheeses = orm.Set(Cheese)     ❻

db.generate_mapping(create_tables=True)
```

❶ A Pony database `Entity` stores an object's state in the database, connecting the database to the object through its existence.

❷ Pony uses standard Python types to identify the type of the column—from `str` to `datetime.datetime`, in addition to the user-defined Entities like `Purchase`, `Customer`, and `Cheese`.

❸ `lambda: Purchase` is used here because `Purchase` is not yet defined.

---

8 Transaction contexts allow you to roll back executions if an error occurs in an intermediate step.

❹ The `orm.Set(lambda: Purchase)` is the first half of the definition of the one-to-many `Customer` to `Purchase` relation.

❺ The `orm.Required(Customer)` is the second half of the one-to-many `Customer` to `Purchase` relationship.

❻ The `orm.Set(Cheese)` relationship, combined with the `orm.Set(lambda: Purchase)` in ❹ define a many-to-many relationship.

With the data entities defined, object instantiation looks like it does in the other libraries. Entities are created on the fly and committed with the call to `orm.commit()`:

```
camembert = Cheese(type='Camembert')
leicester = Cheese(type='Red Leicester')
cat = Customer(name='Cat')
doug = Customer(name='Douglas')


d = datetime.date(1971, 12, 18)
day = datetime.timedelta(1)
Purchase(date=(d - 1 * day), customer=doug, cheeses={camembert, leicester})
Purchase(date=d, customer=cat, cheeses={camembert})
orm.commit()
```

And querying—Pony's tour de force—really does look like it's pure Python:

```
yesterday = d - 1.1 * day
for cheese in (
        orm.select(p.cheeses for p in Purchase if p.date > yesterday)  ❶
    ):
    print(cheese.type)

for cheese, purchase_count in (
        orm.left_join((c, orm.count(p))  ❷
            for c in Cheese
            for p in c.purchases)
    ):
    print(cheese.type, purchase_count)
```

❶ This is what a query looks like using Python's generator syntax.

❷ The `orm.count()` function aggregates by counting.

SQLObject

SQLObject (*http://www.sqlobject.org/*), first released in October 2002, is the oldest ORM in this list. Its implementation of the Active Record pattern—as well as its novel idea to overload the standard operators (like ==, <, <=, etc.) as a way of abstracting some of the SQL logic into Python, which is now implemented by almost all of the ORM libraries—made it extremely popular.

It supports a wide variety of databases (common database systems MySQL, Postgres, and SQLite, and more exotic systems like SAP DB, SyBase, and MSSQL) but currently only supports Python 2.6 and Python 2.7. It's still actively maintained, but has become less prevalent with the adoption of SQLAlchemy.

Records

Records (*https://github.com/kennethreitz/records*) is a minimalist SQL library, designed for sending raw SQL queries to various databases. It's basically Tablib and SQLAlchemy bundled together with a nice API and a command-line application that acts like a SQL client that can output YAML, XLS, and the other Tablib formats. Records isn't by any means a replacement for ORM libraries; a typical use case would be to query a database and create a report (e.g., a monthly report saving the recent sales figures to a spreadsheet). Data can be used programatically, or exported to a number of useful data formats:

```
>>> import records
>>> db = records.Database('sqlite:///mydb.db')
>>>
>>> rows = db.query('SELECT * FROM cheese')
>>> print(rows.dataset)
name          |price
--------------|-----
red leicester|1.0
wensleydale  |2.2
>>>
>>> print(rows.export('json'))
[{"name": "red leicester", "price": 1.0}, {"name": "wensleydale", "price": 2.2}]
```

Records also includes a command-line tool that exports data using SQL, like this:

```
$ records 'SELECT * FROM cheese' yaml --url=sqlite:///mydb.db
- {name: red leicester, price: 1.0}
- {name: wensleydale, price: 2.2}

$ records 'SELECT * FROM cheese' xlsx --url=sqlite:///mydb.db  > cheeses.xlsx
```

NoSQL database libraries

There is also an entire universe of not only SQL databases—a catchall for any database that people are using that's not a traditional relational database. If you look on PyPI, things can get confusing, with a few dozen similarly named Python packages. We recommend searching specifically on the main project's site for Python to get an opinion on the best library for a product (i.e., run a Google search for "Python site:vendorname.com"). Most of these provide a Python API and quickstart tutorials for how to use it. Some examples:

MongoDB

MongoDB is a distributed document store. You can think of it like a giant Python dictionary that can live on a cluster, with its own filter and query language. For the Python API, see MongoDB's getting started with Python page (*https:// docs.mongodb.com/getting-started/python/*).

Cassandra

Cassandra is a distributed table store. It provides fast lookup and can tolerate wide tables but is not inteded for joins—rather, the paradigm is to have multiple duplicate views of the data that are keyed on different columns. For more on the Python APIs, see the planet Cassandra page (*http://www.planetcassandra.org/ apache-cassandra-client-drivers/*).

HBase

HBase is a distributed column store (in this context, *column store* means data are stored like (`row id, column name, value`), allowing for very sparse arrays such as a dataset of "from" and "to" links for websites that make up the Web). It is built on top of Hadoop's Distributed File System. For more information about Python APIs, see HBase's "supporting projects" page (*https://hbase.apache.org/supporting projects.html*).

Druid

Druid (*http://druid.io/*) is a distributed column store intended to collect (and optionally aggregate before it stores) event data (in this context, *column store* means the columns can be ordered and sorted, and then storage may be compressed for faster I/O and smaller footprint). Here is a link to Druid's Python API on GitHub (*https://github.com/druid-io/pydruid*).

Redis

Redis is a distributed in-memory key value store—the point is to reduce latency by not having to do disk I/O. You could store frequent query results for faster web lookup, for example. Here is a list of Python clients for Redis (*http://redis.io/ clients#python*) that highlights redis-py as their preferred interface, and here is the redis-py page (*https://github.com/andymccurdy/redis-py*).

Couchbase

Couchbase (*http://www.couchbase.com/*) is another distributed document store, with a more SQL-like API (as compared to MongoDB's JavaScript-like API)— here is a link to Couchbase's Python SDK (*http://developer.couchbase.com/docu mentation/server/current/sdks/python-2.0/introduction.html*).

Neo4j

Neo4j is a graph database, intended to store objects with graph-like relationships. Here is a link to Neo4j's Python guide (*http://neo4j.com/developer/python/*).

LMDB

LMDB, the Symas Lightning Memory-mapped Database (*https://symas.com/prod ucts/lightning-memory-mapped-database/*) is a key-value store database with a memory-mapped file, meaning the file doesn't have to be read from the beginning to get to the part where the data is—so the performance is near the speed of an in-memory store. Python bindings are in the lmdb library (*https://lmdb.read thedocs.io/*).

Additional Notes

Python's Community

Python has a rich, inclusive, global community dedicated to diversity.

BDFL

Guido van Rossum, the creator of Python, is often referred to as the *BDFL*—the Benevolent Dictator for Life.

Python Software Foundation

The mission of the *Python Software Foundation* (*PSF*) is to promote, protect, and advance the Python programming language, and to support and facilitate the growth of a diverse and international community of Python programmers. To learn more, see the PSF's main page (*http://www.python.org/psf/*).

PEPs

PEPs are *Python Enhancement Proposals*. They describe changes to Python itself, or the standards around it. People interested in Python's history, or in language design in general, would find them all really interesting—even the ones that eventually get rejected. There are three different types of PEPs, defined in PEP 1 (*https://www.python.org/dev/peps/pep-0001*):

Standards
Standards PEPs describe a new feature or implementation.

Informational
Informational PEPs describe a design issue, general guidelines, or information to the community.

Process
Process PEPs describe a process related to Python.

Notable PEPs

There are a few PEPs that could be considered required reading:

PEP 8—Style Guide for Python Code (https://www.python.org/dev/peps/pep-0008)
Read this. All of it. Follow it. The pep8 tool will help (*https://pypi.python.org/pypi/pep8*).

PEP 20—The Zen of Python (https://www.python.org/dev/peps/pep-0020)
PEP 20 is a list of 19 statements that briefly explain the philosophy behind Python.

PEP 257—Docstring conventions (https://www.python.org/dev/peps/pep-0257)
PEP 257 contains the guidelines for semantics and conventions associated with Python docstrings.

You can read more at the PEP index (*http://www.python.org/dev/peps/*).

Submitting a PEP

PEPs are peer reviewed and accepted/rejected after much discussion. Anyone can write and submit a PEP for review. The diagram in Figure A-1 illustrates what happens after a draft PEP is submitted.

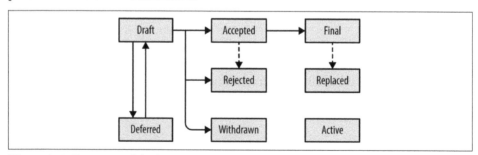

Figure A-1. Overview of the PEP review process

Python conferences

The major events for the Python community are developer conferences. The two most notable conferences are PyCon, which is held in the United States, and its European sibling, EuroPython. A comprehensive list of conferences is maintained at *http://www.pycon.org/*.

Python user groups

User groups are where Python developers meet in person to present or talk about Python topics of interest. A list of local user groups is maintained at the Python Software Foundation wiki (*http://wiki.python.org/moin/LocalUserGroups*).

Learning Python

These are some of our favorite references, grouped by level and application.

Beginners

The Python Tutorial
> This (*http://docs.python.org/tutorial/index.html*) is Python's official tutorial. It covers all the basics and offers a tour of the language and the Standard Library. Recommended for those who need a quick-start guide to the language.

Python for Beginners
> This tutorial (*http://thepythonguru.com*) focuses on beginner programmers. It covers many Python concepts in depth. It also teaches you some advanced constructs in Python like lambda expressions and regular expressions. It concludes with the tutorial "How to access a MySQL db using Python."

Learn Python
> This interactive tutorial (*http://www.learnpython.org/*) is an easy, nonintimidating way to get introduced to Python. It takes the same approach used on the popular website Try Ruby (*http://tryruby.org/*)—there is an interactive Python interpreter built into the site that allows you to go through the lessons without having to install Python locally.

Python for You and Me
> This book (*http://pymbook.readthedocs.org/*) is an excellent resource for learning all aspects of the language and is good for those who prefer learning from a traditional book rather than a tutorial.

Online Python Tutor
> This site (*http://pythontutor.com/*) gives you a visual step-by-step representation of how your program runs. Python Tutor helps people overcome a fundamental

barrier to learning programming by understanding what happens as the computer executes each line of a program's source code.

Invent Your Own Computer Games with Python
This book (*http://inventwithpython.com/*) is for those with no programming experience at all. Each chapter has the source code for a game, and these example programs are used to demonstrate programming concepts to give the reader an idea of what programs "look like."

Hacking Secret Ciphers with Python
This book (*http://inventwithpython.com/hacking/*) teaches Python programming and basic cryptography for absolute beginners. The chapters provide the source code for various ciphers, as well as programs that can break them.

Learn Python the Hard Way
This (*http://learnpythonthehardway.org/book/*) is an excellent beginner programmer's guide to Python. It covers "hello world" from the console to the Web.

Crash into Python
This site (*http://stephensugden.com/crash_into_python/*), also known as *Python for Programmers with 3 Hours*, gives developers who have experience with other languages a crash course on Python.

Dive Into Python 3
This book (*http://www.diveintopython3.net/*) is good for those ready to jump into Python 3. It's a good read if you are moving from Python 2 to 3 or if you already have some experience programming in another language.

Think Python: How to Think Like a Computer Scientist
This book (*http://greenteapress.com/thinkpython/html/index.html*) attempts to give an introduction to basic concepts in computer science through the use of the Python language. The focus was to create a book with plenty of exercises, minimal jargon, and a section in each chapter devoted to debugging. It explores the various features available in the Python language and weaves in various design patterns and best practices.

The book also includes several case studies which have the reader explore the topics discussed in the book in greater detail by applying those topics to real-world examples. Case studies include designing a GUI and Markov Analysis.

Python Koans
This online tutorial (*http://bitbucket.org/gregmalcolm/python_koans*) is a Python version of Edgecase's popular Ruby Koans. It's an interactive command-line tutorial teaching basic Python concepts using a test-driven approach (*http://en.wikipe dia.org/wiki/Test-driven_development*): by fixing assertion statements that fail in a test script, the student progresses in sequential steps to learning Python.

For those accustomed to languages and figuring out puzzles on their own, this can be a fun, attractive option. For those new to Python and programming, having an additional resource or reference will be helpful.

A Byte of Python
This is a free introductory book that teaches Python at the beginner level—it assumes no previous programming experience. There is an a version for Python 2.x (*http://www.ibiblio.org/swaroopch/byteofpython/read/*) and a version for Python 3.x (*http://swaroopch.com/notes/Python_en-Preface/*)

Learn to Program in Python with Codecademy
This Codecademy course (*http://www.codecademy.com/en/tracks/python*) is for the absolute Python beginner. This free and interactive course provides and teaches the basics (and beyond) of Python programming while testing the student's knowledge as she progresses through the tutorials. It also also features a built-in interpreter for receiving instant feedback on your coursework.

Intermediate

Effective Python
This book (*http://www.effectivepython.com/*) contains 59 specific ways to improve writing Pythonic code. At 227 pages, it is a very brief overview of some of the most common adapations programmers need to make to become efficient intermediate-level Python programmers.

Advanced

Pro Python
This book (*http://amzn.com/1430227575*) is for intermediate to advanced Python programmers who are looking to understand how and why Python works the way it does and how they can take their code to the next level.

Expert Python Programming
This book (*http://www.packtpub.com/expert-python-programming/book*) deals with best practices in programming Python, and is focused on the more advanced crowd. It starts with topics like decorators (with caching, proxy, and context manager case studies), method resolution order, using `super()` and meta-programming, and general PEP 8 best practices.

It has a detailed, multichapter case study on writing and releasing a package and eventually an application, including a chapter on using `zc.buildout`. Later chapters detail best practices such as writing documentation, test-driven development, version control, optimization, and profiling.

A Guide to Python's Magic Methods

This handy resource (*http://www.rafekettler.com/magicmethods.html*) is a collection of blog posts by Rafe Kettler that explain "magic methods" in Python. Magic methods are surrounded by double underscores (e.g., __init__) and can make classes and objects behave in different and magical ways.

For Engineers and Scientists

Effective Computation in Physics

This field guide (*http://bit.ly/effective-computation-in-physics*), by Anthony Scopatz and Kathryn D. Huff, is intended for early graduate students who are starting to use Python in any scientific or engineering field. It includes snippets for searching through files using SED and AWK, and provides tips on how to accomplish every step in the research chain, from data collection and analysis to publication.

A Primer on Scientific Programming with Python

This book (*http://bit.ly/primer-sci-pro-py*), by Hans Petter Langtangen, mainly covers Python's usage in the scientific field. In the book, examples are chosen from mathematics and the natural sciences.

Numerical Methods in Engineering with Python

This book (*http://bit.ly/numerical-methods-eng-py*) by Jaan Kiusalaas puts the emphasis on modern numerical methods and how to implement them in Python.

Annotated Algorithms in Python: with Applications in Physics, Biology, and Finance

This tome (*http://amzn.com/0991160401*), by Massimo Di Pierro, is a teaching tool intended to demonstrate the algorithms used by implementing them in straightforward ways.

Miscellaneous Topics

Problem Solving with Algorithms and Data Structures

This book (*http://www.interactivepython.org/courselib/static/pythonds/index.html*) covers a range of data structures and algorithms. All concepts are illustrated with Python code along with interactive samples that can be run directly in your browser.

Programming Collective Intelligence

This book (*http://bit.ly/programming-collective-intelligence*) introduces a wide array of basic machine learning and data mining methods. The exposition is not very mathematically formal, but rather focuses on explaining the underlying intuition and shows how to implement the algorithms in Python.

Transforming Code into Beautiful, Idiomatic Python

   This video (*http://bit.ly/hettinger-presentation*), by Raymond Hettinger, will show
   you how to take better advantage of Python's best features and improve existing
   code through a series of code transformations: "When you see this, do that
   instead."

Fullstack Python

   This site (*https://www.fullstackpython.com/*) offers a complete top-to-bottom
   resource for web development using Python from setting up the web server, to
   designing the frontend, choosing a database, optimizing/scaling, and more. As
   the name suggests, it covers everything you need to build and run a complete
   web app from scratch.

References

Python in a Nutshell

   This book (*http://bit.ly/python-in-a-nutshell*) covers most cross-platform Python
   usage, from its syntax, to built-in libraries, to advanced topics such as writing C
   extensions.

The Python Language Reference

   This (*http://docs.python.org/reference/index.html*) is Python's online reference
   manual. It covers the syntax and the core semantics of the language.

Python Essential Reference

   This book (*http://www.dabeaz.com/per.html*), written by David Beazley, is the
   definitive reference guide to Python. It concisely explains both the core language
   and the most essential parts of the Standard Library. It covers Python 3 and
   Python 2.6.

Python Pocket Reference

   This book (*http://bit.ly/python-pocket-reference*), written by Mark Lutz, is an easy-
   to-use reference to the core language, with descriptions of commonly used modules and toolkits. It covers Python 3 and Python 2.6.

Python Cookbook

   This book (*http://bit.ly/python-cookbook-3e*), written by David Beazley and Brian
   K. Jones, is packed with practical recipes. It covers the core Python language as
   well as tasks common to a wide variety of application domains.

Writing Idiomatic Python

   This book, by Jeff Knupp, contains the most common and important Python idioms in a format that maximizes identification and understanding. Each idiom is
   presented as a recommendation of a way to write some commonly used piece of
   code, followed by an explanation of why the idiom is important. It also contains

two code samples for each idiom: the "harmful" way to write it and the "idiomatic" way. There are different editions for Python 2.7.3+ (*http://amzn.com/1482372177*) and for Python 3.3+ (*https://amzn.com/B00B5VXMRG*).

Documentation

Official documentation

The official Python Language and Library documentation can be found here for Python 2.x (*https://docs.python.org/2/*), and here for Python 3.x (*https://docs.python.org/3/*).

Official packaging documentation

The most current instructions for packaging your Python code will always be in Python's official packaging guide (*https://packaging.python.org*). And remember that testPyPI (*https://testpypi.python.org/pypi*) exists so you can confirm that your packaging works.

Read the Docs

Read the Docs (*https://readthedocs.org/*) is a popular community project that hosts documentation for open source software. It holds documentation for many Python modules, both popular and exotic.

pydoc

pydoc is a utility that is installed when you install Python. It allows you to quickly retrieve and search for documentation from your shell. For example, if you needed a quick refresher on the time module, pulling up documentation would be as simple as typing this into a command shell:

```
$ pydoc time
```

which is essentially equivalent to opening the Python REPL and running:

```
>>> help(time)*
```

News

Our favorite places to get Python news are listed here in alphabetical order:

Name	Description
/r/python (*http://reddit.com/r/python*)	The Reddit Python community where users contribute and vote on Python-related news.
Import Python Weekly (*http://www.importpython.com/newsletter/*)	A weekly newsletter containing Python articles, projects, videos, and tweets.
Planet Python (*http://planet.python.org/*)	An aggregate of Python news from a growing number of developers.

Name	Description
Podcast.__init__ (*http://podcasti nit.com/*)	A weekly podcast about Python and the people who make it great.
Pycoder's Weekly (*http://www.pycoders.com/*)	A free weekly Python newsletter for Python developers by Python developers (it highlights interesting projects and includes articles, news, and a jobs board).
Python News (*http://www.python.org/news/*)	The news section in the official Python website (*http://www.python.org*). It briefly highlights the news from the Python community.
Python Weekly (*http://www.pythonweekly.com/*)	A free weekly newsletter featuring curated news, articles, new releases, and jobs related to Python.
Talk Python to Me (*http://talkpython.fm/*)	A podcast on Python and related technologies.

Index

A

abstraction layers, 66-69
ActivePython, 20
ActiveState, 20
Advanced Message Queuing Protocol (AMQP), 263
Amazon S3, 178
Anaconda, 20, 41
Ansible, 227
Apache HTTP server, 221
Apache licenses, 94
applications, using logging in, 91
Aptana Studio 3, 32
arbitrary argument list, 53
arbitrary keyword argument dictionary, 54
argparse module, 195
argument passing, code style for, 52-56
Atom, 29
Autoenv, 39

B

bbFreeze, 185
bcrypt, 269
Beazley, David, 235, 238
Beck, Kent, 223
Behave, 86
Bendersky, Eli, 258
Berkeley Software Distribution (BSD)-style licenses, 94
Blanks, Hunter, 49
block comments, docstrings vs., 89
Bokeh, 274
Boost.Python, 247
bpython, 36

breaking tests, 78
BSD (Berkeley Software Distribution)-style licenses, 94
buffer protocol, 258
Buildbot, 226
Buildout, 40
built distribution
    defined, 174
    packaging for Linux, 186

C

C Foreign Function Interface (CFFI), 244
C/C++
    Boost.Python, 247
    CFFI (C Foreign Function Interface), 244
    ctypes and, 245
    licensing issues, 179
    SWIG and, 246
__call__() method, 158
Canopy, 20
Cassandra, 298
Celery, 264
CFFI (C Foreign Function Interface), 244
Chameleon Page Templates, 217
Chef, 230
CI (see continuous integration)
circular dependencies, 68
class-based decorators, 156
classes
    custom, user-extensible, 112
    mixins, 159
    new-style vs. old-style, 161
Click, 198-200

duck typing, 156
dynamic typing, 73

E

easy_install, 177
Eby, Phillip J., 146
Eclipse, 32
eggs, 174
Ellison, Larry, 283
Elpy, 28
Emacs, 27
enhanced interactive tools, 35
    bpython, 36
    IDLE, 35
    IPython, 35
Enthought, 20
equality, alternatives to checking for, 56
Eric (the Eric Python IDE), 34
error handling, code style for, 51

F

F2PY (Fortran-to-Python) interface generator,
    245
Fabric, 232
Falco, Gabriel, 86
Fettig, Abe, 262
file formats, programmatically registered,
    125-128
fixture (testing tool), 86
Flask, 162-172, 212
    application-specific defaults, 169
    logging, 167-168
    modularity, 171
    reading code, 163-166
    reading documentation, 162
    routing decorators, 168
    structure examples, 169-172
    style examples, 168
    using, 163
Fortran-to-Python (F2PY) interface generator,
    245
Fowler, Martin, 223, 285, 287
framework (see software framework)
framework, reading code in, 162-166
freezing code, 179-186
    bbFreeze, 185
    comparison of popular tools for, 180
    cx_Freeze, 182
    defined, 179

py2app, 184
py2exe, 184
    PyInstaller and, 181
function arguments, 52-56
function definitions, 62
function names, underscore-prefixed, 103
functional programming, 71
functionality, separating into namespaces, 111
functions, decorators and, 72

G

Gale, Andy, 230
Gallina, Fabián Ezequiel, 28
game development, GUI applications for, 208
gevent, 261
Gleitzman, Benjamin, 51, 99
Global Interpreter Lock (GIL), 234, 242, 258
global state/context, 69
Gondor, 219
GPU libraries, for speed optimization, 242
GTK+, 206
GUI applications, 202-209
    game development, 208
    GTK+, 206
    Kivy, 205
    Objective-C, 207
    Qt, 205
    Tk, 204
    wxWidgets, 207
Gunicorn (Green Unicorn), 221

H

Hansson, David Heinemeier, 223
hashlib module, 266
HBase, 298
Heroku, 219
Hettinger, Raymond, 49
hidden coupling, 69
Homebrew, 10
hooks, version control automation, 77
hosting, 219
HowDoI, 99-105
    compatibility handling, 104
    leveraging data from system, 103
    limiting functions to doing just one thing,
        103
    packaging, 102
    Pythonic coding choices, 104
    reading a single-file script, 99-102

About the Authors

Kenneth Reitz is the product owner of Python at Heroku and a Fellow at the Python Software Foundation. He is well known for his many open source projects, specifically Requests: HTTP for Humans.

Tanya Schlusser is her mom's primary Alzheimer's caregiver, and an independent consultant who uses data to drive strategic decisions. She's delivered over 1,000 hours of data science training to individual students and corporate teams.

Colophon

The animal on the cover of *The Hitchhiker's Guide to Python* is the Indian brown mongoose (*Herpestes fuscus*), a small mammal native to the forests of Sri Lanka and southwest India. It is very similar to the short-tailed mongoose (*Herpestes brachyurus*) of southeast Asia, of which it may be a subspecies.

The Indian brown mongoose is slightly larger than other species of mongoose, and is distinguished by its pointed tail and furry hind legs. Their fur varies from dark brown on their bodies to black on their legs. They are rarely seen by humans, suggesting that they are nocturnal or crepuscular (active at dawn and dusk).

Until recently, data on the Indian brown mongoose was sparse and their population was thought to be vulnerable. Improved scientific monitoring has discovered a fairly large population, especially in southern India, so their status has been upgraded to Least Concern. Another population of the Indian brown mongoose was also recently discovered on the island of Viti Levu in Fiji.

Many of the animals on O'Reilly covers are endangered; all of them are important to the world. To learn more about how you can help, go to *animals.oreilly.com*.

The cover image is from *Lydekker's Royal Natural History*. The cover fonts are URW Typewriter and Guardian Sans. The text font is Adobe Minion Pro; the heading font is Adobe Myriad Condensed; and the code font is Dalton Maag's Ubuntu Mono.

Get even more
for your money.

Join the O'Reilly Community, and register the O'Reilly books you own. It's free, and you'll get:

- $4.99 ebook upgrade offer
- 40% upgrade offer on O'Reilly print books
- Membership discounts on books and events
- Free lifetime updates to ebooks and videos
- Multiple ebook formats, DRM FREE
- Participation in the O'Reilly community
- Newsletters
- Account management
- 100% Satisfaction Guarantee

Signing up is easy:

1. Go to: oreilly.com/go/register
2. Create an O'Reilly login.
3. Provide your address.
4. Register your books.

Note: English-language books only

To order books online:
oreilly.com/store

For questions about products or an order:
orders@oreilly.com

To sign up to get topic-specific email announcements and/or news about upcoming books, conferences, special offers, and new technologies:
elists@oreilly.com

For technical questions about book content:
booktech@oreilly.com

To submit new book proposals to our editors:
proposals@oreilly.com

O'Reilly books are available in multiple DRM-free ebook formats. For more information:
oreilly.com/ebooks